LORD HASTINGS' INDENTURED RETAINERS 1461–1483

THE LAWFULNESS OF LIVERY AND RETAINING UNDER THE YORKISTS AND TUDORS

BY

WILLIAM HUSE DUNHAM, JR.

ARCHON BOOKS
1970

Originally published 1955
Connecticut Academy of Arts and Sciences,
Transactions, volume 39

Reprinted 1970 with permission
in an unaltered and unabridged edition

ISBN: 0-208-00989-2
Library of Congress Catalog Card Number: 76-114420
Printed in the United States of America

1933281

CONTENTS

ACKNOWLEDGEMENTS

To the Trustees of the Henry E. Huntington Library and Art Gallery my especial thanks are due, first, for having made available to the scholarly public Lord Hastings' indentures and the other Hastings Manuscripts; then, for a Research Fellowship during 1941–42 when I transcribed the indentures and the other documents used in this study; and finally, for permission to print the texts in the Appendices and the quotations in the narrative and to reproduce the photograph of one indenture, Plate I.

For the opportunity to locate in British archives the manuscripts used to complement the Hastings collection, for permitting me to spend part of my time as a Fulbright Research Scholar, 1952–53, on this study, and for their gracious assistance in many ways, I thank the United States Educational Commission in the United Kingdom.

The Trustees of the National Gallery, London, have authorized the reproduction of the Wilton Diptych as Plates VI and VII. The Trustees of the British Museum have permitted the reproduction of pages containing the peers' badges, Plates II-V, from MS. Additional 40742, fols. 5, 7, 10, 11, and of Lord Hastings' seal, Plate VIII, from Additional Charter 19808.

The considerateness and cordial assistance, now too often taken for granted, of the staffs of the British Museum, the Bodleian Library, the University Library, Cambridge, the Public Record Office, and the Huntington Library have been much appreciated. The authorities of these institutions I thank for permitting me to read, cite, and print from manuscripts in their collections.

Those of my kith and kin, scholarly and otherwise, who have helped me have been thanked already for their aid and forbearance. To list their names here would serve only to publicize the breadth of my acquaintance, and it might implicate good friends and scholars in faults and opinions not their own.

18 October 1954.   *W. H. D. Jr.*

ABBREVIATIONS USED IN FOOTNOTE CITATIONS

Cal. Close Rolls: Calendar of the Close Rolls, London.

Cal. Patent Rolls: Calendar of the Patent Rolls, London.

Eng. Hist. Rev.: The English Historical Review, London.

Hardwicke State Papers: Miscellaneous State Papers from 1501–1726, ed. Philip Yorke, earl of Hardwicke, 1778.

H.M.C. Report: The Reports of the Historical Manuscripts Commission, followed by the number of the report or the name of the collection when not numbered.

Letters and Papers of Henry VIII: Letters and Papers, Foreign and Domestic, of the reign of Henry VIII, 1509–47, ed. J. S. Brewer *et. al.* 1862–1910.

P.R.O.: The Public Record Office, London, followed by the "Reference" number of the manuscript cited.

Rot. Parl.: Rotuli Parliamentorum, (1278–1503), London. 1832.

Rymer, Foedera: Foedera, Conventiones, Litterae ... ed. Thomas Rymer and Robert Sanderson, 1704–35.

State Papers of Henry VIII: State Papers published under the authority of H. M.'s Commission, King Henry VIII, London. 1830–52.

S.R.: Statutes of the Realm, ed. A. Ludors et al., 1810–28.

Trans. Royal Hist. Soc.: Transactions of the Royal Historical Society, London.

LORD HASTINGS' INDENTURED RETAINERS
1461—1483

THE LAWFULNESS OF LIVERY AND RETAINING
UNDER THE YORKISTS AND TUDORS

WILLIAM HUSE DUNHAM, Jr.

ARGUMENT: THE FEUDALITY OF RETAINING
BY INDENTURE

To dub the politico-military system of feed retainers in fifteenth-century England "Bastard Feudalism" [1] does not seem very enlightening —no more so than to brand Britain's Baldwinian economy "Bastard Capitalism." Actually, neither system was illegitimate, that is unlawful, even though acts of parliament regulated aspects of each. A happier view is to construe the peers' practice of retaining companies of knights, esquires, and gentlemen as a refinement, and not a degeneration, of an earlier feudal custom. Its continuance as an effective social procedure would seem to prove, not decay, but viability. Likewise, the notion that the years 1399–1485 marked "the decline and fall of English feudalism" reflects a pessimistic attitude towards feudal retaining—the result of evaluating the institution from its defects rather than from its purpose and achievements. The misuse, largely through unlawful maintenance, of the power that liveried retainers provided, led to wrongs aplenty. This happens when any institution, like the Stuart monarchy, is abused. But overmuch concern with the evil consequences of these abuses has

---

[1] A Victorian divine, the Reverend Charles Plummer, chaplain of Corpus Christi College, Oxford, seems to have coined this unedifying expression and to have contributed it, along with the unchivalrous term, "pseudo-chivalry," to the English historical vocabulary, *Sir John Fortescue, The Governance of England* (1885), p. 15. K. B. McFarlane resurrected it in 1943, but in 1945 he was willing to qualify it to mean only the "appearance of" or "resembling" feudalism. Helen M. Cam favors Holdsworth's refined, but hardly more historical, term, "new feudalism." Since this study discloses a continuity of feudal principles and attributes, the implication in the word "new" of a revival, or an imitation, of feudalism makes this term misleading. The most significant writings on retaining by indenture are: H. M. Cam, "The Decline and Fall of English Feudalism," *History*, XXV (1940), 216–233; K. B. McFarlane, "Parliament and 'Bastard

produced moral indignation and a denigration of retaining, rather than an historical understanding.

An optimistic point of view towards Yorkist society, and one freed from Tudor propaganda,[2] may lead to a more judicious conclusion. Did not the so-called "pseudo-chivalry" of Edward IV's reign produce, in fact, more sophisticated arrangements for war and politics than had the socially primitive tenurial feudalism of Norman England? After all, the practice of retaining men by oath or indenture was founded upon the most sacred of English constitutional principles—that of contract. Even after the personal relation between a "lord" and his "man" had become separated from the tenure of land, it still rested upon a bi-lateral contract. Whether a contractual arrangement not based upon land and tenure is strictly "feudal" may be a matter of debate; but to Maitland feudalism before 1300 meant:

"a state of society in which the main social bond is the relation between lord and man, a relation implying on the lord's part protection and defense; on the man's part protection, service and reverence, the service including service in arms. This personal relation is inseparably involved in a proprietary relation, the tenure of land . . ."[3]

Once this personal relation has been severed from the proprietary relation, some will argue, it has lost its "feudal" character. But during the fifteenth century, men translated the latin word for fief, *feodum*, into "fee", the thing that had supplanted the land fief. Recent research has traced the *fief-rente* (a fief consisting of an annual payment in pounds, shillings, and pence) back to Henry I's time, the year 1103. Henry II, too, used the *fief-rente* to procure military service from continental nobles, and "literally hundreds" of "feudal contracts" survive

Feudalism'," *Trans. Royal Hist. Soc.*, 4th Ser., XXVI (1944), 53–79; N. B. Lewis, "The Organisation of Indentured Retinues in Fourteenth-Century England," *Idem*, XXVII (1945), 29–39; K. B. McFarlane, "Bastard Feudalism," *Bulletin of the Institute of Historical Research*, XX (1943–45), 161–180; J. C. Wedgwood, "John of Gaunt and the Packing of Parliament," *Eng. Hist. Rev.*, XLV (1930), 623–625; cf. N. B. Lewis, *Idem*, XLVIII (1933), 391; J. S. Roskell, "The Knights of the Shire for the County Palatine of Lancaster," *Chetham Society*, vol. 210 (1937), 6; Bryce D. Lyon, "The Money Fief under the English Kings, 1066–1485," *Eng. Hist. Rev.*, LXVI (1951), 161–193; "The Feudal Antecedent of the Indenture System," *Speculum* XXIX (1954), 503–511; H. G. Richardson, "John of Gaunt and the Parliamentary Representation of Lancashire," *Bulletin of the J. Rylands Library*, XXII (1938), 175–222.

[2] The extravagance of the Tudors' propaganda for authoritarianism, law, and order—doubtless as necessary as useful at the time—has been exceeded only by that of their twentieth-century idolators.

[3] F. W. Maitland, *The Constitutional History of England*, p. 143.

from the reigns of John and Henry III.[4] Here, surely, was an antecedent of, though perhaps not "the model for, the indenture system." By Edward I's time, lords, as well as the king himself, were using *fiefs-rentes* to procure reserves of fighting knights. An agreement in 1297 between Sir Aylmer de Valence, the lord, and Thomas, lord of Berkeley, the man, substituted cash—a £50 annuity—for land as the substantive bond between them.

This use of money, often derived from particular lands named in the indenture, in place of the land itself may have marked a change in the form, but not in the substance of the contractual principle. The reciprocal quality of the contract persisted. On through the fourteenth century cash fees, still called *feoda* in contemporary documents, annuities, and the giving of cloth for livery, *robe,* supplanted land as the nexus between a lord and his retainers, as his "men" came to be styled.[5] N. B. Lewis has already analyzed the organization of these indentured retinues and described the terms of fourteenth-century contracts by which a lord procured military and other services in return for cash annuities, livery, and military equipment. The domestic discord of Edward II's reign and the foreign wars of Edward III's provoked a need for soldiery, at the king's expense, and this prompted lords to increase the number of men they retained in peace as well as for war. The greater amount of money current at this time made it more convenient and more economical to fee a retainer than to endow with land a knight. The lord's control over his retainer was firmer, for how easy to stop payment on an annuity and how cumbersome to recover a land fief either by a private war or through a lawful, but protracted, process in the king's court. As the magnates' revenues became greater on through the fifteenth century, so did the size of their retinues of feed retainers. Even in Edward IV's reign, some peers still were paying cash annuities; but a change was taking place, and only two of Lord Hastings' 69 extant indentures (1461–1483) record money fees. Instead, this peer contracted to be a "good and favorable lord" to his men who were neither tenants nor, literally, "feed" retainers. The final substitution of what medieval men called good lordship—aid, favor, support, and preferment—for the fee created a more refined, certainly a more subtle, relationship, one that could be advantageous and

4 B. D. Lyon, "The Feudal Antecedent of the Indenture System," *Speculum,* XXIX (1954), 503–511.

5 P.R.O. E101/411/13, fols. 36–38, the "account Book" of Sir John Fogge, keeper of the great wardrobe, in 1464 used the heading, *Feoda et Robe,* for the list of annual payments to the chamberlain of England, the steward of the household, the king's chamberlain, and other household officers.

effectual only in a more sophisticated society. And yet, paradoxically, these less tangible gifts by the lord gave fifteenth-century feudal retaining a close resemblance to the Anglo-Saxon institution of lordship. Perhaps there was a continuity through the intervening centuries, by means of things-taken-for-granted, custom, and traditions, which the surviving written records do not make evident. Certainly by 1483 the practice of retaining, replete with good lordship, had become an institution far richer socially than the arid phrase, "the indenture system," can possibly connote.

Parallel to the process whereby fiefs gave way to fees, and fees to favor, was an elaboration of the services rendered by the retainer, no longer a tenant "involved in a proprietary relation." Service in arms, the original *raison d'etre* of Norman and Angevin feudalism, still continued as the essential function of the fourteenth-century retainer. But he performed peace-time services, too, as Lewis has demonstrated, attending the lord at tournaments, parliaments, and public assemblies; joining in the lord's recreations; and being "in the household at the lord's will," though not a permanent resident. This comparatively civil tone is even more conspicuous a century later in Lord Hastings' contracts though they still required the retainers to fight for their lord. But they describe fighting in euphemistic terms—to ride and go, defensibly arrayed, at Hastings' call. By Edward IV's reign, the retainer's commitment to take his lord's part and quarrel against all men, except the king, had come to mean more than just fighting with him on the field of battle.

In actual practice, the retainer now supported the lord in county politics and, occasionally, in the national arena of parliament. The recent identification of some members of the fifteenth-century house of commons as peers' retainers has led to the contention that the lords of parliament dominated the lower house by "placing" therein their "servants." But the history of Lord Hastings' 88 retainers fails to confirm this assertion. His men constituted, at the most, no more than 2.2 % of the members of Edward IV's six parliaments; and seven, perhaps ten (2.4 % or 3.44 % of the whole house) was the largest number of his servants to sit at a single parliament. Furthermore, all but 3 or 4 of Hastings' 14 retainers who sat in any parliament were elected to the house before, and not after, they signed indentures with him. However, his company of knights, esquires, and gentlemen did give Lord Hastings political influence, the "rule" of the midland shires of England. Many of his men were sheriffs and justices of the peace in Derby, Leicestershire, and Stafford. By capturing county offices, they performed political services which complemented their military functions and established their lord's local ascendancy. In the same way the earl of Northumberland's retainers, among whom were 38 knights, account for his dominance in the north. Such a company of gentry, tied by indentures to a peer of the realm, through their position in county society and by their connection, through their lord, with one another, seems a progenitor of those associations of lords and country gentlemen which were to produce the parliamentary factions of the future.

The peers' bands of non-resident retainers survived into the sixteenth century, and even the most order-conscious of the Tudors, Elizabeth I, had to dispense with those acts of parliament that prohibited livery and retaining. She licensed not only the peers, but courtiers and civil servants, even her chief justice, to retain men and to give them liveries. The reason why was that this politico-military system still had a place in Tudor England for it supplied the sovereign with manpower. The royal government needed men for both war and peace; and the lords' retainers provided captains for the contract armies and officials for county governance. There they guarded the king's, as well as the lord's, parochial interests, and on occasion they satisfied the vanity and enhanced the worship of both lord and sovereign by parading, while dressed in parti-colored liveries, up and down the countryside or along the streets of London. Their part in Tudor pageantry disguised, but it did not eliminate, the original military purpose of retaining. Retainers constituted a potential military force in Mary Tudor's time; and even if the threat of force was used more frequently than its application, a company of retainers might enable a peer to speak more forcefully in national as well as local affairs.

The monarch's problem was to control this institution and to use it to his and the kingdom's advantage. To do this, he had to command the lords' allegiance, and this meant a mastery of the art of politics— guiding, checking, driving, and cajoling men high-spirited, ambitious, and selfish. Henry VI's complete inability to do so explains not only his failure but why the lords seized his government and why the practice of retaining got so out of hand. Nevertheless, during the two centuries, 1399–1603, the vast majority of peers usually were constant to the reigning sovereign as were their own retainers to them. Even the Tudors, with all their talk about law, order, and the cult of kingship, condoned retaining. Like the Yorkists, they, too, depended upon the system far too much to try seriously to stop the peers from binding men by oath, promise, or indenture. Militarily, the lords and their companies provided the king with a skeleton, if not a standing, army. They constituted an organization through which the monarch might recruit, under the royal contract system, armed forces to meet domestic emergencies or to make foreign expeditions. Until the Tudor dynasty was secure, if ever it was—certainly not until after Norfolk's rebellion in 1569 or perhaps even Essex's in 1601—the most that the sovereign could hope to do was to control the lords and their retinues. Gradually he gained ascendancy through statutory regulation, through personal politics, and by the centripetal magnetism of his court over a system that determined the structure of both war and politics.

The statute of 1390 was the first major attempt to regulate and control retaining and to restrict it to the presumably dependable members of society, the peers of the realm. Who designed the act is not certain, but its consequence was to give a monopoly on retaining companies of knights and esquires to the lords temporal. Furthermore, to do so lawfully, the lord must retain by indenture, and the retainer must contract for the term of his life and for peace as well as for war. Such a permanent connection, the legislators hoped, would prevent peers from admitting into their companies irresponsible men, wrong-doers, or criminals, and it might even make the lord responsible for his followers. The retainers, too, were to be recruited from the gentry. Only knights and esquires were eligible to be retained, for other than household or legal service, and to wear the livery of a lord's company. The 1390 act not only prescribed the conditions under which peers might retain, but it also determined in large part the terms of the contracts and the course of future legislation.

Subsequent acts of parliament regulated retaining by trying to eliminate the abuses of the institution, chiefly maintenance, champerty, and embracery. They also sought to restrict ancillary practices like the retainer's wearing of livery—badges, cognizances, tokens, jackets,—the insignia which identified the retainer's lord. This later legislation distinguished between maintenance (the evil to be eradicated), livery (the psychological stimulus to many of the abuses), and retaining itself (the institution to be preserved). Statutes repeatedly prohibited unlawful, though not lawful, maintenance; then they restricted the wearing of livery to various categories of persons—household servants, the king's and the prince's retainers, officers in the universities, and the lords' non-resident retainers, but only on those occasions when they went with their lord on the king's service. Actually, not a single act of parliament until that of 1468, despite the commons' petitions and their speakers' requests, denied the peers' right to retain by oath, promise, or indenture. But the act of 1468 forbad any person of whatsoever rank or degree to do so; and when construed literally, this statute would seem to apply to peers. However, not only did the lords temporal continue to retain non-residents, but they drew up elaborate indentures like those signed and sealed by Lord Hastings and his retainers.

Beneath all of these laws, statutes, and contracts, there was of course a code of social conduct, a romanticized version of Edward III's rules of chivalry, to govern retaining in practice. This code, like all unwritten ones, consisted of traditions, attitudes, and convictions all taken for granted. Seldom were the rules written down, and now they are hard to come by. Even Hastings' contracts state so little and assume so much. The very concept of good lordship in Yorkist England needed no definition; and even the "faith and honor of knighthood," by which Sir Simon Montfort swore to be Lord Hastings' servant, were words easier to understand in 1469 than to define today. Fidelity and trust, man to man, was at the heart of the lord-retainer connection. Granted that the promise of faithful service was not always kept in Yorkist and Tudor England, still feudal retaining would not have survived for a decade, let alone two centuries, had not the vast majority of a lord's company been true and stuck to him for term of life. Just this, we know, Lord Hastings' men did until his death at Richard III's command drove them to seek a new lord. The values which governed this politico-military system were honor and integrity, good faith and the keeping of contracts. But its genius was the combining of the high ideals of Plantagenet chivalry with Yorkist-Tudor opportunism. The mutual advantages to both lord and retainer account for its success, and they enabled the institution to survive even Thomas Cromwell's "Revolution in Tudor Government."[6]

The rise and fall of a retainer, as William, Lord Hastings' career may be styled, demonstrates the opportunities that the institution offered an ambitious man on the make. Richard, duke of York, had retained William's father, and he himself first became the duke's servant and then the retainer of his son, Edward, earl of March. When Edward became king of England in 1461, Hastings became his councillor, his chamberlain, and a baron. Thereafter, he went on from power to power and built up his own company of retained knights, esquires, and gentlemen, the well-willers who constituted the true foundation of a peer's prestige. Without his personal attachment to Edward IV and without his permanent position at the Yorkist court from 1461 to 1483,

---

[6] Many of us have been unable to find any evidence that either Edward IV's or Henry VII's monarchy was either "new" or "strong." G. R. Elton, *The Tudor Revolution in Government*, (1953), has provided positive affirmation of my belief that not until 1533–35 did the Tudor monarchy really acquire strength sufficient to distinguish it clearly from its medieval predecessor.

Lord Hastings, a nouveau peer, might not have drawn and held together his company of men; but without their support, both political and military, his career at court might have been less profitable and certainly less long. Ironically, Hastings' fall resulted from his fidelity to his own lord, King Edward IV, and his loyalty to his lord's son, Edward V. A seasoned councillor and no novice at palace politics, this lord balked at Richard III's usurpation of his nephew's throne. Unlike the earl of Warwick's death in battle which ratified his treason to Edward IV, Hastings' execution sanctified with blood his loyalty to his lord. While the fidelity of a single retainer cannot obliterate the bar-sinister imposed upon fifteenth-century feudalism, it may in part redeem feudal retaining from the charge that it was only

"a parasitic institution ... cut off from its natural roots in the soil, and far removed indeed from the atmosphere of responsibility, loyalty and faith which had characterized the relationship of lord and vassal in the earlier middle ages."[7]

[7] H. M. Cam, "The Decline and Fall of English Feudalism," *History*, XXV (1940), 225. Like N. B. Lewis, I feel that the permanency and the legality of the written bond made the indentured retinue "certainly a steadying influence in a society where old institutional loyalties were breaking down ..." This is not to deny the evils obviously resulting from the abuses, defects and human frailties apparent in the institution's operation. But I find it very difficult to follow the argument of the enthusiasts for the twelfth and thirteenth centuries— in view of the civil wars under Stephen, John, and Henry III and the armed opposition against Henry II and even Edward I—that the tenurial tie afforded English society a greater stability than did the "personal ties" in Lancastrian and Yorkist England. N. B. Lewis, "The Organisation of Indentured Retinues in Fourteenth-Century England," *Trans. Royal Hist. Soc.*, 4th Ser., XXVII (1945), 39.

I

LORD HASTINGS AND HIS LORD: A RETAINER'S RISE AND FALL

On Friday-the-thirteenth of June, 1483, "close upon noon," William, Lord Hastings was beheaded. Scarcely an hour before, he, the king's chamberlain, had sat in the Tower of London at a council with the protector of the realm, Richard, duke of Gloucester. There the duke accused him of treason and swore by St. Paul not to go to dinner until his enemy was dead. A squad of armed men hustled Hastings from the White Tower onto the Green "beside the chapel;" a priest near at hand shrived "him apace;" and Hastings' head was "laid down upon a log of timber and there stricken off." Just a fortnight later the impetuous duke seized Edward V's throne and became Richard III.

The nature of Hastings' treason is not yet clear. Supposedly, he refused to go along with Richard's plan to usurp his nephew's crown. "Undoubtedly, the protector loved [Hastings] well, and loath was to have lost him," Sir Thomas More later wrote, for Hastings had supported Richard, after Edward IV's death in April 1483, against Queen Elizabeth and her Woodville kinsmen. First, he had joined the duke's faction which had enveloped the boy-king; and then he had helped to make Gloucester the protector of the realm until Edward V should come of age. However, in order to contain Richard's ever-increasing power, Hastings had effected a reconciliation with the queen. Together with Bishop Morton of Ely and the chancellor, Archbishop Rotherham of York, he sought to maintain a balance between the rival factions. But the chamberlain, like many a moderate in time of crisis, merely made himself suspect to each side and fell victim to their feuds.

However, the protector had given Hastings his chance for he had sent a common friend, William Catesby, to win him over to "their party." But Catesby had "found him so fast [firm] and . . . heard him speak so terrible words" that he dared disclose no more of Richard's scheme. Hastings, doubtless, had learned enough, or perhaps too much.

And so he, with Rotherham and Morton, had to go—the bishops into confinement and the chamberlain, with no cloth to save him, to the block. Later on Richard allowed Hastings' head and body to be buried together in St. George's Chapel at Windsor Castle.

The fall of Hastings, like his rise to power, probably resulted from his adherence to the cult of lordship. He himself had been Edward IV's retainer, and fidelity, good faith, was in theory at the very heart of the system of retaining men by oath or indenture. In the case of Lord Hastings, contemporaries recognized in him an "honorable man, a good knight and a gentle, of great authority with his prince." Here in the personal attachment between lord and man is, I believe, a clue to Hastings' conduct between Edward IV's death in April and his own on 13 June. Otherwise, why should Hastings have stuck at a change of monarchs, one that would advance his own erstwhile friend? Even a stranger, a cynical Italian cleric visiting England in 1483, caught the point of Hastings' fidelity to Edward IV and to his heir. Dominic Mancini, in a cold, Machiavellian analysis of Yorkist politics and personalities, explains that after the protector had gotten into his power all the blood royal, his prospects were not sufficiently secure "without the removal or imprisonment of those who had been the closest friends of his brother [Edward IV] and were expected to be faithful to his brothers offspring." The three most conspicuous of Edward's *fideles,* according to Mancini, were Morton, Rotherham, and Hastings.

However, the chamberlain's relations with Edward IV had been more intimate than those of the bishops. All three men had "helped more than other councillors to form the king's policy and besides carried it out." "But Hastings," Mancini noted, "was not only the author of his sovereign's public policy, as being one that shared every peril with the king, but was also the accomplice and partner of his privy pleasures". Thomas More, too, believed that Queen Elizabeth's special grudge against Hastings resulted not just from Edward's "great favor" towards his chamberlain but from his being "secretly familiar with the king in wanton company," meaning, John Stow explained, "wanton doings with light women." But Hastings was also a "man of great feeling (*sens*) and prowess (*vertu*)," the French chronicler, Commines, declared, and he had "great authority with his master, and not without reason for he had served him well and loyally." Upon his death the *Great Chronicle of London* recorded how "this noble man was murdered for his truth and fidelity which he firmly bore unto his master." And Thomas More, on Bishop Morton's authority, finally characterized

Hastings as "a loving man and passing well beloved. Very faithful and trusty enough, trusting too much."[1]

Trusting too much, perhaps, but the first Baron Hastings was no novice in the sophisticated politico-military machinations of 1483. His own rise to power and wealth proves that. He caught the main chance in 1461 and thereafter he grasped lands, offices, fees, and favours. Ethically, Hastings seems neither better nor worse than his rivals at court; nor was he, a recipient of the king's cast-off paramours, noted for any peculiar moral sensitivity—except for his fidelity to Edward IV, a virtue not wholly distinct from self-interest. Throughout Edward's reign, Hastings had succeeded in manipulating men and women; he had mastered many an intrigue at home and abroad; and in 1471 he had outmaneuvered and outfought his brother-in-law, Warwick the king-maker. Even if Hastings was, as More asserted, "easy to beguile, as he that of good heart and courage forestudied no perils," Mancini looked upon him as a hardened councillor, one "in age mature and instructed by long experience in public affairs." So old a hand in palace politics was not likely to stick quixotically to a boy-king without some strong conviction. Back in 1471, upon Edward IV's restoration to the king-ship, Hastings had accepted Prince Edward to be the "undoubted heir" to the crown of England; and he, "as a true and faithful subject", had sworn to bear to the prince "faith and truth". But so had five dukes, thirty-one other earls and barons, and numerous knights, some of whom went along with Richard III or at least acquiesced in his usurpation.[2]

Hastings' will, dated at London 27 June 1481 when Edward IV still

---

[1] For Hastings' relations with Edward IV and Richard III, and for the analysis of his character, see: D. Mancini, *The Usurpation of Richard III*, ed. C. A. J. Armstrong; Thomas More, *The History of King Richard III*, ed. J. R. Lumby; Philippe de Commines, *Memoires*, ed. B. de Mandrot (1901) I, 205; II, 3, 6; *The Great Chronicle of London*, ed. A. H. Thomas and I. D. Thornley, p. 231; John Stow, *The Annals of England . . .* (1615), pp. 447–51.

[2] In the parliament chamber at Westminster, 3 July 1471, those present swore this oath:

"I, Thomas, cardinal archbishop of Canterbury, knowledge, take, and repute you, Edward prince of Wales etc., first begotten son of our sovereign lord, King Edward etc. to be very and undoubted heir to our said lord as to the crowns and realms of England and France and lordship of Ireland, and promise and swear that in case hereafter it happen you by God's disposition to overlive our sovereign lord, I shall then take and accept you for the very true and rightwise king of England etc. and faith and truth shall to you bear; and in all things truly and faithfully behave me towards you and your heirs as a true and faithful subject oweth to behave him to his sovereign lord etc. So help me God and halidom and this Holy Evangelist." *Cal. Close Rolls, 1468–1476*, pp. 229–30, no. 858.

lived, suggests that conscience was what prompted him to oppose Richard's *coup d'etat*. No copybook testament, this will is an intimate document marked by sincerity and candor. "In witness that this is my last will and testament", it reads, "I did write this clause and last article with mine own hand". The striking feature of the will is the recurrent mention of Hastings' connection with his personal lord, Edward, earl of March, duke of York, and then king of England. After commending his soul to God in a conventional manner, he tells how

"the king of his abundant grace, for the true service that I have done and at the least intended to have done to his grace, hath willed and offered me to be buried in the College or Chapel of St. George at Windsor in a place by his grace assigned in the which College his highness is disposed to be buried."

Hastings then orders his "simple body" to be buried there and bequeaths 100 marks for a tomb and lands worth £20 a year to the dean and canons of Windsor for a "priest to say daily mass and divine service . . . for the king's prosperous estate during his life and after his death for his soul, for the souls of me, my wife, and for all Christian souls". Here is evidence of a special intimacy between Hastings and Edward IV, and of affection towards his earthly lord. For Hastings, not without pride, preferred to be buried at Windsor alongside the king rather than alongside his wife at Ashby-de-la-Zouche.

From Edward, Hastings sought one final favor. In his will he asks the king to care for his son and heir, for his wife and other children, and to "be good lord to" his executors. These last commissions, so reminiscent of Anglo-Saxon wills, conform to the centuries-old code of good lordship. To Edward, as to his personal lord, Hastings appeals for his family's protection. Then for the heir to his barony, his son, Edward (presumably named after the king) he writes,

"also, I in most humble wise beseech the king's grace to take the governance of my son and heir; and as straightly as to me is possible, I charge mine heir on my blessing to be faithful and true to the king's grace, to my lord prince, and their heirs."

Here is Hastings' mandate to his son and successor to bear a true allegiance, not only to the king but also to Edward, prince of Wales. How, then, could Lord Hastings himself, within two years, forsake his lord's heir, Edward V, without becoming in his own son's eyes a notorious faith-breaker? Furthermore, he ends his will by asking the king to be good lord to his wife and children; and, in turn, he charges them to be their sovereign's true subjects. And then, writing the last article with his own hand, Hastings addresses Edward IV "whose good grace in the most humble wise I beseech to be good and tender, gracious lord to my soul, to be good and gracious lord to my wife, my sons and mine heirs, and to all my children whom I charge upon my blessing to be true subjects and servants to you, my sovereign lord under God, and to your heirs, to all your issue; beseeching you, sovereign lord, also to be good lord to my surveyors and executors in executing this my last will and testament as my most singular trust is in your good grace above all earthly creatures, as well for my wife and children as to mine executors and surveyors in executing this my last will and testament. Signed with mine hand and sealed with the seal of my arms the day and year aforesaid."[3]

The temper of this will, admittedly a solem matter made at a solem moment, is that of honest devotion and genuine fidelity. Although "sentiment was not a fifteenth-century virtue, disloyalty to the king was a breach of feudal obligations and a challenge to authority besides which death was as nothing."[4]

If Hastings' fidelity to his lord was a factor in his fall, Edward's good lordship had been directly responsible for his rise. For over twenty years he remained the true friend and confidant, the companion-in-arms and chamberlain, and the faithful retainer of Edward as earl of March, duke of York, and king of England. Why William Hastings fared better than Edward's other retainers remains a mystery, that of personality. William's father, Sir Leonard Hastings, had been a retainer of Edward's father, Richard, duke of York. The duke granted him a £15 annuity for life in 1436 and by 1442 had made him his "beloved councillor." Six years later Leonard was knighted, and in 1449 Henry VI, perhaps under York's influence, granted him exemption for life from serving on assizes or juries and from being appointed sheriff, escheator, coroner, constable or collector. Such were the emoluments of good lordship, and his lord, the duke of York, in 1456 executed Sir Leonard's will.[5]

3 William Hastings' will was proved 12 August 1483 at Maidstone. Contemporary copies are at Somerset House, London, P.C.C., Logge, 7, and at the H. E. Huntington Library, MS. HA, Family Papers, 1464–83.

4 C. H. Williams, in *Cambridge Medieval History,* VIII, 439–40.

5 For Hastings' life and career, see: G. E. Cockayne, *The Complete Peerage,* ed. V. Gibbs; *Dictionary of National Biography;* William Dugdale, *Historical and Genealogical Collections of the Family of Hastings . . .,* an unpublished manuscript history written in 1677, H. E. Huntington Library, MS. HA (hereafter cited as Dugdale, *History of Hastings Family*); cf., Huntington Library Bulletin, V (1934), 52 and *H. M. C. Report,* Hastings MSS., IV, 348–51. Dugdale states (p. 13) that William was "born about the year 1431." For details about Sir Leonard Hastings, *idem;* for the record of the Hastings-Pierpont arbitration, MS. HA Family, 1400–62. *The Cals. of Patent* and *Close Rolls, 1461–83,* record Hastings' appointment to various offices and many were noted in Dugdale, *History of Hastings Family.* For the payment of arrears of Hastings'

The year before, William, then about 24 years old and the duke of York's "beloved servant," was sheriff of Warwickshire and Leicester. York granted him, too, on 23 April 1458, a £10 annuity "in consideration of his good and faithful services done and to be done to the said duke." William agreed to serve York before all other men, except the king, and to attend him at any time. Almost immediately, in 1459, Hastings experienced the advantage of being a great lord's retainer. When Henry Pierpont complained that William and Thomas Hastings and Henry Ferrers were responsible for the slaying of his brother, Robert Pierpont, the duke of York arbitrated the case. To "appease" the variances between them, the parties "were put in the rule, ordinance, and judgement" of the duke. After hearing Pierpont's complaint and the Hastings brothers' "excuse," York made an "award" dated 17 October 1459. This required both sides "to keep the king's peace" and thereby to prevent the "great inconveniences which else were like to grow between them." Further, the Pierponts were to release, by writing, "all manner of appeals" for Robert's death and all "actions of trespass;" in return, the Hastings brothers were to forego "all manner of actions" against the Pierponts and to pay them in 5 installments between Christmas 1459 and Michaelmas 1462 a total of £40. Henry Pierpont was to find a priest "to sing divine service" during 2 years for Robert's soul. Thus the duke of York acted as the good and gracious lord of his retainer, and this arbitration saved the Hastings brothers a more costly, and perhaps a less successful, trial at common law. The Pierponts, too, probably found private mediation cheaper, speedier, and more rewarding than the king's justice might have been.

This same year, 1459, Hastings fought in the duke's army at Ludford, and for this the Lancastrian parliament at Coventry attainted him. The next year, he was with York's son and heir, Edward, earl of March, and so absent from the battle of Wakefield where the duke was killed. Upon York's death, Hastings presumably became Edward's retainer, and he marched with him from Gloucestershire to London where the new duke of York, on 4 March, 1461, was proclaimed King Edward IV. On Palm Sunday, 29 March, Hastings fought for Edward at Towton, and there the Yorkist king knighted him on the field of battle. A few months later, sometime after 13 June and before 26 July when he summoned Hastings to parliament, Edward created him a baron, Sir William Hastings, Lord Hastings.

Already preferment had begun to come Hastings' way. On 11 May,

salary of 12 *d.* a day as constable of Rockingham in 1468, P.R.O., K.R. Memoranda Roll, E159/245/ mem. vii (Trinity Term 8 Edward IV). For the grant of Folkingham Castle, Lincs., *ibid.,* mem. 28 (Michaelmas Term).

1461 the king appointed him and his brother, Ralph, jointly constable of Rockingham Castle in Northamptonshire, and from this office they received wages of 12 pence a day. Lord Hastings also enjoyed many other emoluments—lands, offices, rewards, fees, and annuities granted by the king or by his fellow peers. He stood so high in Edward IV's esteem, Dugdale was to write in his *Historical Collections . . . of the Family of Hastings,*

"that divers eminent persons taking notice thereof accumulated their favors on him. Amongst which John Mowbray, then duke of Norfolk, bestowed on him the stewardship of his manors of Melton Mowbray, Segrave, and others in county Leicester with the fee of £ 10 per annum during his life."

Other peers and peeresses—Anne, duchess of Buckingham, John, Lord Lovell, Lord Rivers, and Jacquet of Luxembourg, duchess of Bedford—favoured him with grants and annuities. Even more durable were the lands—those of Viscount Beaumont, the earl of Wiltshire, and Lord Roos—which the king granted Hastings in 1461 "for the better maintenance of his estate;" and on 17 February 1462, a royal letter patent declared his properties to constitute "the lordship, barony, and honor of Hastings." Edward IV further augmented the chamberlain's growing fortune in August 1467 by bestowing upon him a chain of manors and castles, including Folkingham in Lincolnshire—properties that were to be the territorial foundation of his grandson's earldom of Huntingdon.

Besides lands and annuities, the first Lord Hastings acquired many offices of profit. He was constable of several castles, steward of royal manors, honors, and lordships, a master forester, chamberlain of North Wales, receiver-general of Cornwall, chief steward of the duchy of Lancaster, keeper of the exchanges at the Tower of London and Calais, and master of the king's mints which were to pay him 4d. for every pound weight of gold and silver coined. There is no need to catalogue all the sources of Hastings' income; he had a plenty and his revenues constantly increased as Edward's reign wore on.

The king's favor also led to advantageous marriages for Hastings himself and later for his children. His own marriage, before 6 February 1462, to Katherine Neville, Lord Harrington's widow, the earl of Salisbury's daughter, and Warwick's sister, brought wealth, prestige, political connections, and apparently some degree of happiness. She bore him heirs, three sons and a daughter, who afforded opportunities for marriage alliances with old peerages. His daughter, Anne, her father's will provided, was to marry George, earl of Shrewsbury (whose wardship Hastings held in 1475); and if he should die "before carnal knowledge between the same earl and her had", then she was to marry his brother, Thomas, "if the law of the church will suffer or license it." His own heir, Edward, married, before 18 February 1481, Mary, the heiress of Margaret, Lady Hungerford, and in her own right Baroness Botreaux, Hungerford, and Moleyns. She brought to her husband her baronies and titles which passed on into the Hastings estate for their son, George, the first earl of Huntingdon.[6].

During Lord Hastings' own life, he held two major political appointments. He was the king's chamberlain from 1461 until his death, and in 1471 he was made "keeper, governor-general, supervisor, king's lieutenant of the town and castle of Calais, the tower of Rysbank, castle of Guisnes, and the marches thereabout." The former office brought and kept Hastings close to the king as one of his most secret councillors; while in the latter post, Hastings preserved for the Yorkist dynasty, and for England, the bridge-head to the continent so essential for Edward's expedition in 1475 to France. On this occasion Hastings augmented his estate by a pension of 2,000 *écus* from Louis XI. His refusal to give an acquittance for its payment, lest the English king's chamberlain be called publicly a pensioner of France, won for him, according to Commines, the French king's praise. With less regard for chivalric niceties, Hastings accepted a similar gift from Edward's ally, the duke of Burgundy.

Such gratuities helped Lord Hastings to meet the high cost of serving his king and of living at the royal court. The "robes" and "fees" which he, as chamberlain of the household, received annually were commuted at only £12 a year; but the king supplemented this salary with occasional "rewards". For Hastings' "great charges and costs, as well in his attendance upon our person in the office of our chamberlain as in the attendance and daily labor in our council and otherwise by our commandments," the king in 1468 ordered the exchequer to pay him £100 "by way of reward." The fruits accruing to Lord Hastings from his service to the king enabled him to avoid any financial embarrassment prior to his death. In 1483, however, his widow and his heir had to redeem gold and silver plate pledged for a loan of £360. Of this sum, £40 had been borrowed against "a collar of gold of King Edward's livery".[7]

[6] H. E. Huntington Library, MS. HA Family, 1464–83 (2 June 1475) and William, Lord Hastings' will.

[7] For Hastings' fees and robes as chamberlain, P.R.O. E101/411/13, fols. 36–38, the "Account Book of Sir John Fogge," for the year 4 Edward IV. For Hastings' "reward," 9 Nov. 1468, P.R.O., E404/74/11, a privy seal warrant. For the gold collar, *H. M. C. Report* No. 78, Hastings MSS. I, 305.

This token of Edward's lordship, like the badge a lord gave to his retainer, also signified Hastings' obligations. He served his lord faithfully in a variety of ways, and throughout Edward's reign his loyalty was constant. When the earl of Warwick temporarily restored Henry VI and the Lancastrians to power in 1470, Hastings had managed Edward IV's escape and had crossed with him to Holland. The chamberlain was the man who brought the volatile duke of Clarence back from his defection and who organized the Yorkist return. He landed with Edward at Ravenspur in the spring of 1471, and his retainers, with their followers, were the first to rise in the Yorkist king's behalf. Hastings commanded the third division, said to include 3,000 horsemen, at the battle of Barnet on 14 April; then he marched on west with Edward to fight in the final victory in May at Tewkesbury. There one of Hastings' own retainers, Nicholas Longford, was knighted. Already, on 17 April 1471, the king had licensed Hastings to convert his houses at Ashby-de-la-Zouche, Bagworth, Thornton, and Kirby in Leicestershire and one at Slingesby in Yorkshire into castles. This permission to build walls, towers, pinnacles with holes for shooting, and machicolations points up the Yorkist dynasty's dependance upon those peers whom Edward could trust and also the king's confidence in Hastings' fidelity.[8]

Immediately after Edward IV's restoration, Hastings accepted fresh responsibilities. Right off in 1471, he became the king's lieutenant, the keeper, and the governor-general of Calais. In this post, he recruited soldiers to garrison the castles, clerks and gentry to administer the civil government, and engineers to repair the fortifications—and so prepare the way for Edward IV's French invasion of 1475. The English landings in France led to little more than verbal skirmishes and a truce. But for the next three years Hastings at Calais carried on negotiations with the French. Duties such as these fell to him as an officer of state, the king's lieutenant at Calais and his chamberlain; and yet underneath these formal appointments lay Hastings' close personal connection, as a feudal retainer, with Edward. After the king's death, he was one of the executors of Edward's will; and at once he sought to protect his lord's minor heir, Edward V, from his uncles, Rivers and Gloucester. Finally, Hastings' death at the duke of Gloucester's command—no longed for martyrdom it's true—sanctified with blood his good faith to his personal lord.

Hastings' "great authority with his prince", as Thomas More described it, may explain how he acquired power over other men. Con-

8 Henry N. Bell, *The Huntingdon Peerage* (1820), pp. 15–19, 19 *n.*

versely, his use of lordship—the practice of retaining men by indenture—may account in part for his influence with the king. The constancy and consequences of Hastings' affinity with Edward suppose
something more than mere personal compatability. The chamberlain was
not just a royal favorite, in the seventeenth-century sense, upon whom
the monarch squandered his and England's wealth to slake his emotions.
Nor can the chivalric cult of fidelity alone explain their mutual stead-
fastness. Yorkist England, as the many perpendicular parish churches
still commanding the countryside recall, was a wealthy and a
materialistic England, a land where power was the determinant. Wealth,
both landed and commercial, as Hastings' affluence makes clear, could
make a man powerful; but in fifteenth-century politics, manpower
counted even more in both military and civil affairs. Time and again
a lord's ability to raise men to serve in war or peace proved the decisive
factor. Horsemen and archers in abundance determined which faction,
or alliance of factions, was to gain the ascendancy. Men to staff the civil
offices in shire and borough meant power to maintain both a magnate's
personal sway over the territory where he had "the rule" and the peace
of peaceless kings. Even if Hastings' authority with the king was the
keystone of his power, that authority, in turn, depended upon the
man-power that he could bring to his sovereign's service. No doubt
Edward IV's trust and confidence enabled Hastings to build up a party
of adherents, to reward his own faithful servants, and to hold their
loyalty. However, he seems also to have had the talent to organize, into
an effective political force, his "well-willers". Some of them he retained
formally by written indentures; others were tenants on his lands; and
the services of a few he procured for nothing more tangible than the
hope of preferment to be obtained through the chamberlain's influence
at Edward's court and in his council.

From the king's point of view, the benefits he bestowed upon Lord
Hastings proved a sound investment politically, and politics, after all,
was the essence of the regal enterprise. The king's business was to rule
English society effectively, a thing the saintly and forlorn Henry VI had
failed to do. To accomplish this, Edward IV needed loyal men to serve
him and the kingdom, in effect, both a standing army and a civil
service. In theory, Hastings, like every other peer of the realm was a
counsellor-born; and in practice, he, like other magnates loyal to
Edward, brought to the king's service his own band of faithful
followers. Their collaboration in wartime worked to preserve the king's
government, and in peace they helped to impose the regal policy
throughout the kingdom.

Tudor propagandists dramatized the battles between Yorkists and

Lancastrians and called them the Wars of the Roses. Thus they created the impression of a prolonged period of warfare. Actual fighting probably occupied less than 12 weeks between 1450 and 1485; and the battles, seldom lasting longer than an eight-hour day, were well dispersed among the English counties. So there was really no physical disruption of normal life for over 95 % of the people for about 99 % of the time. Similarly, the mythical red and white roses have supposed a two-party war. Actually English politics throughout the fifteenth century were conducted on a multi-party basis. The apparently dual alignment in the battles to gain possession of Henry VI's person or of the kingly office was illusory and often only temporary. Beneath the surface were many factions. Even when two opposing armies appeared upon a battlefield, the warriors wore neither the red rose nor the white, but the peers' many different badges. Alliances between the lords, many of them merely momentary, merged their bands of soldiers into armies; but their agreements sometimes lasted hardly long enough to win a battle and seldom longer than to serve the individual peer's political advantage. At Bosworth Field in 1485, the earl of Northumberland, who had indented in 1474 to be Richard, duke of Gloucester's faithful servant, withdrew and did not fight; and only towards the end did Lord Stanley and his contingent join battle for Henry Tudor.

Like other fifteenth-century magnates, Lord Hastings used the system of retaining by indenture to maintain a central corps of adherents. Around them he organized the manpower, civil as well as military, to support or to thwart the reigning king. These partisans constituted a body of reservists, men upon whom Hastings could count to champion not only his own quarrels but also his lord's. One of his retainers, Harry, Lord Grey of Codnor, signed indentures dated 30 May 1464 to take Lord Hastings' "full part and quarrel and to be with him against all" persons except the king. He proved faithful, during the critical spring of 1471, to both his lord and to his king by "attending in his own person upon us [Edward IV] in this our great journey [battle] as in bringing unto us a great number of men defensibly arrayed at his cost and charge". For this loyal and effective support, the king, on 24 May 1471, ordered the exchequer to pay Lord Grey of Codnor "£100 by way of reward".[9] As Hastings' retainer, Grey was in alliance with the chamberlain and brought to Edward's aid his own servants. Presumably Hastings' other retainers also brought men "defensibly arrayed", and they probably provided many of the 3,000 men whom he is said to have commanded at the battle of Barnet.

[9] P.R.O., E404/74, a writ of privy seal, 24 May 1471.

A decade earlier, in 1461, Hastings had begun to recruit retainers who were to form his company. As soon as he became a baron, he was eligible to retain men by oath, promise, or indenture lawfully. In the course of his career at least 88 knights, esquires, and gentlemen, and 2 peers, signed and sealed indentures to serve him for life in both peace and war. To prevent Lord Hastings from calling up to London this company of faithful retainers, men who had covenanted to take his part and quarrel, was probably the reason why Richard, duke of Gloucester, in June 1483, struck him down so quickly. Hastings' execution was reported to Sir William Stonor within the week: "with us is much trouble, and every man doubts other. As on Friday last was the lord chamberlain beheaded soon upon noon." And then below his signature, as a postscript, Simon Stallworth noted one immediate consequence in an unadorned statement:

"All the lord chamberlain's men became my lord's of Buckingham men".[10]

Was this rank desertion, a running to cover under the protection of Gloucester's momentary ally? Or did it presage the duke of Buckingham's forthcoming revolt in October 1483 against King Richard III? How many of Hastings' retainers joined the duke is not known. But in 1485 Henry VII was to knight two of them, Humphrey Stanley and James Blount, for fighting against Richard III on Bosworth Field, land that had belonged to William, Lord Hastings.[11]

[10] *The Stonor Letters and Papers,* ed. C. L. Kingsford, II, 161.

[11] Stanley and Blount were made bannerets after the king's victory over Lambert Simnel's adherents at the battle of Stoke, 1487, and 4 of Hastings' retainers were made knights after this battle: Henry Willoughby, Ralph Longford [Langforthe], Maurice Berkeley, and Ralph Shirley, *The Paston Letters,* ed. J. Gairdner, VI, 187.

II
LORD HASTINGS AND HIS RETAINERS:
GOOD LORDSHIP

Hastings' band of retainers constituted only one of the several circles of clients whom a great lord commonly attracted. Like other peers of the realm, he had first of all and close at hand his household servants who, by statute, lawfully wore his livery. They formed an immediate and constant entourage composed of domestics, officers who managed his estates, manned his castles, ran his households, and kept his chancery. Then came the knights, esquires, and gentlemen retained by indenture, and out beyond them was an ill-defined and amorphous group of men called well-willers. Such was Sir John Paston who could boast that he had never been a "lord's sworn man" and yet who intermittently sought the chamberlain's favor and good lordship. The constancy of this outer ring was far from fixed, and the loyalty of such men varied in direct ratio to a magnate's momentary influence with the king or any other source of power and preferment. Finally, the lords had connections, formalized by written agreements, with one another. Lord Grey of Codnor, in 1464, and Lord Mountjoy, in 1480, indented with Lord Hastings in contracts phrased in very different language from that appearing in the 88 commoners' indentures. In return for Hastings' "faithful, true heart, love, and kind cosinage . . . Lord Grey, trusting always of the continuance of the same," promised and bound himself "to bear good will to the said Lord Hastings, always taking his part and quarrel and to be with him against all manner of persons, his liegeance, my lord of Clarence, and Sir Thomas Burgt, knight, only except." Such an alliance, like an international treaty, might be no more than a scrap of paper and no more durable than self-interest might require or allow. Or it might serve to bring the whole system of retaining into play upon the field of battle or in the realm of politics.

The political activities, the county affiliation, and the social status of Lord Hastings' company of retainers exhibit both the purposes and the consequences of retaining by indenture. The names and rank of 90 men retained by Hastings at one time or another between 1461 and 1483 are known, and the indentures signed and sealed by 67 of them survive. Of these men, 20 are described in formal, legal language as "gentlemen", 59 as "esquires", and 9 as "knights", while 2 of them, Henry, Lord Grey of Codnor, and John Blount, Lord Mountjoy, were peers. Not only was none of Hastings' retainers below the rank of gentleman, but all of them bore names of prominent and substantial county families. Gentility marks off these men retained by indenture from the household retainers, domestic officers and servants, and from the liveried men-at-arms who sometimes resided on a magnate's estates. And they certainly were not unemployed veterans back from the French Wars.[1]

However, this body of minor aristocrats did provide a reservoir of potential warriors for Lord Hastings and, through him, for his own lord, King Edward IV. But they lived apart from their lord, upon their own lands, and about a dozen of the extant indentures mention the retainer's residence. Several of the contracts stipulate that Hastings should give the retainer "reasonable warning" when calling upon him for service, and this supposes that he did not normally live in the lord's houses or castles. Many of these men covenanted to come up, at Hastings' summons, "defensibly arrayed;" and each agreed to bring with him as large a number of his own friends, tenants, or "well-willers" as he could raise or as accorded with his rank. These same retainers in time of peace performed civil functions, and their governmental activities prove that lordship was still, as it had been in Anglo-Saxon England, a political as well as a military device.

The peace-time services that many of Hastings' men performed indicate that retaining by indenture was becoming, as the fifteenth century wore on, more and more civil in its purpose. Retainers contracted "to do service", as William Dethick's indenture states, "as well in time of peace as in time of war;" and the perdurability of these agreements, "for term of life," enabled Lord Hastings to maintain so successfully his power in a cluster of midland counties. Although his principal seats at Kirby Hall and at Ashby-de-la-Zouch, were in Leicestershire, where Thomas More said "the lord chamberlain's chief power lay", by far the greatest number, 32 of the 90 known retainers, was associated with Derbyshire. Sixty-five of the 76 men who have been identified

---

[1] Sixty-seven original indentures, the parts signed and sealed by retainers and kept by Lord Hastings, are at the H. E. Huntington Library, HA Family Papers, Box 104. This also contains a list of 87 retainers written on parchment no earlier than Elizabeth I's reign and probably in 1622. The texts of these indentures and 2 from British Museum MS. Cotton, Titus B VIII, with an analysis and tabulation are below, Appendix A. All statements concerning the indentures, the names, and the number of retainers are, unless otherwise noted, based on the evidence contained in Appendix A. See also Plate I.

with counties belonged to Hastings' home-land—strategically the very heart of England—Staffordshire, Derby, Nottingham, and Leicester. Fourteen retainers appear to have been connected with Leicestershire, the same number with Stafford, and 5 with Nottingham. Yorkshire was probably the home of 3 retainers, Warwick and Cheshire of 2 each, while one came from Rutland, Lincolnshire, and Oxford respectively; and William Griffith was from North Wales. The 2 peers, Grey of Codnor and Mountjoy, lived in Derbyshire, and although they and several of the 30 commoners from that county held lands or offices in Staffordshire and Leicester, too, Derbyshire, where Hastings enjoyed the "rule" of the borough, provided over a third of his men.[2]

This corps of retainers constituted a permanent organization through which the chamberlain's influence and power could permeate the midlands.[3] A lord's control over county government by nominating the local officers was, as Plummer pointed out years ago, a foremost objective of retaining. Many of Hastings' servants were sheriffs and justices of the peace; and his company, like a political machine, assured him of the "rule" over his home-land. When the duke of Clarence and the earl of Warwick turned against Edward IV in 1469, they complained, hypocritically, of magnates about the king who, "by their maintenances in the countries where they dwelt or where they have rule, will not suffer the king's laws to be executed upon those whom they owed favor unto".[4] Besides securing Hastings' power in county politics, his retainers also provided him with men who supported him in

[2] The biographical data about each of the 90 known retainers are drawn from a variety of printed sources, too exensive to be cited for each man. Standard genealogical guides, Victoria and other county histories, archeological society publications, Wedgwood's *History of Parliament, 1439–1509,* the *Calendars of Patent* and *Close Rolls* provided most of the information for the collection of which I am indebted to Mr. Jack Upper. Over a dozen of the families concerned appear, with references to printed sources, in G. W. Marshall, *The Genealogist's Guide.*

[3] A lord's company may have been a cohesive, but not necessarily a congenial and compatible, body of men. In 1469 Sir John Gresley, Sir Thomas Stathom, William Babington, esquire, (all Hastings' retainers at various dates) and 6 others sued Thomas Meverell, also a Hastings retainer, for trespass by breaking into their closes and houses. *(Derbyshire Archeological Soc. Journal,* XXX (1908), 18.) Some of the retainers were inter-married. Thomas Curson married Sandria, daughter of Sir Thomas Gresley; William Moton married Sir Robert Harcourt's daughter; and John Davers' son married John Shirley's daughter. Whether marriage increased the degree of compatibility is a matter for speculation, but it indicates a personal and social connection.

[4] These articles were put, in form at least, into the mouths of "the commons." J. Warkworth, *Chronicle of . . . King Edward the Fourth,* Camden Soc. 1839, p. 49.

national affairs—either on the field of battle or, on occasion, in the house of commons. Between 10 and 14 (10 certainly and possibly 4 more) of the retainers, besides the 2 peers, sat in one or more of Edward IV's parliaments. But the names of only 64 % of all the members between 1461 and 1483 are known, so perhaps as many as 17 to 22 (19 %–25 %) of Hastings' 88 commoners actually sat. Of the 10 retainers whose election to the house of commons is certain, 6 were knights before Hastings died in 1483, and Henry VII knighted 3 of the remaining 4. Furthermore, 10 others of the 79 esquires and gentlemen were to become knights after Edward IV's reign, and these honors are proof of the retainers' social prestige and of their military prowess or political dexterity.[5]

However, a comparison of the number of Hastings' servants who sat in Edward IV's parliaments with the total membership of the commons diminishes the impressiveness of these figures. In the first place, there should have been about 1760 members of the 6 parliaments held between 1461 and 1483 of whom the names of only 64 %, 1123 are known. Of this number, 90 identifications are admitted to be doubtful, so when these are deducted only 1033 of the 1760, or 58 %, are certain. The percentage, then, of Hastings' men, whether the 10 certain identifications or the 14 possible ones be used, is very small, either 0.97 % or at most 1.2 % of the 1033 M.P.'s known by name. The 10 certain members all sat as knights of the shire, and Hastings' retainers constituted 2.25 % of the 444 county representatives at the 6 parliaments. Even this figure is not overly impressive; but if each of the 35 to 40 peers normally present at Edward IV's parliaments procured the election of 2.25 % of the county members, then about 80 % of the 74 knights would be accounted for.[6] There is evidence that the lords of parliament procured first the nomination, and then the election, of their "well-willers" as knights of the shire during the century preceding Edward IV's reign; and the Paston Letters tell how Hastings himself was believed to be a broker in parliamentary seats.[7]

[5] For the tabulation of the retainers who were members of the house of commons and of those who were sheriffs, see, Appendix B. The statistics following are drawn from these tables.

[6] Edward IV summoned 45 lords temporal to the 1461 parliament and at least 40 were actually present. *The Fane Fragment of the 1461 Lords' Journal,* ed. W. H. Dunham, Jr., p. 91.

[7] *The Paston Letters,* ed. J. Gairdner, V, 137, 148–52. But cf. V, 178 (26 March 1473) from which MacFarlane concludes Sir John was a member of the 1472–75 parliament: John Paston to Sir John Paston, "I pray God send you the Holy Ghost among you in the Parliament House." K. B. MacFarlane, "Parliament and 'Bastard Feudalism'," *Trans. Royal Hist. Soc.,* 4th Ser., XXVI (1944), 63.

Sir John Paston, that genial young man-about-town and a well-willer of Lord Hastings, wished a seat in the 1472 parliament. His first maneuver was to write from London to his brother, John, to manage his election from Norfolk. But his request came too late, and John the youngest could report only that his brother's election was a thing "impossible to be brought about; for my lord of Norfolk and my lord of Suffolk were agreed more than a fortnight ago to have Sir Robert Wingfield and Sir Richard Harcourt." John then wrote to Yarmouth urging that town to make Sir John a burgess, but their seats had been promised three weeks before. However, he got James Arblaster, the duchess of Norfolk's retainer, to write to the bailiff of Malden in Essex, and his letter discloses how good lordship was used to get a magnate's henchman elected:

"Right trusty friend, I commend me to you, praying you call to your mind that, like as you and I communed of, it were necessary for my lady [of Norfolk] and you all, her servants and tenants, to have this parliament as for one of the burgesses of the town of Malden, such a man of worship, and of wit as were towards my said lady; and also such one as is in favor of the king and of the lords of his council nigh about his person. Certifying you that my said lady for her part and such as be of her counsel, be most agreeable that both you and all such as be her farmers and tenants and well-willers should give your voice to a worshipful knight and one of my lady's counsel, Sir John Paston, which stands greatly in favor with my lord chamberlain [Hastings]; and what my said lord chamberlain may do with the king and with all the lords of England, I trust it be not unknown to you most of any man alive. Wherefore, by the means of the said Sir John Paston to my said lord chamberlain, both my lady and you of the town could not have a meeter man to be for you in the parliament, to have your needs sped at all seasons. Wherefore, I pray you labor all such as be my lady's servants, tenants, and well-willers to give their voices to the said Sir John Paston, and that you fail not to speed my lady's intent in this matter, as you intend to do her as great a pleasure as if you gave her an hundred pounds . . ."

Despite the duchess's sponsorship and his own connection with Lord Hastings, Sir John was not to be a Malden burgess. Yet John the youngest's devotion to his easy-going brother, and his confidence in Hastings' powers were so great that he could write to Sir John: "if you miss to be burgess of Malden, and my lord chamberlain will, you may be in for another place; there be a dozen towns in England that choose no burgesses which ought to do, and you may set in for one of those towns and [if] you be friended."

Whether or not Hastings secured Sir John's election in 1472 is not certain. But evidently he supported his indentured retainers for five of them sat as knights of the shire in this parliament and perhaps two others as burgesses. This number, 5 to 7, was about double the average number of seats held by the chamberlain's men in Edward IV's six parliaments. His retainers secured 25 seats in all, of which 15 can be positively identified with his retainers and possibly 10 others. But they constituted only 1.5 %, or possibly 2.2 %, of the known members of the house of commons between 1461 and 1483.[8] However, an examination of the individual parliaments will change these unreal "averages" to both less and more meaningful statistics. At the first parliament of 1461, John Gresley was the only known member whose name appears among Hastings' company. Again in 1463, only Sir Simon Montfort is listed among the commons; and there are only two retainers, Maurice Berkeley and Thomas Danvers, who may have been the members with the same names at the 1467 parliament. For Edward IV's first three parliaments, at the most only 4, and perhaps only 2, of Hastings retainers were among the known members. Certainly during the 1460's the chamberlain's retainers, so far as the evidence indicates, did not constitute even a bloc, let along a faction or a party, in the house of commons. At the last parliament of the reign, in January 1483, only 1 certain and 2 possible identifications have been found. So at four of the six parliaments Hastings seems to have placed no more than 5, perhaps 7, of his retainers. In these instances the evidence, incomplete at it is, argues against the contention that the fifteenth-century house of commons was dependent upon the peers of the realm.

In the other 2 parliaments, however, the data tend to modify this conclusion. At the 1472 parliament, which had 7 sessions before its dissolution in 1475, 5 retainers certainly sat, and possibly 2 more, out of the 283 known members—1.76 % to 2.47 % of the total. If half a dozen members, as in the eighteenth century, could give the lord or magnate who got them seats influence in the lower house, then Hastings had his spokesmen there. Furthermore, the 5 certain members were knights of the shire—presumably the men of quality in the house— 2 for Derbyshire and one each from Warwick, Lincoln, and Leicestershire. The doubt about the other 2, Maurice Berkeley and Thomas Danvers, names of Hastings' retainers it is true, arises because they sat for Southampton and Downton, Wilts., localities remote from the midlands. But if John Paston was correct when he wrote, in 1472, that the lord chamberlain might put a man in parliament if he wished, then perhaps the M.P.'s, Berkeley and Danvers, and Hastings' retainers were the same men. This parliament was, of course, the first to be elected after Edward's restoration in 1471, and the advantage to the king of having loyal Yorkist supporters in commons is obvious.

---

[8] The average is between 3 and 4 retainers for each parliament; or, if extrapolated figures be used, 5 or 6.

Similarly, the 1478 parliament also met for a particular political purpose—to attaint the duke of Clarence of treason. On this occasion even more of Hastings' servants sat in the house of commons. Seven members, and perhaps 3 more, of the 291 whose names are known belonged to the chamberlain's company, and they constituted either 2.4 % or 3.44 % of the house. Four retainers, 2 certain and 2 doubtful, represented boroughs, Downton and Westbury in Wiltshire, and Stafford and Leicester. The appearance of 4 of Hastings' men as burgesses, while not unprecedented, was unusual. Thomas Danvers, a man of law, sat only for boroughs—Hindon, Wilts. in 1467, and Downton in 1472, 1478, and 1483; and John Staunton, if he was the retainer of that name, represented Westbury. Lord Hastings' dominance in the local government of Leicestershire and Stafford is enough to explain the choice in 1478 of Thomas Gresley as Stafford's burgess and of John Wigston, merchant and mayor of Leicester in 1469–70, to represent that borough. Of the 8 retainers who were burgesses, 1461–1483, only 2 of them seem to have names which can be certainly identified. Therefore it seems as if Hastings' use of his power and influence to procure the choice of his men as burgesses was an exception rather than the common practice. Most surprising is the case of Derby. Sometime before 1474, this town had "granted and ordained the said lord to have the rule and governance of the said town," and in that year James Blount's contract with Hastings stipulated "that the said James shall occupy and have the rule, in his absence, of the said town." And yet not one of Derby's burgesses during Edward IV's reign bore any of the names on the list of Hastings' retainers. His apparent indifference to the opportunity to use the midland boroughs to build for himself and for the king a bloc of henchmen in the house of commons confirms the impression that only seldom did the great lords bother about the choice of burgesses.[9]

[9] M. McKisack, *The Parliamentary Representation of the English Boroughs during the Middle Ages,* pp. 62–63 for the letter (*c.* 1470) from Ralph Neville, earl of Westmoreland, to the mayor of Grimsby requiring him to turn over to him the writ so that he could appoint 2 members of his council to be the burgesses whose expenses the earl would pay. Cf., *H. M. C. Report* XIV, vol. 8, 252; also, *idem,* 250 for Viscount Beaumont's letter to the mayor of Grimsby in *c.* 1459 regarding the election to parliament of his servant, Ralph Chandler. *Idem,* 255–56 for similar instances at Grimsby in 1557, 1558–59, and 1562. In 1597 the earl of Essex asked that he might name the burgesses for Shrewsbury, *idem,* V, 333.

McKisack remarked (pp. 109–114) the exceptional character and higher social status of the burgesses elected to the 1472 and 1478 parliaments; but she presented only a few instances of electing lords' retainers.

An instance of a town profiting from a peer's power occurred in 1467 when

A group of 7, perhaps 10, of the chamberlain's followers in the 1478 parliament provided him with spokesmen in the lower chamber, but it hardly made a faction, let alone a party. Those retainers who were knights of the shire may have asserted leadership and influence, especially if known to be Hastings' men, way beyond their numerical strength which was at best only 3 % of the known members. But if a dozen peers, in league with king and court, contributed a like proportion of M.P.'s, then there would have been a sufficient number of members in the house to direct, and probably to carry through, the government's bills and policies. The parliament of 1478 and that of 1472 are two instances when Lord Hastings seems to have deliberately placed his men in the commons; but even for these parliaments the evidence is by no means sufficient to prove that the lords of parliament, or the court, really determined the composition of the lower house. The year when Edward IV was making his final settlement with his faithless brother was certainly a time when the king needed members whose loyalty to him was beyond cavil. But even if Hastings and other government peers did put a few men into the house of commons on this occasion, and likewise in 1472, their proportion of the total membership was scarcely large enough to destroy utterly that chamber's independence. Other more direct methods of exerting government or baronial pressure upon the members were, of course, available; but to have passed up the chance to have in parliament a man already sworn to be a lord's faithful servant would seem a curious contradiction to the supposed logic of Yorkist politics.

However, a further consideration of the statistics for the parliaments of 1472 and 1478 casts even more doubt upon their significance. The 10 retainers certainly members of these 2 parliaments, where the theory of packing seems most plausible, were without doubt Hastings' men. But the date on which each man bound himself by oath, promise, or indenture to be his "retained servant" is less certain. For those retainers

Lord Wenlock procured a charter of incorporation for the borough of Wenlock by reason of the town's assistance to Edward IV in gaining the kingship. *H. M. C. Report,* X, Part iv, 420–21.

J. C. Wedgwood (*History of Parliament, Biographies,* p. xxxiii) identified 140 members of the house of commons, 1439–1509, as the retainers of 18 lords temporal, of 2 bishops, and one abbess. But 140 is a small fraction of the estimated members of the house during these 70 years. Wedgwood's identification of nearly 50 of John of Gaunt's retainers as members of the 12 parliaments, 1372–82, has been analyzed and its importance minimized by Dr. N. B. Lewis whose skeptical attitude the present analysis of Hastings' retainers confirms. *Eng. Hist. Rev.,* XLV (1930), 623–25; XLVIII (1933), 391.

whose original indentures survive, a date *on* and *after* which they were retained is known. But they may have joined Hastings' company at a previous date by oath or promise without a written indenture, or by an earlier indenture now lost. This was the case with Nicholas Kneveton for whom 2 indentures from 1465 and 1474 survive, and also with John Harcourt who signed indentures in 1474 and 1479.[10] For 2 of the 7 retainers in the 1472 house of commons, no indentures, hence no dates for their retaining, exist; and the indentures of the other 5 were dated in 1474, 1475, 1479 and 1481. Unless lost indentures bearing a date before 1472 be supposed, then these men sat in that parliament *before* they became Hastings' servants. Likewise, 3, and perhaps 4, of his retainers who were elected to the 1478 parliament signed their indentures after the elections were held. And so only 2 of the 7 retainers at the 1472 parliament could have indented with Hastings before they were elected; and in the 1478 house 3 retainers (possibly 6) may have indented before their election, while 4 were M.P.'s before Hastings retained them. In fact, this analysis leads rather pointedly to the converse of a common assumption, that by being a lord's retainer a man might gain a seat in the house of commons. If the date on the indenture indicates accurately just when a man, for the first time, bound himself to Hastings, then 7, or perhaps 8, of the 10 retainers who were certainly M.P.'s in 1472 and 1478 sat in parliament *before* they joined the chamberlain's company. For 2 of the 3 other men no indentures, hence no dates, are known; and they, too, may have been retained after their elections. The third, however, was William Moton, one of the knights for Leicestershire in 1478, three years after he had contracted with Hastings, and he is the only retainer whose indenture is dated before his first appearance in parliament and whose election Hastings may have aided. On the other hand, Sir William Trussell, elected in 1472, did not sign his indenture until 10 March 1475, just 4 days before this parliament was dissolved. At this time, he was in France with Edward's army, and he had contracted with the king on 21 November 1474 for service of war for one year with 6 spears and 60 archers. Trussell's military competence, more than his membership in the house of commons, may have attracted Hastings who agreed to pay him an annuity of £ 10. Furthermore, the payment of a cash fee suggests that Hastings desired Trussell's attachment even more than the knight wanted the peer's good lordship and that the chamberlain had had to bargain with this retainer. Similarly, the unusually detailed contract in 1469 with Sir Simon Montfort, an M.P. in

---

[10] See Appendix A.

1933281

3*

1463, suggests an agreement reached only after extensive negotiation.[11] Likewise, Hastings seems likely to have initiated the agreement with Robert Tailboys. He sat in commons for Lincolnshire in 1472 and again in 1478 and was knighted on the rising of the latter parliament; but his indenture was not dated until 4 October 1481.

As so often in human relations, the impetus, like an alternating current, flowed in both directions. The only safe deduction from this analysis of Hastings' retainers is that many of them, no doubt the majority, and especially the younger men, bound themselves to him of their "own free will and motion" as the indentures often state. But in the case of several others, notably the knights and members of parliament, Lord Hastings very likely was the one who took the initiative and sought their service and support. Another inference, seemingly unavoidable, is that parliament in Yorkist England did not yet hold the allure and attraction for the gentry that it was to have a century later. Nor does the high esprit of Elizabethan and Stuart members of the house of commons, eager to serve without either recompense or reimbursement of their expenses, seem to have prevailed among Edward IV's faithful commons. Certainly that spirit of *noblesse oblige,* so often ascribed with great exaggeration to the eighteenth-century governing class, had not yet become a cult; and several hard-headed or tight-fisted Yorkist members sued, successfully too, to recover their expenses. Indeed, there is no indication that the 20 gentlemen and 59 esquires belonging to Hastings' company rushed pell-mell to gain election to London's best club.

On the contrary, there are hints, besides the inferences drawn from the 1472 and 1478 parliaments, that sometimes the retainer's ambition ran the other way. At least one of them, John Cokeyn, esquire, (retained in 1475) invoked Hastings' good lordship to get him exempted from the onerous burden of royal service. In 1482, this retainer procured a letter patent exempting him from serving on juries and assizes and from being made assessor, collector, mayor, sheriff, constable, bailiff, "or other officer or minister of the king against his will."[12] Similarly, John Paston the youngest urged his brother to have Sir Richard Harcourt, M.P. for Norfolk, and if need be Lord Hastings, get

---

[11] For a copy of Trussell's war indenture, Bodleian Library MS. Dugdale 2, p. 269. *Idem,* p. 270 contains a copy of a similar indenture for war service in Normandy and France for one year between Edward IV and Sir Simon Montfort. Only one of Hastings' indentures, besides Trussell's, carried a cash annuity. That with Nicholas Kneveton in 1465 provided for an annual fee of £ 4, but a second contract without any fee superseded it in 1474. For Montfort's original war indenture, P.R.O., E101/72/2/ no. 1039.

[12] *Cal. Patent Rolls, 1476–1485,* pp. 315–16.

his cousin, John Blenerhasset, "out of that thankless office", collector of taxes. Especially costly was the shrievalty, and writs of privy seal indicate how Edward IV gave indemnities of £160 and £240 to ex-sheriffs for the losses they had sustained. Even "rewards" of as much as £100, such as those Nicholas Kneveton, William Blount, and Harry Pierpont received in 1469 for their services as sheriffs, were hardly the kind of inducement to make men rush after the office.[13] The Yorkist gentry, in their attitude towards politics and government service, do not seem to have had that passionate desire to appear in the house of commons enjoyed by seventeenth-century parliament men. The court of Edward IV, far more than his parliaments, was the pathway to profit and preferment through royal or baronial favor. Real power, the gentry saw, was not at Westminster, but nearer home. Most of Hastings' retainers found it in the midlands where they spent their lives promoting family, friend, and kinsman; and by serving in local offices they acquired for themselves and their lord an ascendancy in the county milieu.

The number of Hastings' men who served as sheriffs, justices of the peace, and in other county offices provides a truer estimate of the political significance of retaining by indenture. Here the evidence, even statistically, is more impressive than the intermittent appearance of a few retainers at parliaments. And here again, as might be expected, most of the shrievalties held by Hastings' retainers were in Derbyshire, Staffordshire, and Leicester. Certainly 19, and possibly 22, of the chamberlain's adherents served as sheriffs during the 22 years between November 1461 and the spring of 1483; and half a dozen others (and also the sons of Hastings' retainers) were to be pricked for sheriff during the next two decades. In Edward IV's reign, 8 retainers in 12 of the 22 years were sheriffs in Staffordshire; 7 of them in 9 of the 22 years held the joint shrievalty of Nottinghamshire and Derbyshire; while 5 retainers in 5 years occupied the office for Warwickshire and Leicestershire. Two others served in Lincoln, each for only one year, and 3 were the sheriffs, for a year, of Northamptonshire, Rutland and Wiltshire.

---

[13] P.R.O., E404/74/2 mem. 86. A writ of privy seal, 9 Nov. 1469, appointed William Blount, esquire, to be sheriff of Nottingham and Derby for the next year; and the treasurer and chamberlains of the exchequer were to give him a tally for £100 to be levied at the exchequer of receipt against the issues of this "sheriffwick" ... "for our reward." Rewards also were ordered for Henry Pierpont, esquire, Nicholas Kneveton, esquire (sheriff 1466–67 and Hastings' retainer), and Sir Robert Clifton, late sheriffs. *Idem,* mem. 87 for similar cases in other counties with rewards from £160 to £240 for losses sustained. Cf. *idem,* mems. 53, 97, 99.

Again, as in the case of his retainers in the house of commons, statistics become more indicative when the specific years—and the political events occuring therein—are considered. Up until Edward IV's expulsion, in 1470, and his restoration the next spring, only 4, perhaps 5, of Hastings' men served as sheriffs. Then with the appointment of Sir Simon Montfort as sheriff of Warwick and Leicestershire on 11 April 1471, three days before the battle of Barnet, and the appointment the next November of 3, perhaps 4, retainers as sheriffs of Nottinghamshire and Derby, of Staffordshire, of Warwickshire and Leicester, and possibly of Wiltshire, the restored government utilized the civil as well as the military services of Hastings' fellowship.[14] The sheriff of Nottingham and Derby was one of the chamberlain's retainers in 1471 and again in 1472, in 1475–1478, and in 1480 and 1482. The sheriff of Staffordshire, too, in 8 of the 12 years, 1471–1482, was a Hastings man, while 5 retainers during the same period served as the sheriff of Warwickshire and Leicester. The essential point that these statistics establish is that both Lord Hastings' concern—and the significance of retaining—was territorial, local more than national. He and his retainers worked to maintain control over the society and the people of the midland counties. Then, secondly, the intensity of the retainers' political activity corresponded chronologically to the increase in Lord Hastings' power and prestige after Edward's restoration in 1471 and until his death in 1483.

However, the question of the dates when these men became Lord Hastings' retainers must be remembered. A collation of the year when a retainer was sheriff with the date of his indenture produces only a neutral result. While 9 men signed their contracts with Hastings *before* they served as sheriffs, 10 (possibly 11) others contracted with him *after* their first shrievalties. For 2 retainers who were sheriffs, neither the indentures nor their dates survive. This equal division suggests that Hastings retained some men because they already had political power in the Midlands, as evidenced by their service as sheriffs, while others, of their own "mere motion" became his retained servants. Once they had become retainers, then their connection with the chamberlain may have helped them to gain, or compelled them to accept, the shrievalty.

---

[14] Richard, earl of Warwick, wrote to the mayor of Southampton in October 1470 to restore a carvel belonging to Montfort which Henry VI's enemies had robbed. Warwick described him as "our servant" and "my right trusty and well-beloved friend." Sir Simon's position and his loyalties in 1470–71 left a confused pattern for posterity. But by April 1471 he was back in Edward IV's camp, if really he had left it; and he may have continued a sincere Yorkist until finally an extravagant loyalty led him to support Perkin Warbeck for which he was beheaded in 1495. *H. M. C. Report,* XI, part iii, 113.

Sir Simon Montfort's affinity with Lord Hastings may explain, in part, his removal by the Lancastrians in 1470 from the panel of the Warwickshire justices of the peace and then his appointment by Edward IV in 1471 as sheriff of that county. But in the last analysis, the motive and initiative in seeking office rested with the individual. Except in the year of crisis when his lord may have put pressure on him to take office, the man himself probably decided whether or not he chose to run and so to incur all the expense and hazard that even county offices entailed. Conclusive answers to such questions would require a biography of each retainer. But Hastings' servants held many local offices, and some of them probably sought, and may have even enjoyed administrative authority and political power. Perhaps a few even aspired to sit in parliament. But for others, office was very likely a burden and rather the fulfillment of a duty to their lord and to their king.

An even larger number of Hastings' retainers, 33, were commissioned between 1461 and 1483 justices of the peace. The 2 peers, Grey of Codnor and Mountjoy, and at least 31 of the knights, esquires, and gentlemen belonged to commissions of the peace, and many of them and their sons were to serve as justices during the decade after Edward's death.[15] Often one man was appointed in the same or different years to serve in 2 or more shires, so an identification of the retainers who were J.P.'s with single counties is impossible. Nevertheless, the lists of commissions assign most of them to Derbyshire, Staffordshire, and Nottingham. Furthermore, several of Hastings' men held various other administrative posts. A few were assessors of subsidies; some served in commissions of array, others as commissioners of dikes and sewers; while half a dozen were stewards or bailiffs of the king's lands and forests, and 4 were escheators. A dozen or more retainers enjoyed remunerative offices, such as constable of the king's castle at Dublin, controller of customs at Southampton, constable of Vernon in Normandy, ranger of Cannock, and lieutenant of Hammes. Such appointments were the rewards which Hastings' followers garnered through his influence at court. They compensated for the unpaid services in county offices in which either the chamberlain's good lordship or their agreement to serve at his command had placed many of his men.

Several of Hastings' company went with him on Edward's expedition to France in 1475, and at least 5 of them brought along men-at-arms and archers. Lord Grey of Codnor and Hastings himself were among the 19 peers serving with the royal dukes, Clarence and Gloucester, who

---

[15] For the names of the retainers commissioned justices of the peace, see Appendix B. The commissions, counties, and dates may be found in the *Cal. Patent Rolls, 1461–1483, sub nom.* of each retainer.

shared the chief command under the king. Sir Nicholas Longford and
Sir William Trussell each brought 6 spears and 60 archers, while James
Blount took with him 3 men-at-arms and 20 archers. John Harcourt
was licensed in 1475 to enlist men to go overseas, and Sir John Stanley's
son, John, with 6 archers went as a man-at-arms. Undoubtedly others
of Hastings' retainers, like Sir Simon Montfort, "accompanied with as
many persons defensibly arrayed as he may goodly make or assemble,"
joined this expedition and enabled the chamberlain to serve his own
lord, King Edward.[16] Here, in time of war, the original *raison d'etre*
of retaining cropped up again. The need for an army was one reason for
perpetuating this system. Thereby the king, through the peers, could
maintain a skeleton staff which could recruit still larger military forces.
Also, some retainers served the king on a temporary basis, doubtless
prompted by their lord to do so. At Calais in 1477, the royal establishment included among the foot-archers 5 of Lord Hastings' indentured
retainers: William Palmer, Henry Columbell, Richard Eyre, Rauf Pole,
and John Shirley. When retainers were on the king's service in time
of war, the 1429 act of parliament provided, their lords might give
them "their liveries." The 40 men-at-arms and the 300 archers whom
Lord Hastings led to France in 1475 wore his badge—a "black bull's
head, raised horns and pys [breast], and about the neck a crown gold."
At other times they may have worn this lord's second badge, a more
belligerent one, the manticora or mantyger, or its alternative form, a
bayon or baboon. The devise of the bull's head was used on the
Hastings' standard; William's grandfather, Sir Ralph, had borne it;
and his own grandson was to give it to his men in 1544 when he went
against France with Henry VIII.[16A]

In return for such services to his lord and to his king, a retainer
sometimes got his reward. Two years after the French invasion, the king
granted to Nicholas Kneveton the lieutenancy of the forest of Kynfare
and the stewardship of the manor with the fees and profits "for his

[16] J. Wedgwood, *History of Parliament, Biographies, sub nom.* (John Harcourt under his father, Sir Robert). *Cal. Patent Rolls, 1467–1477*, p. 515; P.R.O.,
E101/71/6/ nos. 987, 998 and E101/72/2/ no. 1039 for the military indentures
between the king and Trussell, Blount, and Montfort.

[16A] *Edward IV's French Expedition of 1475: the Leaders and their Badges*,
ed. F. P. Barnard, Facsimile, fol. 2, and p. B2; British Museum MSS. Harley
4632, fols. 235, 239, 247v and 992, fol. 98; Additional 40742, fol. 11; Additional Charters 19808 for Hastings' seal. See below, Plates II–V. I am greatly indebted to the Richmond Herald, Anthony R. Wagner, for instructing me on the
heraldic nomenclature and for authenticating these badges. He wrote me that
"it was quite common for a nobleman to have more than one badge at that date"
[early sixteenth century].

good service in all the victorious fields and armies within the realm and beyond the seas." James Blount, too, was rewarded with the lieutenancy of Hammes, in France, perhaps through the good lordship of Hastings, then the governor-general of Calais.[17]

Good lordship, after all, was what Lord Hastings had promised each retainer when he contracted to serve him. No matter how the indenture phrased it—to be good and tender lord, gracious lord, faithful lord, favorable lord, or "to owe his special favor"—the purport was the same. Precisely what good lordship meant, what the term connoted, the indentures do not explain. It was a thing contemporaries understood, something they took for granted and did not stop to define. Nor was good lordship, so exasperating in its vagueness to moderns, limited in practice to men formally retained by oath, promise, or indenture. Even Lord Hastings, who had contracts with 90 retainers, extended his good lordship beyond this formal company to other friends and well-willers, and between them influence and favor flowed back and forth.

Such were the Paston brothers, Sir John and John the youngest, who in the 1470's belonged to Hastings' retinue at Guisnes and Calais. Ever since 1462 when Sir John proudly had claimed to be "well acquainted with my Lord Hastings and my Lord Dacre which be now the greatest about the king's person", he had worked hard to gain, and to use, the chamberlain's good lordship—but without becoming what he called a "lord's sworn man". Sir John, as a man about London and a friend and well-willer of Lord Hastings, constantly sought his favor and influence. This young courtier, several cuts below his brother in character, spent much time at London or with the court, and his unearned knighthood, bestowed before he was twenty-one, turned his head and loosed his morals. Dazzled by the *haut monde* of the capital, Sir John found need to seek aid from men with worldly power. But he let the means, their favor and acquaintance, obscure from his vision the end—the furtherance of the family whose head he was by birth. He was loathe to come to Norfolk, to his mother's great dismay, and win the country folks' affection upon which the Pastons built their local influence. His letters home, though refreshed by wit and humor, were filled with London tittle-tattle and court gossip; in contrast, his

[17] *Cal. Patent Rolls, 1476–1485*, p. 47; J. Wedgwood, *History of Parliament, Biographies*, p. 84; British Museum MS. Additional 46455–6, fol. 14, the muster rolls and lists of officers and men at Calais, 17 Edward IV [1477]. Mr. P. Derek Noton of Sheffield University very graciously allowed me to use his transcript of this manuscript. Three other foot-archers, Thomas Eyre, Ralph Bradshaw, and William Aston, bore the surnames, but not the Christian ones, of Hastings' retainers and were probably brothers or cousins.

brother's earnest reports on crops and litigation exhibit John the youngest's self-reliance. Sir John had lapsed into the protegé's easy dependence on a lord, and his fear of offending the high and mighty made him indecisive. Once, in Hastings' absence from the city, Sir John could only write, "when he cometh, then shall I know what to do". Sir John, like so many petty aristocrats, was angling for an advantageous marriage, one for land not love, but in this too he failed.

More successful was his effort to procure Hastings' good lordship and that of other councillors to recover for his family Caister Castle. This episode, one of vast moment to the Pastons but probably a routine affair to Hastings, demonstrates the working of good lordship—pressure by the man of influence upon one's enemy. The contest over Caister arose because the Pastons' cloudy title had given the duke of Norfolk the chance to gain possession of the manor under cover of the law. Upon the death of Sir John's father in May 1466, the duke "purchased" rights to the property, and by September 1469 he had acquired possession of the great mansion at Caister. For nearly 7 years thereafter, Sir John and his brother tried every conceivable device, except a suit at common law, to force the duke to relinquish the manor, but all to no avail. Sir John, in November 1472, got letters from the king to the duke, and wrote to his mother, "the king hath specially done for me in this case, and hath pitied me, and so have the lords, in right great comfort, that if this fail that I shall have undelayed justice". Lord Hastings, too, was expected to intervene in Sir John's behalf, but his brother impatiently complained "I marvel that I hear no word of the letters that my lord chamberlain should send to my lord and my lady [of Norfolk] for Caister. It is best that my lord chamberlain write to my lady by some privy token between them and let a man of his come with the letters." But letters had no effect upon the duke and he continued in possession. Two years later, in 1475, when Sir John was at Calais, he informed his brother that the marshall and the council there had written to Lord Hastings, and also to the master of the rolls and Sir Thomas Montgomery urging them to "labor both the king and my lord [Hastings] to entreat my lord of Norfolk, my lady his wife, and their council to do for me all that reason will."

Although the Paston brothers persisted in their efforts throughout 1475, they failed to move the king to action. Edward's hesitancy and his procrastination indicate how delicate a balance the king maintained between his litigious magnates. His subjects' conflicts gave the strong king countless opportunities to intervene and to compel them to acknowledge his primacy; but conversely, quarrels such as the Paston-Norfolk feud, were for the weak king occasions to make enemies, rather than to win friends. Even though Edward IV's hold upon the throne in 1475 might seem secure, he dared not take too strong a line towards the duke of Norfolk. However, in October of this year, he opened a pourparler with the duke at Calais. From there, Sir John wrote home that he hoped soon to have the castle again; but the duchess's account of her husband's conversation with the king was less optimistic. She reported to John Paston, the youngest, that King Edward had asked Norfolk, somewhat gingerly, if he actually had said "that the king should as soon have his life as that place" and that the duke had answered, "yea". Thereupon, the duchess declared, "the king said not a word again, but turned his back and went his way; ... and [if] the king had spoken any word in the world after that, the duke would not have said him nay".

This conversation broke down, nothing was effected, and soon Sir John drew up a formal petition to the king. It declares that for 4 years he had referred his complaint to Norfolk's council (instead of to the king's courts of common law) and that the duke ignored his suit. The petition goes on and tells the king how Sir John "now is out of remedy, without your abundant grace be showed in that behalf, in so much as he is not of power to attempt your laws against [one of] so mighty and noble estate [as the duke's] nor to abide the displeasure of him." Fortunately for Sir John, the duke died unexpectedly a few weeks later, in January 1476, and his amiable widow was free to show the good ladyship that she professed towards the Pastons. She agreed to refer the dispute over Caister to the king's council, and in May they rendered a decision in Sir John's favor. He then wrote proudly to his mother that his "matter" had been "examined by the king's council and declared afore all the lords; ... and all the lords, judges, [and] serjeants have affirmed my title good." This long drawn-out contest shows how necessary was the personal influence of lords and magnates, and that even the king's prestige was needed to effect a settlement outside the course of common law.

When Sir John Paston died in 1479, John the youngest again sought Hastings' aid. His uncle William had tried to take over some of his nephew's manors, and John needed a lord to maintain him in his right. Within ten days of his brother's death, John wrote to his mother, Margaret Paston, that sweet matriarch who so sagaciously directed the family's affairs:

"this I think to do when I come to London, to speak with my lord chamberlain and to win by his means my lord [the bishop] of Ely if I can; and if I may by any of their means cause the king to take my service and my quarrel together, I will ..."

Upon reaching London, Paston at once set in motion the mechanism
of lordship, and soon he could report that the bishop of Ely had promised "that he will be with me against mine uncle in each matter that
I can show that he intendeth to wrong me in." John's cousin, William
Lomnor, already had consulted with "carefull" Margaret Paston and
wrote that they thought it expedient for Paston to have the "lord
chamberlain's good favor and lordship;" but they were sceptical towards
John Morton, bishop of Ely and warned, "deal not with him by our
advice for he will move for treaty" [arbitration]. The next month, John
did not yet know Hastings' intent, but he hoped to ascertain it on the
morrow. But the controversy with his uncle was to drag on for at least
5 years, and John's wife, Margery, tried to enlist the duchess of Norfolk's good ladyship. She had been advised to get Lady Calthorp, her
mother-in-law, and her mother to go together to the duchess and ask
her to be "good and gracious lady" in this dispute. For, she was told,
"one word of a woman should do more than the words of 20 men."[18]

Dame Alice Rotherham was another woman whose good ladyship
had weight in men's affairs. She wrote in behalf of a poor house of
nuns at Grimsby to the mayor asking him "to support them in their
right and to be favorable unto them . . . . . as you will that I do any
thing for you in time to come; and also I shall pray my lord my son
[Thomas Rotherham, bishop of Lincoln and lord chancellor] to be
good lord to you in any matter that you have to do." This petticoat
influence in Edward IV's reign was not new. Back in Henry IV's time,
Margaret, countess of Warwick, had asked the bishop of Norwich for
his good lordship "to aid and support" her poor tenants living in his
territory "as need may be in right and reason for love of me."[19]

Whether it be styled good ladyship or lordship, the use of influence,
social pressure, and favor in behalf of one's friend, kinsman, or protegé
was much in vogue in Yorkist England. For several centuries such
persuasion had worked to make society and politics function smoothly;
and it continued to do so on through the eighteenth century and, perhaps, the nineteenth and twentieth. In the form of aid, support, or
maintenance, good lordship was considered "lawful" when the beneficiary's cause was "rightful"—or, as Hastings' indentures stated, in
accord with "law, conscience, and reason". Here was an appeal to a
higher, though undefined, law of ethics, morality, and custom. No
exception need be taken to Lord Hastings' guarding the lands and minor
heir of his deceased retainer, Sir William Trussell in 1481, the very
year when he, in his will, asked the same favor of his own lord, the

[18] *The Paston Letters*, ed. J. Gairdner, IV, 61; V, 137, 195, 204–05, 215,
253, 256–58, 270; VI, 28, 30, 32, 57, 59.
[19] *H.M.C. Report* XIV, vol. 8, 251.

king. But when good lordship meant that a lord arbitrated his retainer's dispute, thereby cutting out the common law, then these private procedures constituted a secondary system of adjudication. The whole elaborate cult of influence, formalized by covenants between a lord and his retainers, was doubtless in disrespect of the courts of common law. Yet it was a very human way, and at times a more efficient one, for a man to bring his "matter" to a successful conclusion. Custom and usage, surely since the tenth century, sanctioned such extra-regal justice. All save a few squeamish moralists and, of course, the common lawyers, approved a man's maintaining a kinsman, a friend, a well-willer, or a retainer in his "lawful" and "rightful" cause.

At the same time, however, Hastings' retainers, and presumably those of the other peers, worked with the king's government to administer county affairs. The data about them presented above, fragmentary as they are, prove the point that Hastings' servants were men of consequence in their shires. They accepted, whether with avidity or grudgingly is hard to tell, responsibilities as civil rulers in county governance. Then as occasion might require, they came up at Lord Hastings' command, "defensibly arrayed" as their contracts stipulated, to fight for both lord and king. The dual character, civil and military, of the Yorkist retainer may explain why Edward IV tolerated, perhaps even encouraged, the lords' practice of retaining. This king, perforce, depended upon those peers loyal to him and to his regime to raise men to administer county government and to form a home-guard of, quite literally, territorials. These basic needs prevented the Yorkist government from trying sincerely to eradicate an institution which, when a great lord forsook his allegiance, as did the earl of Warwick in 1470, could be so dangerous and disastrous to the monarch.

Perhaps sheer necessity, or perhaps administrative lethargy, prevented Edward IV from devising new ways to staff a standing civil service to rule the counties or a constabulary effective against peers of wealth and power. This king still relied upon the feudal formula, *noblesse oblige* and *largesse*—grants and favors for past or future services—distributed through his own or his officials' good lordship. But Henry VII did so too. In return for Sir Robert Plumpton's help in suppressing the 1489 Yorkshire insurrection, the Tudor king promised him, in writing, future "preferment and advancement." To man the county offices, Edward had recourse to the refined feudalism of his day, a feudalism neither "bastard" nor "new", but one that had changed to meet changed circumstances. The increased availability of money, an extension of political patronage, and more subtle values of social prestige, notably the royal court's attraction, had produced a system of procedures by which the individual peer maintained "the rule" in his

shire. Peers, like robins, sought to mark out their territories, and in
Edward VI's reign the earl of Rutland was told that "in Leicestershire
Lord . . . . and the earl of Huntingdon have the rule; in Lincolnshire,
Lady Suffolk. If [the duke of Norfolk?] have all the shire, there is
but Nottinghamshire for you".[20] Even the Tudors had to depend upon
these lords of parliament for military and political support, and the
king in time of crisis, still called upon loyal peers to take his "full part
and quarrel". Then the peer would produce on the field of battle, as
Hastings had done in 1471, or in the house of commons as in 1472 and
1478, his own faithful retainers. When Henry VII went to York in
1485–1486, the earl of Northumberland met the new king "with a
right great and noble company . . . with 38 knights of his feedmen,
besides esquires and yeomen." And even so late as in Napoleon's time,
the duke of Northumberland maintained 1500 riflemen, cavalry, and
artillery to meet the threatened French invasion; and he called them
the "Percy Tenantry Volunteers."[21]

However, the top was where the chain of command was most vulner-
able. In theory, it was all very simple and direct: from the king to his
"counsellors born", the peers, to the individual lord's retainers who
would rally their adherents as either shire electors or men-at-arms and
archers. Edward IV's main problem, and Henry VII's too, was to preserve and strengthen the essential loyalty between the lords and their
king. The alternative was to strip the peers of their military force and to
reduce their excessive political power, a practical impossibility for
Edward IV so long as Henry VI remained alive. Even after his death
in 1471, the peers' allegiance continued to be a problem that required
at least a century of deft Tudor governance to solve. Instead, Edward IV
banked on the allegiance of his own baronial clients and through them
upon the fidelity of their retainers. This is why every one of the 69
surviving indentures signed and sealed between Lord Hastings and
his men reserved the retainer's "faith and liegance" to King Edward
and after 1471 to his son and heir, the prince.

[20] *The Plumpton Correspondence,* ed. Thomas Stapleton, Camden Soc., 1839,
pp. xcvii–xcviii; *cf.,* pp. 26–27 where the earl of Northumberland requests his
retainer, Sir William Plumpton, to appoint the earl's "beloved servant, Edmund
Cape," to be bailiff of Sessay and promises to "be as well-willed to do things
for your pleasure." *Cf.,* p. 106, where the earl asks Sir Robert Plumpton for a
couple of "running hounds" and his "tame hart" and promises a reciprocal favor.
H. M. C. Report XII, vol. 4, 32.
[21] The names of 25 of the earl's knights are recorded. *The Plumpton Correspondence,* Camden Soc. 1839, pp. xcvi-xcvii, 61. Alnwick Castle, Northumberland,
contains a hall full of arms designated as belonging to the Percy Tenantry
Volunteers, 1802–1815.

III

LORD HASTINGS' CONTRACTS: RETAINING BY INDENTURE

The 69 extant indentures containing the contracts between Lord Hastings and 67 of his 90 known retainers exhibit a variety of terms and forms. These contracts are quite distinct from the medieval military indentures which the English kings used to raise armies for foreign wars. Furthermore, Hastings' indentures, when they are compared with other lord-retainer contracts drawn between 1297 and 1483, reveal a refinement of both the legal form and the institution of lordship. The flexibility, and the vitality, too, of the connection between lord and man may account for the diversity of details in the 26 different forms of contract. Only a single indenture survives for each of 16 forms. Eight other forms are represented by 2, 4, 5, and 6 examples of each, and 2 forms include 7 indentures, the largest number to follow the same pattern. Although the indentures assigned to a single group vary in minor details, each contains the same essential terms common to the others.[1]

All of Hastings' contracts with his retainers were written in English and were formally attested by both signatures and seals. Each of the extant indentures contains the retainer's sign manual, and several of them state that Lord Hastings signed the counterpart which remained with the retainer as William Griffith's declares. The retainer's signature usually is written in a coarser hand than that of the indenture itself which one of Hastings' clerks presumably inscribed. In addition, red wax seals still remain on all but a few of the indentures which have red stains where seals once were. In many of them, the seal is on a narrow tag of parchment put through a slit in the indenture; in others, it is attached to a strip of the indenture itself cut halfway across the bottom; and in only a few is the seal *en placard*. The use of so legalistic and formal a document as a signed and sealed indenture is in itself evidence

---

[1] The 26 forms of the extant indentures are printed in Appendix A which provides the documentation for this chapter where not otherwise annotated.

that the practice of retaining was a very earnest matter, one on which both parties staked their honor. In a few contracts, the retainer used special words of attestation—"by the faith of his body", "upon his faith and honor of knighthood," and "by his oath made upon the Holy Evangelist;" but there is no indication that every one of Hastings' retainers swore such an oath. However, the indenture alone was sufficient to create and to sanction that relation between lord and man which the king's statutes described as retaining by writing, oath, or promise and to bring the covenant within the conditions prescribed by law.

The terms of the various agreements differ extensively in particulars, but all have a common purport and many contain several basic stipulations. The retainer regularly promised to do Lord Hastings' service in peace and in war, within England, and for the term of his life. Also, he commonly agreed to ride and go with Hastings, to aid and succor him, and to take his lord's part and quarrel against all others, his liege lord, the king, excepted. The retainer consented to come, upon reasonable warning, with as many men defensibly arrayed as he could assemble, or as accorded with his social rank and degree. In return Hastings contracted to be good lord to each retainer and to aid, succor, favor, or support him in all things reasonable so far as right, law, and conscience might require. From this composite pattern, individual contracts vary in detail according to the circumstances and the status, or the power and prestige, of the man retained. But each of them is readily distinguishable from the many other types of indenture used in medieval England for commercial, governmental, and military transactions. The longest and most elaborate of the 69 agreements, that with Sir Simon Montfort, reads:

"This indenture made the xxii day of November the ix year [1469] of the reign of King Edward the IV between William, Lord Hastings, on the one part and his entirely beloved cousin, Sir Simon Montfort, knight, on the other part, witnesseth that the said Sir Simon of his mere motion and free will granteth, and by these presents faithfully promiseth for term of his life to be retained and withholden with the said lord as his servant, and his full part and quarrel to take against all others during the said term, the allegiance of the said Sir Simon only except and reserved; and over that the said Sir Simon granteth and promiseth to be ready at all times and places within this realm of England to attend upon the said lord or there as he shall by the said lord be appointed by his writing or commandment, as well in time of peace as war, upon reasonable warning accompanied with such people as thereto shall be requisite and as accordeth to the worship that the said Sir Simon is of or shall be called unto. And in consideration of the premises, the said lord accepteth and taketh the said Sir Simon according to his desire and promiseth him to be his good and faithful lord and him aid, assist, comfort, and fortify in all lawful and reasonable causes as belongeth a lord to do. And moreover the said lord granteth by these presents to pay and satisfy the reasonable expenses of the said Sir Simon and company so laboring with him in time of war or otherwise coming to the said lord by his commandment or writing. And the same Sir Simon promiseth again to the said lord upon his faith and honor of knighthood to perform the premises and every part of them, never in his life to attempt the contrary. In witness whereof to the one part of these indentures remaining with the said lord the said Sir Simon hath set to his seal and sign manual; and the said lord to the other part of these indentures remaining with the said Sir Simon hath set to his seal and sign manual the xxii day of November, the said ixth year of the reign of our said sovereign lord, King Edward IV.

[signed] Simon Montfort, k.
[seal attached]

Montfort's contract exhibits the essential features of the bond between Lord Hastings and his retainers, and, presumably, of that between other English peers and theirs. First of all, Sir Simon's indenture, like every one of the 69, reserved his allegiance to the king in order to bring the agreement within both the code of chivalry and the law of the land. Some contracts, made after Prince Edward's birth in 1470, went further and excepted the retainer's allegiance to Edward IV's heirs or to "the prince". The same operative words, "to be retained and withholden", that appear in Montfort's indenture, are used in several other contracts; but synonyms, such as *belaft, belast,* and *bindeth,* also were used to retain a man "for the term of his life". The perpetuity of these commitments is stated in all but 6 indentures which make no mention of the contracts' duration, nor of their termination. They were, presumably, to continue on indefinitely.

The stipulation that the retainer was to be ready "to do him service," as William Dethick's indenture states, "as well in time of peace as in time of war", appears in 26 indentures. Fifty-four of them use the phrase, "at all times," or its equivalent.[2] This peace-as-well-as-war clause, and the for-term-of-life phrase mark off these indentures from the military ones used to hire soldiers for a specific campaign and for a limited period of service. In 42 contracts, including Montfort's, the retainers obligation to attend Lord Hastings was restricted to service "within the ground [land or realm] of England;" and the same territorial limitation was probably understood in the remaining 27. The retainer, according to 45 contracts, took the initiative and entered

---

[2] Forms H, Q, S, and V (19 indentures) contain both the "peace and war" and the "all times" clauses. This means that 35 indentures use only "at all times" or an equivalent phrase. Only 8 indentures, Forms A, B, O, Y, and Z, contain no temporal term although Lord Grey's (Y) uses the words, "always" and "from henceforth."

Hastings' service "of his own desire and motion," "at his own request and desire", or at "his special desire and prayer." These were by no means just words of common form, and they probably reflect accurately the retainer's ambition to become Hastings' servant. Back in Richard II's reign, one man, W. Bawdewyn, not only sought out a lord, but even specified the terms for his contract.[3] Alice, dowager countess of Kent, wrote to her son, Thomas, earl of Kent, that Bawdewyn had told her of the "desire that he has to serve you before any other person". All Bawdewyn asked for, in view of Kent's current expenses, was for a refresher [refresser] or bonus of 10 marks, bouche of court for himself and his servants, livery of silk and provender for 2 hackneys. For 2 years he would take nothing more of the earl; then he would expect an annual fee of 20 marks or more with other perquisites. In the case of Hastings and his retainers, he was able, so far as the indentures show, to acquire their services without any monetary fees (except in 2 cases) or other material inducements.

Nonetheless, the lord chamberlain made with his men just as binding, though less tangible, commitments. First of all, he promised to be their "good lord", "good and tender lord", "good and favorable lord", or "good and faithful lord." Sometimes these were the only words used to describe Hastings' obligation, but by 1461 the meaning of good lordship was universally understood. Twenty-two indentures record that Lord Hastings promised to support, aid, assist, comfort, fortify, or succour the retainer in his right. To Sir John Gresley he agrees "to help him to his power in all matters and causes lawful and reasonable as far as right and conscience shall require." The limitation here imposed upon Hastings' commitment also appears in over half the extant indentures. They provide that the lord is bound to support the retainer only so far "as right, law, and conscience requireth." By Edward IV's reign, statute and custom had come to sanction this reservation and to restrict a lord's activities in his retainer's behalf to what was "right." In 10 contracts, Hastings' responsibility was limited to aiding his man in only those things that belonged to him of right "according to the law" which one indenture (I) defined as "the king's laws". Another commitment, found in all but a few of the agreements, required Hastings to pay the costs and expenses of the retainer and his company when he came at his lord's command. Even the promise of good lordship was left out of 18 contracts though it may have been in the retainer's copy of the indenture. Be that as it may, no Yorkist lord would have dared to deny that he ought to be good lord to a man bound to him by formal

---

[3] *Anglo-Norman Letters and Petitions*, ed. M.D. Legge, pp. 260-261, no. 186.

indenture; for by 1461 the practice of retaining was deeply rooted in the structure of English society.

The retainer's commitment to serve Lord Hastings faithfully was expressed in various ways: "to do him service," the commonest phrase of all, or "to be towards and owe my service to" Hastings, or "to be his true and faithful servant." In Montfort's case, his primary responsibility was to take his lord's "full part and quarrel", but most contracts used the shorter expression, to "take his part." However, each of them conveyed, in one way or another, the essential idea that the retainer was to "assist and aid" Lord Hastings against "all manner of men," or "all earthly creatures", save the king and his heirs. The retainer might fulfill this obligation in several ways, the most obvious being to be "ready at all times" to answer Hastings' call and to come with a company of as many men as he could assemble. Montfort agreed to bring with him "such people" as were appropriate to a knight, and if he should be made a banneret or baron, then to come with as many men as that rank required. "To ride and go" with Hastings, as many a retainer agreed to do, meant that in time of war, or when war seemed imminent, he and his company would come up "defensibly arrayed;" but Hastings' retainers also rode with him in time of peace, and then they formed a retinue to enhance his worship and prestige. So besides supplying Lord Hastings with military force in time of need, his retainers also satisfied his vanity by surrounding him with an entourage at public meetings—in the shire courts or at London and Westminster. The retainer was to perform still other services. To take Hastings' part might mean to give him aid, counsel, or support in various ways: in or out of the courts of law, in local or national politics, or in promoting the material and social well-being of the lord's family, his kinsmen, his friends, and himself.

Even though Hastings' contracts differ greatly from the early fourteenth-century ones, they are by no means stereotyped. A few of the 69 indentures favor the retainer with special considerations, and these indicate their individual character. Two men, but only 2, were to receive cash annuities of £4 and £10 each; but even the £4 fee granted to Nicholas Kneveton in 1465 for the term of his life was omitted from a second contract made with him in 1474. Another retainer, James Blount, was to have, in his lord's absence, the "rule" which the town of Derby had granted to Hastings; and Lawrence Lowe was to be of his lord's "counsel learned".

Other stipulations in Lord Hastings' contracts disclose the complexities that often existed between a lord and his retainers. Three men found it necessary to reserve their loyalty to other lords because of

4*

previous commitments. Upon their service Hastings could obtain only
a second lien. The contract (C) of one of them, Sir Thomas Stathom,
starts out:

"This indenture witnesseth that I, Thomas Stathom, knight, am retained, withholden, and promised to William Hastings, Lord Hastings, for to be towards
him before all other lords, my ligeance and also Harry, Lord Grey, lord of
Codnor, only except. And if it fortune the same Lord Grey to decease, which
God defend, then I, the said Thomas Stathom, knight, promise and bind me
by this same my present writing to be towards and owe my service to the said
Lord Hastings next my ligeance before all other lords . . ."

John Davers, likewise, was obligated under a previous agreement, and
his indenture (L) reserved his service to Dame Elizabeth Ferrers, then
the wife of Sir John Bourchier, for the term of her life. After her death,
he would assume his full responsibility to Hastings and do him exclusive service. The third case, indenture (I), anticipated the young
Edward, Lord Mountjoy's coming "to full age," and his uncle, James
Blount, esquire, excepted his nephew, when of age, from his promise
to take Hastings' part against all earthly creatures. However, Edward
had died 11 days before the date, 12 December 1474, on Blount's
indenture, but John, the next Lord Mountjoy, James' brother, later
(23 February 1480) became Lord Hastings' retainer, (indenture Z).
Lord Grey of Codnor, likewise was bound to him by indenture (Y),
and so long as these 2 peers maintained their fidelity to Hastings, he
had no need to worry about the divided loyalties of Stathom and
James Blount.

Fidelity was the very foundation of lordship, and the continuance
of the institution depended upon the value to both parties of their
mutual assistance. In return for the retainer's services and good faith,
the lord owed him "his special favor", that influence in English society
which was the dynamic of good lordship. Just as the lord's aid, support,
and counsel worked to further the retainer's affairs, so, too, did the
retainer repay his lord in kind with counsel, aid, and service, both
military and political. And the relationship created through their joint
activities enhanced their respective "profit and worship"—the condition
of being held in high esteem. In this respect the character of lordship
in Yorkist England resembled the Old English institution more than
it did the intervening Norman-Angevin feudal tenancy. Feudal tenants,
by the fourteenth century, were paying money-rents for their fiefs,
rather than military and judicial services; and so a lord needing military
or political aid sought it elsewhere. Many a lord resorted to feed men
bound by cash annuities which enabled him to avoid the alienation of

his lands. Then in Edward IV's reign, and perhaps before, good lordship—influence and favor—supplanted cash annuities as the common fee (*feodum*) that bound the retainer to his lord.[4] Here, surely was a refined, or at any rate, a more sophisticated form of feudalism and not a degenerate or "bastard" brand. This transition from land to cash to favor paralleled the broader refinement of Edward I's essentially military and agrarian society into the commercial and comparatively civil community of the Tudors.

The contrast between the fourteenth-century retainers' contracts and those of Lord Hastings reflects this transformation. General terms replace the strictly military specifications found in the earlier indentures. Likewise, the military indentures by which Edward IV raised an army for his 1475 French expedition are quite distinct from Hastings' contracts. The opening paragraph of an indenture, sealed by Sir Richard Tunstall, 20 August 1474, and written in English, states that he "is retained and belaft" to do King Edward "service of war in his duchy of Normandy and in his realm of France, for one whole year, with 10 spears himself accounted, and 100 archers well and sufficiently abled, armed, and arrayed, taking wages for himself of 2 shillings by the day." Right here basic differences appear: the service is for war

---

[4] According to strict feudal law, fiefs, long before 1400, had become hereditary. This seems to preclude the fifteenth-century retainers fee, Latin *feodum*, whether a cash annuity or good lordship, from being considered a "fief" in the legal sense. The "Account Book" of Sir John Fogge, treasurer of Edward IV's household, has page captions, *Feod* [*a*] *et Rob*[*e*], (P.R.O., E101/411/13/ fols. 36-38). Also, it may be remarked, several of Hastings' retainers' sons were bound to him during their fathers' lives; and, conversely, William, Lord Hastings' son, Edward, continued a few of his father's men as his retainers. Through family continuity, retaining by indenture had then, in fact if not in strict law, an hereditary nature.

Bryce D. Lyon has done much to illuminate the antecedents of the indenture system in his recent articles *(Eng. Hist. Rev.,* LXVI (1951), 161–193; *Revue du Nord,* XXXV (1953), 222–232; and *Speculum,* XXIX (1954), 503–511.

In view of the promises to be a faithful servant or retainer, in peace and war, for term of life, occurring in Hastings' contracts and in the earlier mixed ones, I cannot agree with Lyon's assertion: "Under the indenture system the grantee performed no homage or fealty for the yearly cash fee; the only nexus between grantor and grantee was money and mutual military respect." This statement obviously holds for the temporary and limited military contract; but not for the retainer's lifetime agreement. Homage, the placing of hands, perhaps was not literally performed, yet fealty (fidelity) was expressly stated probably both by oral oath and written contract. The statutes concerning livery and retaining repeatedly refer to retaining "by oath or indenture," and the use of written express contracts, in lieu of the physical act of homage, was surely a refinement over the more primitive Norman and Angevin sanctions.

and in time of war, and not in time of peace; it is to be done in Normandy and France, and not in England; the number of men that the retained knight is to bring is specified precisely and is not left to his estimate of the number appropriate to his rank or his ability to raise; and, finally, the purpose—to provide an army for a single particular campaign—differs from the permanent aid and support, whether military, social, or political, which Hastings' retainers agreed to render.

The remainder of Tunstall's contract—a very long one compared to Hastings'—contains the minute specifications normally found in the fifteenth-century English kings' military contracts. Tunstall and his men were to equip themselves with horses, harness, and victuals; and they were to enjoy and retain two-thirds of their winnings of war. One third of Tunstall's take was to go to the king who also was to receive the "third of thirds"—a third of the third that Tunstall's men paid him. He, himself, enjoyed the right to any prisoners taken, except the king of France, his sons, or lieutenants and "chieftains". In return, the king was to pay the wages, a shilling a day plus a sixpence bonus, of each spear and sixpence a day to each archer. Transportation to France, and return, was the king's responsibility, and he was to provide the soldiers with letters of protection during their absence from England. The dates and places for payment of wages, in both England and France, are stated; but the day of muster and the port of embarkation were left for future notification. All these details, so foreign to Hastings' contracts, covered the points which normally were included in the fourteenth-century military indenture between king and captain: the strength and composition of the contingent to be brought; the period and place of service; the rate of wages and the bonus; the compensation to be given for horses lost in war; the liability for the cost of transportation; and the division—the "thirds" and the "thirds of thirds"—of the "advantages of war", the ransom of prisoners, and the tenure of castles captured.[5]

Among the earlist "purely military" indentures now known, is a sub-contract of 1287 between Edmund Mortimer, a "squadron-leader", and Peter Maulay, a "troop-commander". Maulay contracted to bring, *in expeditione guerre Wallie contra Resum, filium Mereduci,* a troop

---

[5] Tunstall's indenture is printed from a bundle in the Tower by Rymer, *Foedera*, XI, 817–19. Two similar indentures are on pp. 819–22. In 1462, a letter of Edward IV's under the signet and "signed with our own hand" written at Lichfield to Robert Stillington, keeper of the privy seal, ordered him to make indentures of war according to the terms indicated in an enclosed schedule. P.R.O., E101/71/5/ no. 940. For the origin of the "thirds of thirds", D. Hay, "The Division of the Spoils of War." *Trans. Royal Hist. Soc.,* 5th Ser., IV, 91–109.

of 10 men—3 knights and 7 troopers mounted on horses whose quality and value was carefully specified. This contract in Latin (perhaps only in its exemplification on the Close Roll) was sealed by the parties. The initiative in this case seems to have been taken by Mortimer, presumably at Edward I's behest, who was under contract with the king to raise troops for his Welsh campaign. This limited the agreement in place to Wales and in time to the summer of 1287. Its purpose was to meet an immediate military exigency as was the case in the military contracts of the next two centuries.[6]

The military indenture was used to acquire a variety of military services, but in the fourteenth century the services were specified in their particularity. It was not an open contract in the broad, general terms found in Hastings' indentures. Whether between the king and a captain, or a captain and a man-at-arms, the purely military agreement was limited, limited in both time and place of service. In length and extent, these indentures increased, as one dated 30 May 1416 and written in French, between Henry V and Nicholas Montgomery, Richard Hastings, and John Osbaldeston, knights, makes evident. The three knights "retained" to accompany the king in his own person oversea and to do war service. Each was to bring 9 men-at-arms and 18 archers, armed and arrayed, for a quarter of a year beginning 22 June. Their wages are specified and assigned against the tenths and fifteenths voted by parliament. Their muster in a ship assigned for them at Southampton is designated; and the contract described the king's share of the winnings of war. A receipt for the wages of £ 42. 9. 4$^{1}/_{2}$ paid to Sir Richard Hastings for his service and that of 5 men-at-arms and 18 archers for half a quarter, though dated 12 April, 1419, attests the fulfillment of this, or another, contract. Two years later, 1 May 1421, Sir Richard Hastings again contracted with the king for half a year's war service. For this campaign, he agreed to bring 10 men-at-arms and 30 archers, all of them at the king's wages of a shilling a day for the men and 6 pence for the archers. Hastings was to report with his retinue at Dover on 23 May and to hold their muster "on the downs nearby."[7] At the end of the century, an indenture under privy seal in 1492 which "retained and belaft" Edward, Lord Hastings, to serve Henry VII "in his wars beyond the sea" for one whole year shows that the military contract still followed the old form.[8] However, 50 years later Henry VIII, for his invasion of France in 1544, used a letter grandiloquent in phraseology and more mandatory in tone. This

---

[6] *Bulletin of the Institute of Historical Research,* (1935–36) XIII, 85–89.
[7] See Appendix A.
[8] H. E. Huntington Library MS. HA Seals, 142.

order, under the signet and bearing the royal stamp, to the earl of Huntingdon was in effect a uni-lateral contract. The earl was "appointed" to come in his "person" with "150 able footmen", 29 to be archers, and also 70 horsemen "furnished on able horses or geldings". Though the place of service, France, was named, no mention occurs of the length of time, and Henry VIII's power to "require and command" the allegiance and the military support of his peers supplanted the bilateral spirit of the early military indentures.

Parallel to this development of the purely military contract from Edward I's days, is the transformation of the retainer's indenture from one predominantly bellicose into Lord Hastings' semi-civil agreements. Among the earliest retainer indentures is a covenant (*covenaunt*) dated Saturday 21 August, 1311, in French between Sir Ralf Fitzwilliam, Lord Greystock, and Sir Nicholas de Hastings. Sir Nicholas agrees to "stay with" Sir Ralph "in peace and in war for the term of their 2 lives". He promises to "go with" Fitzwilliam, in war, where he goes in his own person and to come to him each time it is reasonable. In wartime, Sir Nicholas was to furnish 2 squires with their accoutrements and 10 grooms—in peace the 2 squires but only 4 grooms. Sir Ralph agreed to supply suitable equipment for Hastings himself, 2 robes a year, and a saddle fit for a knight, and to pay compensation, as appraised by 2 men, for any great horse-of-arms lost by Sir Nicholas while in his service. Further, Fitzwilliam undertook to pay the wages of Hastings' attendants in both peace and war and to reimburse Sir Nicholas's expenses while en route from any place in Yorkshire to join Sir Ralph. "In witness of which covenant each of them has put his seal to the other's indenture." [9]

---

[9] N. B. Lewis has located other retainer indentures dated in the 1290s. One which he cites [*cf.* note 6 above and quoted by J. E. Morris, *The Welsh Wars of Edward I*] (P.R.O., E101/68/1 no. 1) is between Aymer de Valence, son and heir of Sir William de Valence, and Sir Thomas de Berkeley and dated Sunday 7 July 1297. By this "writing indented," Berkeley agreed to "stay with" Valence *de son mennage a banere* with 5 knights, himself included, and 24 horses "as well in peace as in war, in England, in Wales, and in Scotland." This covenant does not contain a specified term of service, but Berkeley was to receive by the year, "so long as he may stay with him," £ 50, robes, and bouche of court for himself, the knights, and their 6 esquires and 3 grooms. Valence was to provide wages in time of war, shipping, and compensation for any horses lost. This is the earliest appearance of the "peace and war" clause known to me, but the agreement, apparently of indefinite duration, does not include the "term of life" stipulation that was used in 1311. The tone and tenor of the Valence-Berkeley covenant is predominantly military; but it is not limited to a specific campaign or place—other than England, Wales, and Scotland. The retention of Berkeley "in peace" and for a £ 50 annual fee and robes shows the divorcement of mili-

This contract is of a mixed character. First, it includes many of the terms found in the purely military indenture, and then it also contains the two key clauses, "in peace and war" and "for term of life," which the statute of 1390 will prescribe for a retainer's indenture. Lacking, however, is any mention of being retained, belaft, or bound as servant or retainer; nor is Sir Nicholas's service limited to England. The tenor of this contract is conspicuously military, and there is nothing to indicate which party initiated the agreement. Nevertheless, the retainer's *quid pro quo* does include more—the 2 robes given him annually for life and the expenses for his service in peace-time—than he would receive under a military indenture. This 1311 contract, like many others in the fourteenth century, was in its conception and purpose essentially military; but as the system of retaining for life and in time of peace developed in England, civil functions came to complement, though they did not eliminate, the original martial duties of the indentured retainer. The form of the mixed indenture (as I have styled the military contract for term of life and in time of peace, as distinct from the indenture for a single campaign) recently has been traced back to the reign of John. This king, in 1213, contracted with continental nobles to supply him with troops, and to some he paid "a fief of 400 m. per annum." In return, the retained noble not only promised a specified number of warriors, but also homage and service, and he became John's "liege man." Still earlier than John's "feudal contracts" with these continentals were the conventions [*conventiones*] involving "fiefs" of £500 a year and 400 *m. in feodo* between Henry I and Robert II, count of Flanders, in 1103 and between Henry II and Thierry of Alsace in 1163. The substance and the principle of these twelfth and early thirteenth-century feudal contracts were the same as in the mixed indentures of the fourteenth and fifteenth centuries. If these later contracts did not prescribe homage and fealty according to Norman-Angevin ritual, they did contain their counterpart in the retainer's sign manual and seal and by such phrases as "by the faith of his body," "by his oath made upon the Holy Evangelist," "faithful service," "faithful servant," or to be "faithful and true unto him"—to say nothing of the express contract

tary service from land tenure and the substitution of cash and livery for land fiefs. Receipts for wages paid to Berkeley at Castle Aberkorn, Scotland, 1297–98, are in P.R.O., E101/68/1/ nos. 2 and 3. The superb analysis by N. B. Lewis of the fourteenth-century indentured retinues makes it unnecessary to discuss in detail the nature and development of the retainer contracts, 1300–1400. To repeat what he has described so well would be gratuitous, but the fourteenth-century indentures mentioned here may complement his remarks. N. B. Lewis, "The Organisation of Indentured Retinues in Fourteenth-century England," *Trans. Royal Hist. Soc.*, 4th Ser., XXVII (1945), 29–39.

itself. Such sanctions, derived directly from earlier feudal forms and doubtless with unbroken continuity, identify the retainer's indenture more closely with the feudal contract than with the later limited military agreement for a specific war.

By the fourteenth century, the practice of keeping "companies" of men in England was already well-established. In 1305 Edward, prince of Wales, could write and ask Sir John Hastings to "retain in his company" Martin Shench, the prince's yeoman, until he could provide for him other livelihood. This was the very year when Edward I's parliament defined retaining with robes [livery] *for maintenance* as conspiracy; and it was nearly a century after 1218–19 when the giving of livery of company by earls and barons was referred to obliquely. About 1240, King Henry III himself gave the first badge now known, an "R" in silk, and by 1307 Prince Edward had supplied his men with uniforms.[10] The duke of Norfolk, in 1282, had agreed to pay an Irish nobleman an annual retaining fee of 20 marks, and the author of the *Mirror of Justices,* from the 1290's, erratic as his book is, considered as existing practice alliances among the nobility through retaining by "oath of bodily service," by fee and, perhaps, by writing.[11] Certainly by Edward II's accession the system of retaining companies of Englishmen by indenture existed. The king's councillor's oath of 1307 required the swearer to tell the king of any "alliance in lordship" [*a seignurage*]

---

[10] Hilda Johnstone, *The Letters of Edward, Prince of Wales, 1304–05,* p. 62 [23 July 1305]; *idem,* p. xxvi; D. M. Stenton, *Rolls for the Justices in Eyre for Yorkshire,* 1218–19, (Selden Soc. 56) p. 424, no. 1149. Here is told how John of Thornton went about the country with 15 horsemen and at Christmas came to Richmond Castle "with 100 marks' worth of cloth and clothed his men therewith as if he were a baron or an earl." Sir Maurice Powicke called to my attention two items in the *Curia Regis Rolls,* VII, 170, 172, 173 (1214) and VIII, 381 (1220): In an appeal against Baldwin Tyrell for having said the king had been murdered, Henry de Pomereia and Alan de Dunstanville declared, *quod illi fuerunt de privata familia domini regis, jurati quod, si illi aliquid audirent quod fuisset contra dominum regem, domino regi illud intimarent;* "and two men accused of murdering their lord were described as of his household, *de manupasto suo.*" In these instances, as in the Anglo-Saxon period, the men were obviously household retainers, not non-residents.

[11] E. Curtis, *Richard II in Ireland,* p. 11. W. J. Whittaker, *The Mirror of Justices,* (Selden Soc. 7) p. 21. Under *Definition of Treason,* the author of the *Mirror* describes those "allied by blood, affinity, homage, or oath, which oath is sometimes an oath of fealty issuing by way of service from the fee *(fieu)* and sometimes an oath of bodily service." "By fee *(loier)* is to be understood fee *(fieu),* possession, robe, seal, pension, church, rent, or any other thing given, including meat and drink, during the service." *Cf.* p. 101 for alliances by courtesy, and p. 117, "the oath of fealty issues ... sometimes from a retainer in the service of another" *(e ascune foiz en autrui service).*

by which he could not "do or keep" his promise "without breaking such an alliance"; and that thereafter he should "not make alliance by oath to anyone without leave of the king" [*sauntz conge le roy*]. The oath of 1310 for councillors in Gascony prescribed that "they shall openly excuse themselves from counselling when it concerns matters touching those persons to whom they are obligated by their other oaths." And Piers Gaveston, in 1311, was accused of "making alliance of people by oaths to live and die with him against all people," thereby lording it over the estate of the king and of the crown.[12] This was the same year when Sir Nicholas de Hastings contracted with Sir Ralph Fitzwilliam, and there can be no doubt that the practice of alliance and retaining flourished, as it was to do in times of weak kings, during the unhappy reign of Edward II. In 1314–15, the earl of Pembroke had received £2,888.12.2 for "having in his company 100 men-at-arms in the king's service" to keep the Scottish marches.

Upon his accession, Edward III approved a statute condemning his father's misguided practice of binding men to him "by writings to come to the king with force and arms at any time they were commanded on pain of life and member". The new sovereign considered that such writings were "to the king's dishonor since everyone was held to do to the king, as to his liege lord, that which belongs to him without writing". Even though Edward III was strong enough to compel his councillors to swear that they "will make no alliance with anyone," the military exigencies of his foreign policy undoubtedly accelerated retaining. Even he, the king, indented with Sir Henry Percy to stay with him in peace and war for Percy's whole life. This retainer was to receive an annual fee of 500 marks, "in time of peace and of war," in return for bringing with him a fixed number of men-at-arms. However, at the 1331 parliament, the king, with the assent of the magnates, granted to Percy and his heirs forever, in place of the annual fee, the castle and manor of Warkworth and the manor of Rothbury for the good service he had done and "will do in time to come."[13] Despite

---

12 For the oath of 1307, J. F. Baldwin, *The King's Council*, pp. 347–48. Articles 10 and 11, about alliances, were not included in the 1257 oath form. This indicates the years between the Provisions of Oxford, 1258, and Edward I's Confirmation of the Charters, 1297, as the period when the use of feed retainers rapidly increased. The requirement in 1307 of the king's leave suggests the line of policy the kings pursued on through Elizabeth I's reign. But in what form the king's permission to retain was granted, unless by word of mouth, remains uncertain. See below, chapters IV and V. *S. R.,* 5 Edward II, c. 20.

13 *S. R.,* 1 Edward III, Stat. 2, c. 15; J. F. Baldwin, *The King's Council*, pp. 351–352; E. C. Lodge and G. A. Thornton, *English Constitutional Documents, 1307–1485*, p. 101; *idem*, p. 112 (Wardrobe Accounts, 1338–40, list

this substitution of land for a cash annuity (here a special favor), the converse process of retaining men by money fees instead of land was becoming the more common practice.

When Henry, duke of Lancaster, died in 1362, his son-in-law, John of Gaunt, took over both his dukedom and his company of retainers. One of them was Sir Ralph Hastings who had promised to stay with the duke "in time of peace as of war." In return, he was to receive "an annual rent of 40 marks sterling for the term of his life," and Gaunt, as the duke's heir, confirmed this contract in 1362. He agreed that he and his heirs would pay the annuity during Sir Ralph's life and assigned it against the revenues from his manor of Pickering. The same year Hastings, too, renewed his own contract with John de Kirby, of Wigginthorpe, Yorkshire, to serve him for term of life, and he doubtless retained other men to bring to Gaunt's service. Hastings' "annual fee" was still being paid in 1391 when he sealed a receipt for a semi-annual installment of 20 marks. Another of Gaunt's contracts retained Sir John Neville, lord of Raby, in 1370 for term of life with a fee of 50 marks in peace-time and free living at the duke's court for himself, one bachelor, 2 esquires, 2 chamberlains, and their grooms and horses. In time of war, Neville's annuity was to be 500 marks plus whatever wages the king might allow Gaunt for Neville's service with 5 knights, 20 men-at-arms, and 20 mounted archers. By Richard II's accession, the feed retainer had surpassed the tenant as a source of manpower for military services; and John of Gaunt's *Register,* 1372–1383, lists 227 men—2 earls, 3 barons, 96 knights, and 126 esquires—bound to him by indentures for term of life in time of peace as well as of war.[14]

Gaunt's retainers, mainly knights and esquires, were men of property

expenses of £1,390 for *feoda militum* and £2,082/15/4 for *robe et calciatura; Rot. Parl.,* II, pp. 62–3.

[14] For the Gaunt-Hastings confirmation, see Appendix A; for Gaunt's other retainers, *John of Gaunt's Register, 1372–1376,* ed. Sydney Armitage-Smith, Royal Hist. Soc., 3rd Ser., XX and XXI; *idem, 1379–83,* ed. E. C. Lodge and R. Somerville, 3rd Ser., LVI and LVII.

Several indentures with feed retainers, some for military service, others with bachelors of his chamber, are recorded in *The Register of Edward, the Black Prince, preserved in the Public Record Office,* Parts i–iv (1930–33). One (iv, 259) in 1358 with Sir Baldwin de Frevill, "retained him to stay with the prince for the term of his life" in both peace and war with a £40 annual fee. Only this indenture conforms to the normal pattern of the later retainer contracts. Another with Sir John de Scully is also for term of life, in peace and war, with a £40 annuity; but he was to be bachelor of the prince's chamber, and he already belonged to the "prince's special retinue both in peace and war." *Idem,* iv, 80 and ii, 45.

with their own estates which provided them with homes and livelihood. The annual cash fee, from £5 to £100, supplemented their private incomes, and many retainers also received food and wages while at Gaunt's court. Their peace-time duty was to attend the duke, to ride and go with him on progresses and so enhance his and their prestige. On occasion, they might perform administrative services, as Sir Ralph Hastings did when he joined the chief forester and steward in investigating trespasses in Pickering Forest. But far more conspicuous than such civil services were the military ones his retainers performed. Events during Richard II's reign indicate that the primary purpose of retaining by indenture in the fourteenth century was to maintain a standing corps of men available for fighting. Gaunt's contracts still specified in detail the retainer's military accoutrements, the number of men he was to bring along, the compensation due him for horses lost in battle, and his share of the prizes and ransoms. His annuity was stated, and if his status improved—if an esquire became a knight or a knight a banneret—the fee was to be increased. The war-time wage was to be met by the king who would pay for the services of Gaunt's contingent. Here in the king's necessity for warriors is, perhaps, the clue to the royal tolerance, even encouragement, of the system of retaining.

The peers' companies of feed men, in Richard II's reign, formed what amounted to a peace-time standing army. At the least they constituted a reserve of warriors experienced, organized, and subject to call. From the lord's point of view, to retain men for cash annuities was more advantageous than granting them land for future services. Even though a lord might encumber a piece of his property, as Gaunt did, with a fixed obligation for the retainer's life, still he possessed the land and its profits and did not lose permanently his capital. Furthermore, in time of foreign war the magnate with a band of retainers at his disposal could fulfill his duty to king and kingdom more efficiently, and the monarch, in turn, could raise his armies more speedily. Actually, the king relied upon both systems—the indentured retainers and contract armies. The lords would call up their adherents to serve at the king's wages; but they also hired additional soldiers under temporary contracts. When the government anticipated war with the Scots in 1380, John of Gaunt sent to his receivers-general in Yorkshire and Lancaster 2 sets of letters. Those in one batch were addressed to his own knights and esquires, men whom he retained for life. But he also sent letters "not addressed" which the receiver-general was to inscribe with the names of "other knights and esquires" suitable to go with Gaunt against the Scots. For a foreign campaign of this sort, the king provided the wages for the lord's retainers, as so many of Gaunt's contracts stipulated; and then the lords supplemented these forces with troops raised at the king's expense under strictly military contracts.

Henry V likewise used both methods to raise armies in 1415 for his conquest of France. He sent out writs to all the sheriffs to call up all the knights, esquires, and *valleti* who held fees, wages, or annuities of the crown, whether granted by himself, Henry IV, Richard II, or Edward III, and all men who were of his "livery and retaining". Any man who failed to come was to forfeit his annuity, fee, or wage, and no excuse was to be accepted. Only those of the king's retainers who were to serve as captains of the men-at-arms to be hired especially for this expedition were excepted from the general summons. Here, Henry V acted like any lord and called upon his feed men, his own retainers, for the military service that they were expected to perform. But as king, he went further and also hired other men as soldiers on limited military contracts. Henry V's need for warriors may explain why he, like his predecessors and successors, permitted the peers of the realm to retain men by indenture in time of peace. For, so long as the king of England had enemies to fight, whether the Welsh, the Scots, or the French, he needed more men than he alone could afford to maintain. From the king's point of view, the military and financial advantages to be gained by allowing the lords to retain what amounted to an army of territorials outweighed the inconveniences the practice imposed upon civil society.

Henry IV's wars with the Welsh and with his own rebellious earls had created ample opportunity for the system of retaining to thrive. The king's son, Henry, prince of Wales, and his ally, Ralph Neville, earl of Westmoreland, regularly retained men by indentures which still survive. Two, in French and dated in 1406 and 1408, bound 2 esquires, John de Thorp and Richard Otway, to the earl for terms of life "in time of peace as of war." Although these were not the military contracts limited in time and place, they struck the same war-like note so evident in John of Gaunt's contracts and so conspicuously absent from Lord Hastings' later in this century. In war-time, Thorp and Otway were to receive the wages that the earl paid to other men of their rank; and the lord was "to have the third of all winnings of war to be won or gotten by" them or their men. These 2 retainers also agreed to serve against all persons save the king of England and his heirs, and each had un annual fee, Thorp's £2 and Otway's 4 marks, to be paid by Westmoreland's receiver at Cockermouth.[15]

[15] Thomas Madox, *Formulare Anglicanum* (1702), p. 97, no. CLXXVI; *H. M. C. Reports*, X, part 4, 226.

Three indentures, also in French, contain similar agreements between Prince Henry and Walter Dewrose [Devereux] and Geoffrey Arden, esquires, and Richard, earl of Warwick. The earl was retained in October 1410 to stay with the prince "as well in time of peace as of war," in or out of the realm or on the sea, "for the term of his life and . . . against all people of the world" except the king. He was to receive 250 marks a year and bouche of court for himself, 4 esquires, and 6 grooms. The prince was to have the third and the third of thirds from the earl and his men when they served at Henry's wages; but the number of the earl's warriors was not prescribed. The arrangements with Dewrose and Arden were the same except for 2 particulars. Neither of these esquires was to receive bouche of court, and their annuities were, quite naturally, much lower—10 marks a year each. Dewrose's indenture required him "to come to" the prince at his command, whether Henry was in or out of the realm or on the sea. The prince would pay Dewrose's men the wages appropriate to their status. Contracts such as these, despite their bellicose intent, are quite distinct from the temporary military indenture; but they provided the lord with retainers whose service still was performed, for the more part, by force and arms.

When Henry V became king, his princely brother, John, duke of Bedford, kept his own retinue for both peace and war. A mixed indenture, in French and dated 15 October 1415, bound to the duke Sir Robert Plumpton, and its detailed terms describe the retainer's functions. Sir Robert was retained and bound "for term of his life to serve him, as well in time of peace as of war," and the military commitments were conventional: to serve with his own men at the duke's wages, to remit the third of his winnings of war and of prisoners, and the third of the thirds remitted to Plumpton by his followers, reserving for Bedford any chieftain or great lord he or his men might capture. Plumpton's peace-time duties were to travel with the duke "in his company in time of peace, or come to his household," under which circumstances the duke was to provide bouche of court for the knight, one squire, and 2 bachelors [*vallets*], all this in addition to his 20 mark annual fee.[15.A] The system of feudal retainers functioned well in Henry V's reign, and the terms of most contracts had become conventionalized though by no means uniform.

Another mixed indenture from 1448, similar except that it is written in English, bound Walter, the son of Sir Thomas Strickland, to serve

---

[15.A] *The Plumpton Correspondence*, Camden Soc. 1839, pp. xlii–xliii, *n. g.*

Richard Neville, earl of Salisbury.[16] This agreement required the retainer to be "horsed, armed, and arrayed and always ready to ride, come, and go" at Salisbury's costs "against all folks saving his ligeance." Strickland's fee was 10 marks a year to be paid from the lordship of Penreth. Even though this retainer had been knight of the shire for Westmoreland in 1441–42, Salisbury probably cared more for his muster roll of 290 men living on his lands—69 bowmen and 74 bill-men horsed and harnessed, and 71 bowmen and 76 billmen not so equipped. All of these Lancastrian indentures emphasize military details, and the desire to procure fighting men was undoubtedly the lord's chief purpose in making these agreements. As late as 1448, it seems clear, little change had occurred in the contract's terms or in its purpose.

Even after Edward IV's accession, the same war-like spirit appears in 4 indentures contemporaneous with Hastings' earliest. Three of them dated 27 April 1462 between Richard, earl of Warwick, and 3 esquires —Thomas Blenkinsop, Christopher Lencastre, and Robert Warcop— contain exclusively military arrangements.[17] What the king-maker wanted is all too obvious, warriors who would bring with them their "servants" to fight at the earl's wages. His retainers were to be "well and convenably horsed, armed, and arrayed" and ready to ride and go with the earl "at all times and into all places." Warwick was to have the usual third of "all winnings of war" and the third of thirds from the retainer's men. In Lencastre's case, his annual fee was to be 5 marks during his father's life, and then after his decease a £5 annuity, while Blenkinsop was to have £3.6.8 sterling. The inclusion of the old familiar military phrases marks off these indentures from Lord Hastings' 69 which omit such minatory details.

Closer to Warwick's contract than to any of Lord Hastings' is one dated 9 December 1467 between Ralph, Lord Greystock and Wem, and John Fleming, esquire, of Rydal in Westmoreland. Fleming was "retained and behest" for term of life "as well in war as in peace" against all men saving his allegiance. Thus far his contract resembles those of Hastings; but in addition to a £4 annual fee "of lawful money of England," he was to have war-time wages such "as the king gives to men of such degree." Then follows the standard provision about Grey-

[16] For Henry V's indentures, see Appendix A; for Strickland's, see Joseph Nicolson and Richard Brown, *History and Antiquities . . . of Westmoreland and Cumberland* (1777), I, 96, 97 *n.*, 98.

[17] P.R.O., Ancient Deeds, E327/6415; *Eng. Hist. Rev.*, XXIX (1914), 720 and P.R.O., E101/71/5 no. 945; T. Madox, *Formulare Anglicanum* (1702), pp. 104–05, no. CLXXXV P.R.O., E237/185. Dr. N. B. Lewis directed me to the Blenkinsop indenture.

stock's right to the third of Fleming's prisoners and to the third of the
thirds acquired from his servants "if he go with the said lord over the
sea or into Scotland." Whenever Greystock should send for Fleming
"to ride with him to London or for any other matter," the lord was to
pay his expenses and to give him and his company bouche of court.[18]
Except for this comparatively pacific service, Fleming's obligations
were distinctly war-like. His agreement is like those that ante-date
Hastings' indentures which substitute for the elaborate military specifications the retainer's simple promise to bring with him men defensibly
arrayed to ride and go with his lord. The new provisions in Hastings'
contracts mark a change in both form and substance—a change of which
the chamberlain's chancery was undoubtedly aware.

The new features in Hastings' agreements concern 3 aspects of retaining: the relation between the contracting parties, the purpose of the
covenant, and the limitations imposed upon their respective obligations.
These indentures are the earliest of those now known to use the words,
lord and servant, as corelatives; and they apply the adjectives, true and
faithful, either to the servant or to his service. Two of them also speak
of the retainer's "faith of his body" and of "his faith and honor of
knighthood." Then, too, in more than half of Hastings' indentures, the
retainer initiates the agreement "of his own desire and motion;" and,
in turn, he is to enjoy Hastings' "good lordship" in whatever words
it may be described. This compensation supplants the annual fee in cash
(in all but 2 contracts), and it reflects a change of purpose on the
retainer's part. What he desired was aid, succor, and support in his
"matters", not just revenue and a chance to fight for the winnings of
war. In return, he agreed to take his lord's "part and quarrel," a duty
that might entail social, political, or legal aid as well as military support.
True, 61 retainers agreed to come at Hastings' call with as many men
as they might assemble, and 51 of them were to bring along their
adherents "defensibly arrayed".[19] Although the old peace-and-war
clause appears in 25 contracts, 33 others read "at all times". Of course
contemporaries understood full well the import of the retainer's commitment "to ride and go" with his lord; but even this implicit recourse
to armed force was euphemistically expressed.

The limitations imposed on each party's obligations and the re-
strictive conditions under which the agreement became operative also

[18] J. Nicolson and R. Brown, *History and Antiquities . . . of Westmoreland
and Cumberland* (1777) I, p. 158.
[19] The phrase, "to take his part," appears in all but 5 indentures which substitute "assist and aid," etc. The words, "defensibly arrayed," are used in 52
indentures (for 51 retainers).

5

point to a conscious effort to couch Hastings' contracts in a civil tone. The retainer limited his service to the realm of England in nearly two-thirds of the indentures; and, in the rest, since they make no mention of serving outside the kingdom, this reservation was probably understood. Hastings' promise to be good lord, to aid and support the retainer in his affairs, was expressly restricted in 14 forms comprising 41 indentures.[20] Twenty-six of these include the illuminating clause, "as far as law and conscience requireth"; and the other 15 require the lord's support in only "lawful and reasonable causes", or "in all things reasonable", or "in his [the retainer's] right", or "according to the law", and in James Blount's case "according to the king's laws."

So novel a deference to law, conscience, right, and reason strikes an unprecedented note. These words alone would distinguish Hastings' contracts from those of Warwick and Greystock so laden down with martial matter. Was King Edward IV's chamberlain trying to bring his agreements within the letter, and perhaps the spirit, of the prevailing law? Were there, then, circumstances or conditions under which retaining by indenture between 1461 and 1483 was lawful? And did not Lord Hastings retain his company of 90 peers, knights, esquires, and gentlemen in conformity with, rather than in defiance of, the king's laws and the acts of parliament? To answer these questions the statutes, ordinances, and proclamations made to regulate livery, maintenance, and retaining by oath, promise, or indenture must be consulted.

[20] Hastings' promise of good lordship, or the like, is omitted from 19 contracts. Possibly it appeared in the retainer's counterpart, but it was certainly understood and assumed during the 1470's. Montfort's contract (D) explains the lord's duty to aid his retainer in all lawful and reasonable causes "as belongeth a lord to do."

IV

THE LAWFULNESS OF RETAINING BY INDENTURE: STATUTES AND PROSECUTIONS

The lawfulness of the contracts between Lord Hastings and his retainers is, first of all, a question of chronology. The earliest surviving indenture, that with William Griffith of North Wales, was signed and sealed at Westminster 6 November 1461. Four other contracts, Lord Grey of Codnor's in 1464 and 3 from 1465, all fell under the laws in force before 1468. In that year Edward IV, "by the advice and assent of the lords spiritual and temporal, and of the commons of this realm ... ordained and established" a statute to regulate livery and retaining.[1] The law concerning retainers prior to 1468, however, rested upon several statutes and ordinances made between 1305 and 1429. These acts distinguished clearly between the 3 practices, unlawful maintenance, the giving or wearing of livery, and retaining or being retained by oath, promise, or indenture.

Retaining, though it may have fostered the use of livery and prompted an increase in unlawful maintenance, must not be confused, as too often it has been, with the other 2 practices. Even maintenance, it must be emphasized, might still in the sixteenth century be construed as lawful. In 1503 German de la Pole could beseech his father-in-law, Sir Robert Plumpton, "for the reverence of Jesu to be so good father unto me and my wife as to maintain it that is my right and to see a remedy for it."[1A] Likewise, the use of livery was under certain circumstances legal. The earliest relevant legislation, from the thirteenth century forward, sought to prevent and to punish conspiracy, embracery, champerty, and maintenance. However, according to the code and custom prevailing since the tenth century, a lord was expected "to maintain" his "man" when someone had done him wrong. The lord's duty was to support him in his right, even in court; and in Anglo-Saxon England it was only when a lord opposed right, "by taking the part of one of

---

[1] S.R., 8 Edward IV, c. 2.
[1A] The Plumpton Correspondence, Camden Soc., 1839, p. 179.

his men who has done wrong," that he was to pay a 120 shilling fine
to the king for his offense.[2] In 1259, justices in eyre were instructed to
investigate cases of "the reception by any magnate or other person, in
return for a gift or a rent, of anyone 'who was not his man, to be under
his advocacy or protection against the king or his neighbour or anybody
else'".[3] The maintenance of one's man or retainer in a lawful and reasonable cause was an accepted part of the social code—"as belongeth
a lord to do" to quote from Montfort's indenture of 1469. "The right
of a lord to protect his own man," Powicke has written, "was bound
up with feudal practice." But by the fourteenth century the word
'maintenance', because of obvious abuses, had acquired an evil con-
notation, too, one comprehending embracery, champerty, and bearing,
and as the bad meaning gained currency it drove out the good.[4] To
tighten the law against these evils and to improve judicial processes,
parliament enacted statutes to stop maintenance, embracery, champerty,
and bearing. None of these offences was new; they had been for long
against the common law; but some men were aware that the custom of
giving livery, signs, badges, or tokens, which identified the wearer as a
man attached to a magnate and enjoying his protection, encouraged
maintenance in its unlawful sense.

Edward I's parliament of 1305 defined as conspirators those who
"retain [receivent] men in the country in their liveries or their fees to
maintain their malicious enterprises".[5] This statute linked together, for
the first time, maintenance (the evil to be eradicated) with livery (the

---

[2] *The Laws of the Earliest English Kings,* ed. F. L. Attenborough, p. 129,
II Aethelstan, c. 3.

[3] Quoted by F. M. Powicke, *King Henry III and the Lord Edward,* p. 405.

[4] The law today still distinguishes between unlawful and lawful maintenance. H. C. Black, *A Law Dictionary, sub* "Maintenance": "Maintenance is
where one officiously meddles in a suit which in no way belongs to him. The
term does not include all kinds of aid in the prosecution or defense of another's
cause. It does not extend to persons having an interest in the thing in controversy, nor to persons of kin or affinity to either party, nor to counsel or
attorneys, for their acts are not officious, nor unlawful."

Professor G. O. Sayles considers it unlikely that maintenance, as an unlaw-
ful act, was an offense at common law before the thirteenth century. The 1294
Yorkshire eyre roll refers to "influential maintainers of false plaints", but the
Ordinance of Conspirators, 1293, does not use maintenance *stricto sensu. Select
Cases in the Court of King's Bench,* III, liv, lvii.

A commons' petition of 1381 expressed the fear that the realm would be
destroyed "by the grievous oppressions in the country, by the outrageous multi-
tude of embracers of quarrels, and maintainers who are like kings in the country." *Rot. Parl.* III, 100, no. 17.

[5] *S. R.,* 33 Edward I [I, p. 145]: the "ordinance and final definition of conspirators" by the king and council in parliament.

psychological stimulus) and retaining (the institutional basis). However, subsequent legislation by Edward III's parliaments concentrated exclusively upon decrying maintenance. An act in 1327 did no more than declare it unlawful "to maintain quarrels or parties in the country to the disturbance of the common law". Three years later a statute prescribed new procedure for hearing suits against "alliances, confederacies, and conspiracies to maintain parties, pleas, and quarrels;" but it said nothing about livery, let alone retaining. An act of 1346 went no further than to require the magnates to oust from their retinues, [retenance] fees, and livery, all bearers and maintainers "without showing to them any aid, favor, or comfort." But such laws were only pious hopes and noble ideals, and no one in 1346 contemplated stopping a peer from retaining men and from giving them fees and livery.[6] Probably so heretical an idea was never even dreamed of, and only in Richard II's reign did a statute seek to restrict the use of livery and to regulate retaining.

This king's first parliament in 1377 declared that "people of small revenue" were enlisting retinues of esquires and others by "giving to them caps and other liveries of one suit a year . . . by such covenant and assurance that every of them shall maintain other in all quarrels, be they reasonable or unreasonable".[7] To check such confederacies by little people, the act of 1377 forbad the giving of "such livery . . . for maintenance of quarrels" but not for lawful maintenance. The justices of assize were to enquire about those who "gather them together in fraternities by such livery to do maintenance." The stress in this statute was clearly upon the little men and upon their agreement to maintain one another in unreasonable quarrels; and it made no attempt to regulate or control the peer's practice of retaining.

Retaining by indenture was, indeed, the very remedy employed in 1390 to eliminate the evils resulting from the giving of livery by the wrong men—those below the rank of banneret. A statute of this year devised a scheme that was both snobbish and practical.[8] It restricted livery of company to only those knights and esquires retained by peers, and it put the responsibility for their good conduct upon the theoretically dependable members of society. First of all, because many men

[6] *S. R.,* 1 Edward III, Stat. 2, c. 14; 4 Edward III, c. 11; 20 Edward III, c. 5. Cf., *S. R.,* I, p. 305, the oath prescribed in 1346 for the king's justices—"that you shall take no fee, as long as you shall be justice, nor robes from any man great or small except the king himself."

[7] *S. R.,* 1 Richard II, c. 7 (p. 3); See also, *Rot. Parl.* III, 23a.

[8] *S. R.,* 13 Richard II, Stat. III, c. 1. Issued under the great seal at Westminster, 12 May 1390. See also, *Rot. Parl.* III, 265a; Seldon Soc., vol. 16, xcvi–c.

were "the more encouraged and bold in their maintenance and evil
deeds" when they belonged to "the retinue of lords and others of our
said realm with fees, robes, and other liveries called liveries of company", all lords spiritual and temporal and others were to oust utterly
"from their service, company, and retinue" any "maintainers, instiga-
tors, barrators, procurors, and embracers of quarrels"—a modest proposal. But this act went still further in trying to cope with the threefold
problem of livery, maintenance, and retaining. It layed down the rules
for the lawful giving of livery and badges, the lord's insignia. Only a
duke, earl, baron or banneret might give livery of company and only
to a knight or an esquire. But a lord was not to give such livery to a
knight or an esquire "if he be not retained with him for term of life,
for peace and war, by indenture, without fraud or evil design". The act
also forbad the lords spiritual, prelates, and clergy, bachelors, esquires.
and men of lower rank to give livery of company as distinct from
livery for their household servants. Except for the domestic residing in
a household, a man to be retained lawfully after 1390 must have an
indenture for term of life, in peace and war — the very phrases found in
Hastings' as well as Gaunt's indentures. In effect, the statute of 1390
restricted livery of company to those knights and esquires lawfully retained by indenture with the lords temporal, and it reserved for the
peers themselves the right to retain, thereby preserving an aristocratic
monopoly over force and arms. In principle, this act placed upon the
peers the responsibility for keeping the practice of retaining within the
law of the land; and it was constructive in that it determined both the
substance and the form of future contracts.

The assumption underlying this "ordinance" to be published in every
shire was that livery of company, and not retaining, was what encouraged
unlawful maintenance and other evil-doings. The principle which the act
invoked to cure such abuses was characteristically English, neither the
abolition nor the prohibition, but the regulation and control of existing
practices. The efficacy of this legislation in reducing illicit maintenance
may be doubted, but it enabled the government to prosecute men with
small revenue who indulged in the habit; and certainly it secured for
the lords temporal their right to retain. This is clear from the way
Richard II's council revised the original petition proposed in 1390. The
commons had asked that "no lord temporal or spiritual" should give
livery to anyone outside his menage; but to this request the king answered that he would "advise" with his council and then ordain a suitable
remedy. The forthcoming ordinance, though entered on the Statute
Roll, was given under the great seal "by the king himself and the
council" who safeguarded successfully the peers' practice by altering the

original petition. Instead of making the giving of livery, let alone retaining, unlawful, the act required a lord, if he was to give livery lawfully to anyone residing outside his household, to retain that man for term of life, in peace as well as war, and by indenture.

Although the statute of 1390 was the foundation of later acts regulating livery and maintenance, none of them until 1468 applied directly to retaining. They dealt primarily with maintenance, embracery, and similar causes of disorder, and secondarily, with the use of badges and livery. Because little men—tailors, tanners, drapers, butchers, and other artisans—wore signs and liveries, an act of 1393 forbad yeomen and others "of lower estate than an esquire", except those "continually dwelling in the house" of a lord, to wear any livery at all.[9] A bolder course of legislation followed close upon the Lancastrian revolution. Henry IV's first parliament of 1399, perhaps to appease the commons, passed what at first appears to be a drastic law "to eschew maintenance and to nourish love, peace, and quietness".[10] This act declared that "no lord" was to give livery or sign of company to any knight, esquire, or yeoman; but not a word was said about the practice of retaining. The lord's right to maintain men by indenture lawfully, as defined in 1390, continued unchallenged as good law as well as current practice. Even the proviso in the 1399 statute to permit the king to give the royal livery to lords, knights, and esquires, both menial and of his retinue, used the old terms and limited the recipients to those who "take of the king yearly fee for term of life". Subsequent statutes of 1401, 1406, 1411, and 1429, confirmed previous acts, modified them, or prescribed more efficient judicial processes for their enforcement.[11] Though they proscribed unlawful maintenance and restricted the use of livery to household servants and officers, and to a lord's council and counsel learned in the law, not one struck directly at the well-established institution of retaining non-resident knights and esquires; and all consistently recognised, at least tacitly, the lord temporal's right so to do.[12]

---

[9] *S. R.,* 16 Richard II, c. 4 (p. 84). See also, *Rot. Parl.* III, 307a.

[10] *S. R.,* 1 Henry IV, c. 7 (pp. 13–14); See also, *Rot. Parl.* III, 23a.

[11] *S. R.,* 2 Henry IV, c. 21; 7 Henry IV, c. 14; 13 Henry IV, c. 3; 8 Henry VI, c. 4, which allowed lords, knights, and esquires in time of war to give "their liveries" to their soldiers in the king's service for the war's duration.

[12] The *Year Book* for Michaelmas Term, 8 Henry VI [1429] (fols. 9b and 10b) reports Thomas Harington's action against R. Rokley brought on the statutes of livery. The defendant's pleadings indicate that the alleged offense was not retaining, but the giving of livery. Four accused receivers of the livery admitted the giving, but each claimed to be Rokley's household retainer or other officer. One was the steward of Rokley's court of the manor of R.; another a parker in his park of L.; a third was the receiver of monies from certain lands

Upon his accession in 1461, Edward IV took cognizance of the evils
produced by maintenance and livery. At his first parliament in 1461,
"articles" in English were drawn up against maintenance; and the king
commanded the lords and all other men not to give signs or livery of
company—except at the king's order.[13] No lord or other person was to
"give any livery of sign, mark, or token of company, but only in such
time as he hath special commandment by the king to raise people for
the assisting of him, resisting of his enemies, or repressing of riots
within his land". Here is a direct statement of policy, the government's
policy towards the use of livery, and underlying it is the assumption
that the peers of the realm had retained, were retaining, and would
continue to retain by indenture men whom the king would call up,
through their lords, in time of need. The giving of livery by a lord to
his retainers was to be, however, in the nature of a royal boon, a fran-
chise or privilege to be acquired only by the king's grace and command
and for the sovereign's benefit. Without the practice of retaining,
King Edward IV's right to command the lords "to raise people" who
would ride and go with them and with their liege lord, the king, would
have been a most fanciful fiction. The *Rolls of Parliaments* add after
these articles,

"And also all lords being at this present parliament [of 1461], have promised
openly before the king in the parliament chamber, that they and each of them
shall help and aid all men that any such [thieves, robbers, murderers] will
take ... though so be that such misdoers be belonging or pertaining to them or
any of them ..."

The lord's right to have retainers, men "belonging or pertaining to
them," was not just tacitly understood, it was expressly stated, as of
record, on the rolls of the 1461 parliament.[14]

in D.; and the fourth his *"meniall home"* in his house to ride and go with him
and to serve him as groom. Since Rokley was not a peer nor a banneret, he
could defend himself only under the clause of the statutes that permitted the
giving of livery to household servants and officers.

[13] *Rot. Parl.* V, 487–88.

[14] The next year, in April 1462, the indenture between Richard, earl of
Warwick, and his retainer, Christopher Lencastre, was entered for better surety
on the King's Remembrancer's Roll. Here again, Edward IV's tolerance of, and
dependence upon the system of non-resident retainers seem manifest. *Eng. Hist.
Rev.*, XXIX, (1914) 720. A letter of Queen Margaret, dated 20 May 1449,
assumes the peers' right to keep retainers but not to give them their liveries.
After telling how the retainers of Lords Beaumont and Ferrers of Groby had
beaten up William Neuby and others, the queen's tenants of Leicester, for
having presented to the king's commissioners that certain persons had taken
livery, the author described three categories of retainers, each apparently law-

Five of Hastings' indentures, those dated between 1461 and 1468, were, then, not only not unlawful, but they were required by the law as layed down in the 1390 statute and subsequent acts of parliament. Only the peers' use of livery without the king's command and, of course, unlawful maintenance were illicit. The retaining of non-resident knights and esquires—to which ranks usage had added, by 1461, gentlemen—was recognized as lawful prior to the parliament of 1468. The statute against liveries of that year, at first sight, appears to be a drastic innovation. It contains what seems an outright prohibition of not only the use of livery and badges, but of retaining non-residents by oath, promise, or indenture. The pertinent part of this act reads:

"And over, that no person of what estate, degree, or condition that he be, by himself or any other for him, from ... [24 June] 1468 give any such livery or badge, or retain any person other than his menial [household] servant, officer, or man learned in the one law or the other, by any writing, oath, or promise; and if he do the contrary, that then he shall incur penalty and forfeiture for every such livery or badge given [of] 100 shillings; and the receiver or acceptor of such oath, writing, or promise or retaining by indenture, for every such retaining or acceptance of every such oath or promise or retaining by indenture shall incur penalty and forfeiture of 100 shillings for every month that any such person is so retained with him by oath, writing, indenture, or promise; and also that every person so retained ... for every month that he is so retained shall forfeit and lose 100 shillings."[15]

This section of the act, when taken alone and at its face value, seems to prohibit the non-resident retainer. Also, it appears to deprive the lords of their right, authorized by the act of 1390 and sanctioned by statutes and long usage, to retain knights and esquires by indenture.

However, 64 of Hastings' indentures are dated after 24 June 1468 when the act became effective. Only one of these retainers is described as "counsel learned" and none as an officer or resident household servant—designations which would bring them within the law. Nevertheless, each of Hastings' contracts exhibits a meticulous regard for legal

ful: "some of the household of the said Lord Ferrers, and some of the clothing of the said lord, with other well-willers to the said lord ..." Besides awarding 100 marks to Neuby, the queen ordered Lord Ferrers not to give any clothing or livery to any person in her lordship of Leicester nor to maintain or support him. But she did not challenge Ferrer's right to retain "servants and tenants and all other that be toward him ..." Mary Bateson, *Records of the Borough of Leicester*, II, pp. 256–257.

Back in November 1433 when the lords swore to keep a set of articles drawn up against wrong-doers, each agreed not to receive, knowingly, nor to hold in his household, "nor maintain" any evil-doer "till his innonce be declared"—after which, presumably, the lord might maintain him in his right. *Rot. Parl.* IV, 422, no. 14. cf., idem, V, 434–35, no. 19.

[15] *S. R.,* 8 Edward IV, c. 2.

niceties, and this suggests that his clerks in drafting the indentures sought to bring the terms within the spirit, if not the letter, of the law. In fact, only in and after 1469 do his contracts contain the limiting phrases, "lawful and reasonable causes", "as right, law, and conscience requireth", and "according to the king's laws". These reservations imply the clerks' awareness of the statute and a conscious effort to prevent the 64 post-1468 indentures from being illicit. The very use of so formal and legalistic a document indicates that Hastings' retaining of non-residents was not clandestine. Actually, several indentures start out like letters patent, open and above-board: "To all men to whom this present writing shall come, Richard Saville, gentleman, sendeth greeting" and "Be it known to all Christian people to whom this present writing shall come." Openness such as this would be the acme of impudence and hypocrisy unless Lord Hastings, and many another peer too, felt assured that he was acting within the law. Was there not, then, some way by which a lord might "aid, help, succor, and support his retainer in all his matters", and do so, as Henry Willoughby's indenture of 1477 added, "according to the law?"

The statute of 1468 contains in itself only one apparent loop-hole for the peers, what may be called a "lawful service" clause. The phrase, "for lawful service done or to be done", occurs in 2 exceptions to the act, one placed in the body of the statute, the other in a proviso. If the phrase "lawful service," be given a broad construction, then Hastings' deftly phrased contracts may be construed as within the terms of the 2 exceptions. The first declares, retroactively, all retainings by indentures made before 24 June 1468 to be void "other than to be the household servant or officer or of his [the lord's] council or for lawful [*loialle*] service done or to be done". If Hastings' non-resident retainers' commitments were considered to be "lawful service", then this exception would have legalized those contracts made before 1468. Furthermore, the proviso contains an exception for "lawful service" which might have authorized indentures drawn after 24 June, 1468. It reads:

"Provided always that this act extend not nor be prejudicial to any gift, grant, or confirmation made or to be made of any fee, annuity, pension, rent, lands, or tenements by the king or any other person or persons to any person or persons for their counsel given or to be given and their lawful service done or to be done and for any other cause not unlawful [*et pur nulle autre cause desloialle*] and to any other intent not unlawful [*ne a nulle autre entent desloialle*], albeit that the person or persons to whom such gift, grant, or confirmation is or shall be made be not learned in the one law or in the other . . ."[16]

<hr/>

[16] *Ibid.*, p. 428 and *n.* 1; Rot. Parl. V, 633–34, in English to the same effect: "lawful service done or to be done, and for none other unlawful cause, nor to none other unlawful intent." A collation of the text of c. 2 as printed

The extension of this "lawful service" exception to "any other cause not unlawful" or "intent not unlawful", stresses, by contrast, the lawfulness of certain services. The meaning of the "lawful service" clause is at best ambiguous—perhaps it was so intended. Had only Edward IV's council defined the clause, or had his justices applied it in court, then the meaning of this exception—whether it exempted the lords of parliament and their retainers from the penalties of the statute—might be ascertained. No such evidence has been found; nor has extensive search revealed a single instance, before the case of Lord Burgavenny in 1506, of the prosecution of a peer under the act of 1468.[17] The "lawful service" clause may have been sufficient to allow the peers the right to retain non-residents by indenture lawfully. Even in 1472, "unlawful retainders" seems still to have meant the retaining of "riotous persons and maintainers." The speaker followed the well-worn convention of

in the *Statutes of the Realm* with the original on the Statute Roll [C74/8 mem. 1] discloses no variant readings in these clauses. The *Nova Statuta*, printed by Pinson in 1501–02, included the phrase, *au ascum person ou persones*, in the text as does the English version in the Rolls of the Parliaments; but the Statute Roll omits it, and the *Statutes of the Realm* carries it only as a footnote taken from the printed statutes. Neither the inclusion nor the exclusion of the phrase is of moment to the present argument.

A final proviso allowed the use of even signs and livery on certain ceremonial occasions (the king's or the queen's coronation, the installation of bishops, and the "marriage of any lord or lady of estate") and "in the defense of the king and of this realm."

[17] The prosecution of Hastings' retainer, Hugh Peshale, an esquire, (described below, p. 83) charged that he had retained others, not that Hastings had retained him. Peshale's indenture with Hastings is dated in 1479, and so his indictment in 1477 appears to have no relevance to the present argument. The act of 1390 had prohibited esquires from retaining men; hence for Peshale to have done so was illegal.

An ordinance in parliament, 6 October 1472, allowed the king's first-born son, Edward, prince of Wales, "to retain and to give his honorable livery and sign at his pleasure" and "the persons so retained" to "receive, wear, and use the same livery or sign," the various statutes (including Edward IV's) "notwithstanding." This act may seem to imply that the prince was prohibited from retaining by the previous statutes. Although an insoluble ambiguity exists in the phrasing, the stress is more upon the giving of livery than upon retaining. The preamble refers to previous princes' "liberties to give their liveries and signs at their pleasures" and to "divers statutes against givers, takers, and receivers of liveries and signs;" it admits that Prince Edward "is as well as any other person restrained of giving of such liveries and signs." But it makes no mention of retaining until the positive statement: "the king also willing that . . . the prince should be at his liberty in retaining any person and giving his signs and liveries . . ." Was not the reason for mentioning the prince's liberty to retain in order to designate those persons to whom he would give livery rather than to enable him to retain lawfully? *Rot. Parl.* VI, 157; *S. R.*, 12 Edward IV, c. 4; *Cal. Patent Rolls, 1467–77*, p. 449 (6 July 1474), contains an exemplification of this ordinance. See below, pp. 103–05.

asking, in the commons' name, the government to enforce many old statutes, from Westminster I (1275) on, forbidding "maintenance, extortions, oppressions, liveries, signs . . . and retainders" and "in especial 20 Edward III [1346]". That "noble progenitor", according to the 1472 speaker, had "caused unlawful retainders of riotous persons and maintainers . . . to be left" [stopped]. To him, these were the "misgoverned persons" against whom the statutes had been passed. Do not the speaker's remarks imply that he, and his listeners, too, recognized the lawfulness of the peers' practice of retaining not only household servants but as well non-resident knights, esquires, and gentleman?[17A] What the lords probably took to be a right in Edward IV's reign, it must be remembered, had begun as a duty layed down by the statute of 1390. That act had allowed the lords temporal to continue to retain knights and esquires, but only in accordance with the terms prescribed in the act itself—all of which still appear in Lord Hastings' indentures.

The close parallel between the reservations in Hastings' post-1468 contracts—"according to the law", "law, right and conscience", and "lawful and reasonable causes"—and the phrases in the 1468 act, "not unlawful cause," "intent not unlawful", and "lawful service", seems more than coincidental. It suggests that Lord Hastings and his clerks, perhaps advised by Lawrence Lowe "of his counsel learned", were trying quite deliberately to phrase the contracts in language that would keep them within the terms of the statute. Certainly up to 1468 the notion was current, and accepted, that a lord's protection and, in return, his retainer's service might conform to right, law, and conscience. Reason, equity, and conscience were invoked constantly to justify one man's aid to another both in and out of court. Back about 1400 an anonymous writer sent a letter in behalf of an esquire of the king's body to a man, seemingly a judge, and asked that the recipient "will be aiding, favouring, and succoring by all the means which you well can by law and reason [*de loy et raison*] to the end that he [the esquire] will be able to feel that this my prayer be of worth to him . . ."[18] Because men "of small conscience" had been impanelled as jurors, an act of 1484 required the sheriffs to call up only men "of substance" and "of good conscience.[18A] A few years later (1485—1491) the duke of Suffolk pro-

---

17A *Rot. Parl.* VI, 8; S. R., 20 Edward III, c. 1.

18 M. D. Legge, *Anglo-Norman Letters and Petitions,* p. 129, no. 77.

18A Thus Frowicke, C. J., in 1500 explained the purpose of, and the reason for this statute: *pur le mischief qe le viconte impanell' simple persons et de small conscience . . . ou de substance . . .* S. B. Chrimes, *English Constitutional Ideas in the XV Century,* pp. 391–92, from *Year Book* 15 Henry VII, Mich. plea 1.

tested to Richard Roos, esquire, that his servants had been "grievously distressed and amerced in [Roos's] court there against right and good conscience;" and about the same time a lesser man begged Roos "to do as reason and right requireth".[19]

Right, reason, equity, and conscience, undefined but understood, were the criteria that nobility and gentry used to justify their matters, causes, or intents. The king, too, used these terms in discharging his treasurer from his obligations in 1469, and a writ of privy seal declared he did so "according to right, equity, and conscience." Even influence might be lawful, as when R. Sheffield, an M. P., extended his "lawful favor" to the City of London. The moral measure of "deeds done," as John Trevelyan described them, was whether they were "contrary to right and conscience," hence bad, evil, and to be punished; or whether they accorded with right, equity and conscience and so were within both the law and the moral code. Perhaps Lord Hastings, too, believed sincerely that by limiting his aid to only the retainer's "lawful and reasonable causes" he had brought his contracts within the intended spirit, if not the letter, of the law.[20]

In actual practice, Edward IV and the lords of his council not only allowed peers to retain, but they even used the lord-retainer contract as a peace-making device. At Nottingham on 13 May 1474, they persuaded Richard, duke of Gloucester, and Henry, earl of Northumberland, to settle their differences by a legal contract. This they embodied in a lord-retainer indenture, dated 28 July 1474, which witnessed that Northumberland promised to be Gloucester's "faithful servant" and "to do service unto the said duke at all times lawful and convenient when he there unto by the said duke shall be lawfully required." In return, Gloucester granted and promised to be Northumberland's "good and faithful lord at all times, and to sustain him in his right afore all other persons," except the king, the queen, and Prince Edward. Then follows the particularity which presumably prompted this alliance. The duke promised not to ask for, nor lay claim to, any offices or fee that the earl had of the king's grant of anyone else. Also, Gloucester agreed not to "accept nor retain into his service any servant . . . that was . . . with the said earl retained of fee, clothing, or promise according to the appointment taken betwixt the said duke and earl by the king's highness and the lords of his council." Here is proof that the king and his

---

[19] *H. M. C. Report* XII, part iv, 10; cf., *The Plumpton Correspondence,* Camden Soc., 1839, pp. 64–65, 73.

[20] P.R.O., E404/74/2 mem. 62; J. Wedgwood, *History of Parliament, Biographies,* p. 70 *n.* 2; *The Trevelyan Papers,* Royal Hist. Soc., 1st Ser. vol. 67, pp. 81–22.

councillors both condoned the practice of retaining and used it—in form at least—as a device to keep the peace. Furthermore, the phrases, "times lawful" and "lawfully required," support the conclusion that certain services by peers' retainers, and hence the peers' practice of retaining itself, were considered in the 1470s to be within the law.[21]

However, the king's justices, and others too, were coming to realize that the practice of retaining was the root from which liveries and badges blossomed into the fruit of maintenance and embracery. To suppose that the lords justices or the house of commons, to protect the justices of the peace from obstruction by lords and their retainers, had petitioned for the act of 1468 at first seems natural.[22] But actually, the bill which became this statute, Gray has disclosed, was not a commons' petition but "an official or government bill" and, presumably, one "drafted in council".[23] Edward IV's council, in which Hastings was so prominent and influential a member, apparently approved the bill; and its technical details about new judicial processes presume that the judges

[21] For this indenture, see Appendix A. Dr. N. B. Lewis very generously provided me with a transcript of the original. Among the earls of Northumberland's retainers were at least two generations of Plumptons. (*The Plumpton Correspondence,* pp. lxv–lxxv.) Edward IV also used the good-lordship formula in 1476 when he settled with William, Lord Berkeley. Berkeley conveyed to the king's son, Richard of York, any right he might have to the lands of the late duke of Norfolk. The agreement then stated: "and after security so made, the king on his part promiseth to be his [Berkeley's] good and gracious lord according to his laws." Though the king's laws might limit even King Edward IV's good lordship, still good lordship itself was assumed to be within, and not against, the law. John Smyth, *Lives of the Berkeleys,* II, 118–19.

[22] The intrusion of armed men into the courts appears in a letter from Margaret, countess of Warwick, to Henry, bishop of Norwich, in 1402. She asked the bishop to punish Parson of Beeston for having held a hundred court in the earl of Arundel's name in her hundred of Wayland *"ove cent archiers pur la mainteigner."* M. D. Legge, *Anglo-Norman Letters and Petitions,* p. 100, no. 52.

In the reign of Henry VIII, perhaps *c.* 1530, Sir William Gascoigne, of Yorkshire, was said to be "of such power and strength in those parts, and hath of the most part of the common jurors in those parts, and other maintainers and oppressors of your subjects in his retinue, badge, livery, and unlawful confederacy, and is himself at every sessions of the peace..." The writer asked for writs of *sub poena* to compell Gascoigne and the rioters to appear before the king in the star chamber. Against such incidents, which were all too prevalent, must be projected the efforts to regulate and control lawful retaining to procure a proper perspective on the practice. In the case of Gascoigne, who was only a knight, he was, of course, breaking the law at any date after 1390. *Yorkshire Archeological Soc. Record Series, XLV, Star Chamber Proceedings,* no. 17, p. 56.

[23] H. L. Gray, *The Influence of the Commons on Early Legislation,* pp. 132, 259 and *n.* 125, 62. The original bill does not appear to be in the P.R.O., and Gray deduced its designation as an "official bill" from the form of the statute.·

drafted its terms and perhaps inspired it. The prelates, too, in both council and parliament may have pushed through the act of 1468. Even so, those lords temporal present, of the 46 peers summoned to the parliament of 1468, either failed to defeat the bill or gave it their assent. Why should the lords' temporal, mighty as they were in 1468, have approved the enactment of a law which would have been, had it applied to them, a self-denying ordinance? Such things were to happen in England's parliaments, but the record of the Yorkist magnates and the cynicism that streaked their politics hardly encourage a belief in such self-sacrifice. Either hypocritically they passed a law that they had no intention to abide by; or else they understood that the "lawful service" clauses would permit them to have non-resident retainers.

Furthermore, Edward IV in 1468 had to rely, for military and political support, upon peers loyal to him and upon their retainers. Just the year before, in January 1467, Sir John Howard (Lord Howard in 1470, the duke of Norfolk in 1483) advised King Edward that he would go with him over-sea. Howard agreed to lead as many men as the king might assign to him and pay for; but, he added, "beside that I will bring with me a hundred good men and at mine own cost and charge, to do the king service in his wars for half a year and cost the king nothing." Sweet words surely to every English king in any year of his reign. Edward IV's reliance on the magnates was such that the king, himself, stood to lose immediate strength and power if the new statute were to be enforced against the lords. For the king and lords to have allowed, let alone sponsored, the passage of a bill so much against their advantage seems unlikely. The political situation in 1468 made Edward IV especially dependent upon the system of retaining. Already, the earl of Warwick's defection had been rumored, but discounted, in October 1467. In November, near Derby, several men [*gentes*] of Lord Grey of Codnor, Hastings' retainer at the time, were murdered. Unrest was not only in the air, but on the land. Back in September 1467, the mayor and aldermen of London had ordained "that no freeman or officer of the City shall take or use the livery of any lord or other magnate under penalty of losing his freedom [of the City] and office for ever". Warwick's suspected hostility towards Edward IV, the modern editor of the *London Letter Books* suggested, prompted this ordinance. The City fathers thought the wisest way to preserve the peace of London was to avoid entangling alliances with baronial factions which seemed about to resume the Wars of the Roses.[24]

24 *The expenses of Sir John Howard* ... *1462* ... *1469*, ed. B. Botfield (Roxburghe Club, 1841) pp. 172–73; William of Worcester, *Annales rerum Anglicarum*, ed. Thomas Hearne (1774) II, 512.
Lord Herbert in October 1467 reported to Edward IV a rumor that War-

The next spring, at the opening of the second session of parliament on 12 May 1468, the chancellor, the bishop of Bath and Wells, declared that the king's "intent final was to minister law and justice, and to plant, fix, and set peace through all this his realm". To further this end, and perhaps to divert the belligerent instincts of the peerage from the shires of England, Edward proposed an "outward peace" to be had through the recovery of "his right and title to the crown and land of France."[25] For this war, parliament granted money, and although seven years were to pass before his expedition set sail across the channel, Edward's eye was doubtless upon military resources some of which the peers and their retainers could best provide. With Warwick flirting with Henry VI's Queen Margaret and her Lancastrians in exile, with the Londoners fearful of domestic discord, and with the king wishing to call up an army for service overseas, to put upon the Statute Roll an act authorizing the government to repress retaining by the lords, and so alienate their loyalty, would seem utterly quixotic. In years to come Tudor justices, and perhaps prelates and townsmen, too, were to take a different view of the statute of 1468. Queen Mary's chancery named this very act as one prohibiting lords and councillors from retaining men and giving them livery and badges; but she, like each Tudor sovereign, dispensed with its application and issued, by letters patent, licenses to lords and councillors to keep a specified number of retainers.

Had Edward IV used the same procedure and granted, under the king's dispensing power, a license to Lord Hastings to retain non-residents, there would be no doubt about the statute's application to the peers. The chamberlain's familiarity with the king and his membership in the council would have enabled him readily to procure such a permit; and this would, of course, have made his contracts lawful. However, no such license remains among the Hastings Manuscripts in the Huntington Library; nor has one been found elsewhere. And yet copies of Edward VI's license to Hastings' great-grandson, Francis, earl of Huntingdon, to keep 100 retainers and to give them his livery, badge, or cognizance, survive at both London and San Marino. The earl's retainers might, the patent reads, "grant to do unto him their service

wick was favoring Queen Margaret's party; but the king considered this a frivolous charge. In November 1467, "those around the king favored Lord Grey [of Codnor]. And the duke of Clarence favored the earl of Shrewsbury and Vernon," an esquire under suspicion whom the king ordered to be tried. R. R. Sharpe (*Calendar of Letter Books ... of London,* L, p.73 and *n.* 1) remarked that Warwick's attitude towards Edward IV and the queen's family necessitated the ordinance of 23 September 1467; and he implied that the act against livery, passed in May 1468, resulted from the fear of Warwick.

[25] *Rot. Parl.* V, 622b.

when he shall appoint and require the same for [the king's] better service." These last words disclose the royal rationalization of the system of retaining, whether by Edward VI or Edward IV. Eternal hope that lords and their retainers would remain true and constant to their liege lord, the king, may explain the prolonged tolerance of the practice. For Edward IV to have licensed his chamberlain to retain 90 peers, knights, esquires, and gentlemen would have been an easy and a natural thing to do. Yet searches in the Patent Rolls of Edward IV and among the few extant writs of privy seal and signet failed to disclose a single license, or even an allusion to one, for either Hastings or any other Yorkist peer.[26] Hazardous as the argument of silence always is, it is hard to avoid the tentative conclusion that Edward IV did not grant licenses to permit peers to keep non-resident retainers. Or if he did, such licenses were not issued through the conventional administrative agencies that the Tudors were to use and that Henry VI's council had used for similar purposes.

A council minute, dated 23 July 1454 when Henry VI was *non compos mentis,* indicates how Richard, duke of York, "protector and defensor of England," procured such a license. This record tells that "the king by the advice of his council willed and granted" that the duke

"should have power and authority to give the king's livery of colors to 80 gentlemen after his discretion, they and every of them to be sworn to be afeed without [with] no man but with the king, without his special license; and that hereupon letters under the privy seal and great seal be made in due form."[26A]

On this occasion, the king's council, but in the king's name, gave York permission to give the king's livery, not his own, to a specified number of men. Then the council authenticated their act "in due form," to wit, through a writ of privy seal ordering the issue of a letter under the great seal. Although this was obviously an extraordinary situation and the council granted an extraordinary privilege, the prescribed procedure was conventional and routine. Also, this minute mentions, as a matter of common knowledge, the king's use of a "special license" to allow his own feed retainers to be feed by other men; and this license was, presumably, to be procured through the same administrative process— a privy seal warrant for a letter under the great seal.

Furthermore, when Edward VI, Mary, and Elizabeth I licensed their

[26] Licenses for other purposes, *e. g.* to become a denizen, were ordered under warrants of privy seal as were Queen Mary's licenses to retain. Also, the privy seal office kept one part of "a roll indented" of knights whom Henry IV and Henry V retained to serve in war for one year. British Museum MS. Additional 24062, fols. 9v, 10, 50v.

[26A] H. Nicolas, *Proceedings and Ordinances of The Privy Council of England,* VI, p. 209.

lords, knights, and civil servants to retain men and to give them liveries, they, too, issued letters patent by warrants under the privy seal. And in Edward VI's case the council originated these permissions. Hence the conventional course for Edward IV to have followed would have been the same one used by both Henry VI and the Tudors. Yet neither the Patent nor the Close Rolls, nor the few extant writs of privy seal that have been examined, reveal any evidence that Edward IV used this procedure for licensing lords either to give their retainers liveries or to keep non-resident retainers. Possibly this king granted some peers, like Lord Hastings, permission by word of mouth with or without his council's advice; possibly the long lost records of the Yorkist council contained licenses to give livery; or possibly the lords gave their retainers badges and insignia without Edward IV's permission; or perhaps the peers complied with the statutes and gave livery to their retainers only when they were on the king's service. After all, the special grant in 1454 to the duke of York to give 80 men the king's livery assumed that he already had the lawful right to retain his own men. Only for the 80 men to use Henry VI's colors did the duke, apparently, seek a license. The tantalizing absence of any evidence, even after 1468, that Edward IV granted the lords licenses either to keep retainers or to give them livery creates an argument of silence, but a strong one, that the act of 1468 was not intended to apply to the peers of the realm.

A second argument of silence—the absence of to-be-expected evidence—also favors the contention that the "lawful service" clause in the act of 1468 sufficed to enable the peers to retain non-residents legally. Had Edward IV's government prosecuted peers guilty of retaining, a few cases should be recorded on the Plea Rolls. A sampling of the King's Bench Rolls of 1469—70, the year after the statute went into effect, failed to reveal any prosecutions of peers for retaining; nor have any such cases been found on several rolls of this court from Henry VII's reign. However, the King's Bench Rolls do record indictments, before justices of the peace, of men accused of violating the statutes of livery, maintenance, and retaining. These indictments were called up before the king's bench where they were heard and determined. The striking feature in these cases, brought on the statute of 1468 and the earlier ones, is the social status of the defendants. All were little men, very little men, except for the knights and esquires who had retained them. Their inferior social rank brought them clearly within the terms of all the acts since 1390 against livery, maintenance, and retaining. These cases show that the statutes were actually and not infrequently enforced; they show for what offences, and against whom—little men, not lords of parliament—they were applied; and in so doing, they create a third argument favoring the proposition that the peers were not originally, in 1468, intended to fall within the terms of the act.

The King's Bench Rolls from 1469—70 contain several prosecutions for maintenance brought against small men, a draper, a scrivener of London, and the like. Such men, who had no apparent connection with retaining, were accused of "trespass and contempt against the form of the statute [*singular*] of maintainers and sustainers of quarrels recently edited." The charge in each of these cases was for having committed maintenance in the king's courts and was not for using livery, nor for retaining or being retained.[27]

Seven years later, however, during Trinity Term 1477, an indictment was brought before the justices of the peace at Ludlow against Hugh Peshale for having given liveries of cloth and robes to 14 men.[28] Peshale, an esquire, of Knightley in Staffordshire, was presumably the Hugh "Percehale", esquire, of Staffordshire, who signed an indenture with Lord Hastings on 28 April 1479. Later, in 1488, Percehale became sheriff of Stafford and was subsequently knighted. Back in 1477, however, the grand jury accused him of having given and delivered to 8 men at Newport, Shropshire, ($11\frac{1}{2}$ miles south-west of Stafford,) on 10 August 1476, 3 liveries "against the ordinances and provisions of divers statutes in this case established and provided and against the king's peace." The 8 recipients included Thomas and Reginald Peshale and 6 men of Newport; and Hugh also provided livery for 6 men from Edgmond, a Shropshire village about 3 miles away. The 14 recipients included 2 weavers, 1 hewster, 1 saddler, 1 tailor, 3 husbandmen, 1 hosteler [or hostler?], 1 fisherman, 2 yeomen, and 2 laborers. All of these men were below the rank of esquire, or even gentleman, and the statute of 1390 and the subsequent acts prohibited them from receiving livery of company. Peshale himself was only an esquire,

---

[27] P.R.O., KB27/838 fols. 39v, 25v, 6v, 5, 35, 39. Michaelmas Term, 49 Henry VI [1470]. The "recently edited" statute was probably not the 1468 act for it does not mention maintenance, only livery and retaining. KB27/833/ fol. 140, Trinity Term 9 Edward IV [1469] contains a prosecution for maintenance in which the defendant admits to having helped his cousin in her appeal for the death of her husband by hiring for her a lawyer at Westminster and advising her. Another defendant claimed to be in the woman's menial service. KB833/ mems. 35 and 43 contain actions against small men for the maintenance and sustenance of quarrels.

[28] P.R.O., KB8/1/ mem. 19 [a small sheet of parchment containing the return of the inquest at Ludlow]; KB27/865/ mem. 123v [for the record of the case in the king's bench]. For extracts from the record, see Appendix C. Cf. *Third Report of the Deputy Keeper of the Public Records* (1842) Appendix II, p. 215, no. 6.

not a baron, and so it was unlawful for him to give them livery. The indictment before Sir Richard Grey, the queen's son and later Hastings' enemy, Sir Thomas Littleton, Sir Richard Ludlow, and 4 other justices of the peace was sealed by Grey and delivered to the king's bench by John Sauston during the fortnight after St. John [24 June]. Even more miraculous, the defendants appeared in that court through their attorney, Simon Hadington, the next term, Michaelmas 1477. They answered, severally,

"that the aforesaid indictment is not sufficient in law to put them, or anyone of them, to answer the same indictment, for this [reason] to wit, that the same indictment does not make mention of how much livery of cloth or robes the aforesaid Hugh Peshale gave to the aforesaid Thomas Peshale and the others; nor that the same Thomas Peshale and all the others had received the same livery of the aforesaid cloths and robes from the aforesaid Hugh Peshale, as ought to be done according to the law; and for this insufficiency they severally ask that thence they be dismissed by the court etc."

The court then perused the indictment. They found that it was not sufficient in law, and they adjudged Hugh Peshale and the 14 alleged recipients of livery to go thence without day. So ended this attempt by the Shropshire quarter sessions to enforce the statutes of liveries against these little villagers to whom Peshale, perhaps even then retained by Lord Hastings, had given cloth or robes.

The Yorkshire quarter sessions held in 1496 at Tadcaster before John, Earl of Suffolk, Sir John Saville, William Fairfax, and John Chaloner, justices of the peace for the West Riding, indicted Sir Thomas Darcy and James Stanley, clerk, for having given livery against the form of the statutes.[29] Stanley, the jurors charged, had presented, on 4 January 1496 at Manchester, a livery or sign commonly called the eaglesfoot to John Lacy, gentleman. He, too, was indicted for having received and worn it openly at various places in Yorkshire from 4 january until the inquest on 28 March. The indictment explained further that Lacy "was never retained in the service of this James [Stanley] as his household servant or man learned in both laws against the form of the statutes of liveries established as in this case provided." Stanley also was accused of having given his silver eaglesfoot to more than a dozen other men including 7 labourers, 2 millers, 2 shearmen, 2 yeomen, a gentleman, a husbandman, and a slaymaker. These men put the insignia in their caps, put the caps on their heads, and wore them in various villages, "the royal license in respect thereof not obtained." Two other lists of men, allegedly recipients of Stanley's eaglesfoot, were included

29 P.R.O., KB8/3/ part I mems. 5, 6, The *Baga de Secretis. Third Report of the Deputy Keeper* ... Appendix II, p. 219, no. 6.

in the indictments which asserted that they had never "been household servants of the aforesaid James Stanley, nor retained in his service, nor men learned in both laws." Before the end of Henry's reign, Stanley was fined £145,610 and his retainers £58,644 for "retainders."[29A]

The same quarter sessions also indicted Thomas Darcy, knight, of Yorkshire for having given, on 1 December 1494 at Temple Newsome in the West Riding, his sign, a silver buckshead, to a number of yeomen and laborers.[30] These men had received and worn the token in their caps until 28 March 1496 "against the form of the established statutes of livery of cloth where none of the aforesaid [6 men] nor any one of them, were ever household servants of this Thomas Darcy, or retained in his service, or learned in both laws."

The clause, "retained in his service", which appears also in the charge against Stanley, implies that men might be so retained and that such retaining, as distinct from being retained as household servant or man of law, was considered lawful. These two cases from 1496, and that of Peshale in 1477, show that knights and esquires were indicted, along with the recipients of their liveries or tokens, for having violated the various statutes established in this case. The acts against livery and maintenance were not, it seems, the dead-letters that many historians have supposed them to have been. Plenty of indicments, carefully phrased to meet the technicalities of the law, Peshale's excepted, were made at quarter sessions. Then, as the statute of 1468 provided, they were called up to the king's bench. The statement in 1496, that Stanley had not obtained the royal license to give his badge, implies that such dispensations might be had—at least in theory. But what is so conspicuously absent is any case, or any allusion to one, against a lord of parliament.

The same silence about the peers of the realm prevails in the case of prosecutions brought for having retained men against the form of the statutes of retainers. Though no indictment has been found from Edward IV's reign, 2 men, Thomas Neville, esquire, and William Bassett, esquire, were indicted in 1501 for retaining.[31] A writ signed by Fineux

---

[29A] C. G. Bayne, *Select Cases in the Council of Henry VII*, (Selden Soc.), p. cxxi, *n. 1*, based on P.R.O., S. P. 1, vol. I, fols. 104–107, last item. Bayne states that the fine was levied at the Lancaster assizes.

[30] P.R.O., KB8/3/ part I mems. 6, 7.

[31] For Neville's case, P.R.O. KB8/3/ part IV/ mems. 40,41. Cf., *Third Report of the Deputy Keeper . . .* Appendix II, p. 225, no. 6. For Bassett's case, KB27/960/ membranes not numbered, but the 12th recto from the end marked X⁰, Trinity Term, 16 Henry VII; also KB27/962/ mem. 112, Hilary Term, 17 Henry VII.

The case of the Abbot of Eynsham v. Sir Robert Harcourt in 1503 was for riots done by him "and divers other evil-disposed persons to him belonging and

J., on 6 May 1501, ordered the indictment of Neville taken 23 October 1499 at Kidderminster, Worcestershire, before the justices of the peace, to be sent up to the king's bench in Trinity term. The record tells that a grand jury of 12 men said that Thomas Neville, esquire, of Childeswikwane, Gloucestershire, had retained 4 men, including 2 yeomen and a painter, to stay with him and to cling to him in all his affairs against anyone soever, the lord king alone excepted. The men, too, were indicted for having "retained themselves" with Neville "against the form of the statute of retainers established and provided in this kind of case."

The same charge was brought the same year against William Bassett of Blore, Staffordshire, who was perhaps, Hastings' retainer of the same name and county. Fineux issued a writ of *venire facias* 11 July 1501 to the sheriff of Staffordshire to bring before the king's bench in Michaelmas term Bassett and Giles Button, Richard Hood, Thomas Joly, and John Starkey, all 4 described as yeomen. They were the tenants of the abbot of Blessed Mary, Rochester, of Prince Arthur's foundation, and they, too, were accused of trespass and contempt "against the form of the statute of retainers." In Hilary Term, 1502, they appeared in court through their attorney, Richard Askam, who asked for a day in court in Easter term. This was granted. Then at Easter, the defendants repeated this manoeuvre and were given a day in Trinity term when they were conceded another postponement until Michaelmas. Again their request for a day in court in Hilary Term 1503 was conceded, but at this point in the Plea Roll, the record stops, and the lower half of the membrane remains blank. Had the defendants worn down the prosecution to the point of giving up, or had they purchased a pardon? Their indictment states that the 4 men were retained and had confederated with Bassett on 20 March 1499 at Blore where they pledged "their mutual faiths and at the same time gave oaths and swore their oaths on the Bible that in high and low justice, and in injustice to us [the king] and not of right, they held themselves to one another." They also had "confederated at the special request of William Bassett" from 20 March 1499 to 6 April 1500.

The attemps to prosecute Neville and Bassett for having violated the statute of retainers show that the common-law courts, quarter sessions and king's bench, did use the judicial processes provided in the statutes

retained." But the editor considered that the statute alluded to was more likely 3 Henry VII c. 12, against the retaining of the king's tenants, than the act of 1468. In any event, Harcourt's having retained men was only incidental to the main charges brought against him. *Select Cases in the Star Chamber,* (Selden Soc. vol. 16) ed. I. S. Leadam, pp. 137–162 and xcv *et seq.*

against persons alleged to have retained, or to have been retained, unlawfully. But as in the actions brought for maintenance and livery, here, too, the defendants were men whom the act of 1390 forbad, because of their low rank and degree, either to give or to receive livery, to retain or to be retained.[32] If the facts alleged against the defendants in these cases were true, then they were clearly guilty of breaking the laws against livery, maintenance, and retaining that had prevailed since 1390. Furthermore in none of these indictments was any distinction, by date or designation, drawn between the numerous statutes against the three offenses. However, lawyers in Queen Mary's reign singled out the act of 1468 and construed it as applying to all men; then individuals procured licenses by letters patent to dispense with its penalties. But there is no evidence that in 1468 and immediately thereafter Edward IV's statute was interpreted to make the peers' practice of retaining non-residents unlawful.

An alternative explanation is to assume that Lord Hastings and the other peers who retained men by indenture after 1468 broke the law but relied for their protection upon Edward IV's tolerance, or his courts' inability to indict them, or the royal clemency. Possibly they purchased general pardons, a traffic in which flourished during Edward's reign, to escape the statutory penalties for retaining. General pardons included, among the many wrongs forgiven, trespass and contempt against the statutes of liveries and retaining. These offenses head the list of wrongs, and at first sight this seems to support the view that the lords first defied the statute of 1468 and then bought pardons. However, the general pardon embraced a whole repertoire of crime—from murder, rape, rebellion and insurrection to conspiracy, maintenance, routs, riots, and unlawful assembly. The form of pardon used in 1462 specified trespasses and contempts committed "against the form of the statutes of liveries of cloth and caps;" but after the statute of 1468 was enacted, this clause comprehended retaining, too. Pardons granted in 1469—70 substituted the more detailed phrase, "the statutes of signs, liveries of cloth and caps, and retainings." What these pardons

[32] In Henry VII's reign, other small men, not peers, were prosecuted. Oliver Stockdale of Thorp, a Yorkshire yeoman, was distrained in Michaelmas 1496 to answer for trespasses against the statute of liveries, KB27/941/ mem. xvj [second series of numbers]. Robert Throgmorton, esquire, of Worcestershire, was indicted 25 June 1499 for having retained men and was summoned before the king's bench in Hilary Term 1501, KB8/3/ part III/ mems. 14, 15, cf., *Third Report of the Deputy Keeper* ... Appendix II, p. 223, no. 6. John Danncer of Haggely, Worcs. husbandman, fined with the king in Michaelmas 1501 for trespasses and contempts against the statute of retainers, KB27/961/ membranes not numbered, this one is dorso of "Fines and Amercements."

did was to remit suit of the king's peace (*sectam pacis nostre*) against the many common-law offenses; but the purchaser was still to "stand to right in the king's court if anyone should wish to plead against him." Outlawry, which might lie for many of these offenses, was pardoned, too, and to the recipient of a pardon the king granted his "firm peace". However, the real purpose of the general pardon, high authority now holds, was to make a man secure against the forfeiture which outlawry entailed.[33] In any event, the great variety and the number of crimes included in these pardons show that they went way beyond livery, maintenance, and retaining.

Furthermore, the social status of the men who bought general pardons ranged from that of husbandman, mariner, or fishmonger to the peers of the realm. The *Supplementary Patent Rolls, 1461—1483,* once called Pardon Rolls, record literally hundreds, if not thousands, of pardons granted to men of every rank and degree. Most of them were certainly not retained by the lords of parliament. Although a peer's possession of a general pardon may have made him feel secure for past offenses against the statutes, it did not legalize his current and future retaining. In any event, a pardon after the fact was hardly a proper or satisfactory formula by which to cloak the practice with legality. Custom with the force of law, established by a century's usage, seems the most likely sanction of retaining by the lords, the king's "counsellors born". Their status in society was exceptional, and without express mention of the lords in the act of 1468, as was done in the 1390 statute, probably no one contemplated its application to the peers. Until positive evidence be found that the parliament of 1468 intended to deprive the lords of their customary right and statutory duty to retain men for term of life, in peace as well as war, the negative conclusion, that the acts against retaining were not intended to apply to peers, seems unavoidable. The frequent attempts to prosecute men of lower rank and degree also serve to support this proposition. Its validity would mean, then, that Lord Hastings' contracts with his retainers were not unlawful.

Howsoever Hastings may have justified his retaining of knights, esquires, and gentlemen after 1468—perhaps by faith in Edward IV alone—he died a forgiven man. He purchased, on 12 March 1483, a general pardon of all offenses including trespasses, misprisions, and con-

---

[33] Upon finding the addition of the words, "and retainings," taken from the statute of 1468, in general pardons in and after 1469, I hoped that the use of pardons, purchased by many peers, might explain how Hastings and other lords avoided the penalties of that act. But Professor C. H. Williams advises me that the general pardon was obtained in order to avoid the dangers of outlawry and forfeiture.

tempts committed "against the form of the statutes of signs, liveries of cloth and caps, and retainings." The *additio* identifying him on the Pardon Roll, entered exactly three months and a day before his execution, reads like an obituary prepared to insert into a Yorkist *Who Was Who:*

"William Hastings, knight, Lord Hastings; *alias* the said William Hastings, knight, Lord Hastings; *alias* the said William Hastings of Hastings, knight; *alias* the said William Hastings, knight, Lord Hastings, our chamberlain; *alias* the said William Hastings, knight, Lord Hastings, our councillor; *alias* the said William Hastings, knight, Lord Hastings, keeper, governor-general, supervisor, and our lieutenant as well of our town of Calais, our Castle of Calais, our Tower of Rysbank, and our Castle of Guisnes as of our Marches near or around the aforesaid Town and Castle of Calais, the Tower of Rysbank, and Castle of Guisnes lying in whatsoever way within our obedience there; *alias* the said William Hastings, knight, son and heir of Leonard Hastings, knight; *alias* the said William Hastings, knight and etc. In whose etc. Witness the king at Westminster the 12th day of March. By the king himself."[34]

[34] *The Supplementary Patent Rolls, 1461–1483* Pardon Rolls, P.R.O., C67/50/ mem. 1 [12 March 1483] and m. 6 for the terms contained in the pardon [John, Lord Howard, February 1483] of offenses committed before 21 January 1483. For the form of pardons current before the act of 1468, C67/45/ mems. 47,49 [17 February and 9 January 1462]: *contra forman statutorum de liberatis pannorum et capuciorum.* For the form used after the act of 1468, C67/47/ mem. 9 [22 February 1470]: *contra forman statutorum de signis liberatis pannorum et capuciorum ac retentionibus.* C66/552/ mem. 5, a pardon to Sir Ralph Hastings, knight of the body to Edward IV, [18 August 1483] follows the same form.

V

TUDOR EPILOGUE: REPRESSION
AND SURVIVAL

At the outset of his reign, Henry VII displayed no more originality
in coping with retaining than had the Yorkist kings. He, perforce, pro-
ceeded cautiously and used the same devices to prevent or to limit the
practice. Like Edward IV, Henry VII persuaded both lords and commons to swear oaths that they would not retain men unlawfully. Like
Richard III, he issued proclamations to shire and borough officials to
enforce the existing laws against livery and retaining; and like many a
medieval king, he had, or let, parliament pass new acts against the institution and its abuses.

Only gradually during the two decades after 1485 did there emerge
what may be called a royal policy towards retaining. In principle, it
was one of repression; but in practice it amounted to connivance and
control. Orders-in-council, royal proclamations, and acts of parliament
expounded principles which underlay policy and constituted its goals.
Henry VII's foremost objective was to make each subject's allegiance to
the king transcend his every other loyalty. Next, he sought to restrict
retaining to the king and to the prince, and to convert it into an exclusive
kingship right. Finally, some statutes and proclamations set forth as their
purpose an outright abolition of retaining. However, political expe-
diency, provoked by military necessity, required all the Tudor sovereigns to permit peers to retain non-residents; but they rationalized this
breach of principle with the hope that the retainers' services would be
for the king's better surety. By the dispensing power, he might license,
through placards, letters missive, and letters patent, individual peers
and knights to retain men other than household servants; and this act
of grace gave to the sovereign, at least in legal theory, a control over
the lords and knights who kept companies of retainers. Towards the
rest of his subjects, the Tudor monarch applied a policy of repression.
First, he sought to prevent men from retaining or being retained illicitly;
and then, when they did so, to prosecute the offenders in the courts of
common law.

At Henry VII's first parliament, in November 1485, the commons took an elaborate oath not to retain men unlawfully. Then the chancellor, Bishop Alcock of Worcester, challenged the lords of parliament to follow the commons' example. They answered "with one voice" that they would do so; and with their hands upon the Holy Evangels, 2 dukes, 8 earls, 1 viscount, and 7 barons (including the second Lord Hastings) swore the oath. The form used was, presumably, that sent out in January 1486 to be sworn before royal commissioners by all knights, esquires, gentleman, yeomen and others giving liveries and retainings *(dantes liberatas et retentiones)*. They were to swear, first of all, not to retain, aid, or comfort any murderer, felon, or man outlawed for felony and known to be such; and then not to "retain any man by indenture or oath, or give livery, sign or token contrary to the law."[1] Right here, of course, was the crux of the matter, the question yet unresolved: what kinds of retaining in 1486 were, and which were not, contrary to the law?

The common-law judges, apparently, considered the retaining of anyone other than household servants and men of law to be illegal. The *Year Book* of 1485—86 reports the cynicism of Sir William Hussey, C. J., about the value of swearing oaths—a sign of weakness in any age— as a means to eliminate retaining. He told the court how the lords in Edward IV's reign had sworn oaths, and that then

"he saw, within an hour while they were in the star chamber, divers of the lords make retainments by oath and surety and other things which were directly contrary to their said sureties and oaths; and so oaths and sureties are to no pur-

[1] *Rot Parl.* VI, 287–288; Rymer, *Foedera,* XII, pp. 280–281. The final paragraph of the oath was against making, or assenting to, any unlawful maintenance, embracery, riot, or assembly. The diary of the Colchester burgesses, Thomas Christmas and John Vertue, at the 1485 parliament also records the oath, and three times it uses the phrase, "contrary to the law of this land," or its equivalent. The diary also records, for 18 November, that the king sent down to the commons "a bill" concerning "an oath that no man should support... [un?] lawful maintenance by the means of the liveries giving, neither by none other means." *The Red Paper Book of Colchester,* ed. W. G. Benham, pp. 61–62.

According to the records of the city of York, its mayor produced, on 25 October 1485, the king's writ of 16 October prescribing an oath of fidelity or allegiance. The Dean, as the king's commissioner, received oaths of fidelity in York minster. The conclusion of that oath reads:

"You shall make no retainder nor be retained, otherwise than the law will, by oath, indenture, or promise, to no manner persons contrary to the king's laws, so help you God and all saints, and by that Book."

If the date, October 1485, is correct, then oaths against illicit retaining were exacted before Henry VII's first parliament met. *Gentleman's Magazine,* New Ser., XXXV (1851), 168, *cf.* C. G. Bayne, *Select Cases in the Council of Henry VII,* p. 80, a denial of giving livery "to any mis-ruled man" (1487).

pose while they are in the aforesaid purpose [state of mind]; and he [chief justice] said that he would tell this to the king himself."[2]

This judge believed, or wished to believe, that the retaining of any but household servants was unlawful; but whether the peers and politicians shared his view is another matter. Certainly, if the lord chief justice had in mind the oaths sworn to Edward IV in 1461, he was reading into that event a meaning that he, in 1485—86, would gladly give it, but one that the Yorkist lords probably never dreamed of. What they had sworn at King Edward's first parliament was only not to give livery, without the king's consent, and not to harbor criminals in their companies. But they did not swear away their traditional right to retain men lawfully. Even the oath of 1485—86 required of them no more than not to retain and not to give livery "contrary to the law".

The judges, seemingly, were trying to extend the meaning of the statutes in an effort to get at the root of those disorders which the lords' retinues provoked. In 1490, Wood, J., in the court of common pleas went behind the facade of livery to retaining itself. He vigorously rejected the casuistic plea that a defendant, who had received livery, had not worn it and therefore was not guilty of having broken the law. The judge declared, "if a man takes livery and does not use the livery, still he is named his man". The real damage, Wood saw clearly, was that the one who gives livery "will have a great company at his command, and for this men do not dare to execute the law on any of them."[3] Here was the issue between the custodians of the law and those who, like the king himself, were responsible for meeting the military requirements of the realm. Only after Henry VII had despatched Lambert Simnel, Perkin Warbeck, and the young earl of Warwick, and after his peace with France in 1492, could the king entertain an exclusively civil policy, one that would permit the repression of retaining. Until his government escaped from a dependence upon the peerage for military forces, Henry VII could do little more than ask the lords to swear oaths and then trust to their fidelity.

Towards the commoners, however, the king pursued a more agressive policy, one sanctioned by proclamations under the great seal and by statutes made by authority of parliament. Both statutes and proclamations asserted and reasserted the supremacy of the subject's allegiance. Actually, the principle itself was not new for each of Lord Hastings'

[2] *Year Book,* 1 Henry VII, plea no. 3. C. L. Scofield, *The Life and Reign of King Edward IV,* II, 381, dates this incident in 1461; but C. G. Bayne, *Select Cases in the Council of Henry VII* (Selden Soc.), p. l., *n.* 5. believes it to have occured in 1472 or later because Hussey was appointed attorney-general only in 1471.

[3] *Year Book,* 6 Henry VII, Michaelmas, plea no. 13.

contracts had reserved the retainer's allegiance to Edward IV and after 1470 to Prince Edward. In fact, this rule was clearly understood in Yorkist England, and one of the reasons given for the duke of Clarence's execution in 1478 was that he had caused men to swear "to be true to him and his heirs without any exception of their allegiance".[4] But Henry VII sharpened the focus, by sharpening the phraseology of the statutes, upon this principle. An act of 1495 expressly states the proposition "that every subject, by the duty of his allegiance, is bounden to serve and assist his prince and sovereign lord at all seasons when need shall require." Then it applies the rule pointedly by adding, "and most especially such persons as have by him promotion or advancement, as grants and gifts of offices, fees, and annuities." Any of these men who failed to attend the king in his wars, "as their said duty bindeth them", were to forfeit their offices and fees.[5] Seven years later, in 1502, Henry VII's regal position seemed secure; and he extended his demand for the supremacy of allegiance by contending, in a royal proclamation, that he had "reserved from the beginning of his reign the retainder to himself of all his subjects". This order, sent to the sheriffs of Kent and Sussex and to the cities of Rochester and Canterbury, charged his subjects not to

"presume, or take upon them, to use any retainders or to be retained by livery, wages, cognizance, or promise, but to reserve them wholly to his person and to be ready to serve him like as they shall be commanded . . ."[6]

An act of parliament in 1504 further refined this principle by differentiating a third degree of allegiance. Persons enjoying the king's gifts and grants of honors, castles, manors, lands, and tenements were to be, by reason thereof, the "more bounden to give their attendance upon the king's most royal person" in his wars than were those men who had of his gift only fees, offices, and annuities—to say nothing of the ordinary subject.[7] Regardless of the category to which a particular man might belong, Henry VII had made it as clear as mere words could that allegiance to the sovereign was to supersede all other obligations.

[4] T. B. Howell, *A Complete Collection of State Trials,* I, 276. The purpose alleged against Clarence was "to begin his usurpation."

[5] *S.R.* 11 Henry VII, c 18 [1495]. Cf. *The Statutes at Large . . . in Ireland,* ed. J. G. Butler, 10 Henry VII, cc. 6 and 10 [1495] against retainers, livery, and wages. These repeat similar sentiments about allegiance to the king, denounce retaining by lords, and forbid livery, wages, or promises by indenture. The acts excepted the marches of Ireland and allowed the marchers to have men in their retinues whose names they were to certify by indenture to the king's lieutenant.

[6] P.R.O., Patent Roll, 17 Henry VII, part II, mem. 5v. [10 March 1502]; *Cal. Patent Rolls, 1494–1509,* pp. 286–87.

[7] *S. R.* 19 Henry VII, c. 1 [1504].

A natural corollary to this principle was to reserve for the king and the prince exclusively the right to retinues with livery of company. Henry VII's first step towards this goal was to bring those enjoying royal favors back under royal discipline. Here he followed Sir John Fortescue's advice: that every man who held a royal office should swear to be servant to the king alone and not to take from any other man his fee or livery.[8] Already, Richard III had put Fortescue's precept into practice. He had instructed Sir Marmaduke Constable, steward of the king's honour of Tutbury, Staffs., to have all the inhabitants of the honour swear oaths that "they shall be true and faithful liegemen unto the king and not to be retained to any lord or other but immediately to the king's grace".[9] A statute of 1487 went further and enabled Henry VII to seize those lands, fees, or offices held of him by a tenant who became another man's retainer. Some officials had failed to give Henry, "in his great troubles" between 1485 and 1487, their loyal support; and they had "absented them from his grace contrary to the duty of their allegiance and against all truth and kindness". Hence this act empowered the king to recapture from men with divided loyalties their royal emoluments.[10]

Another chapter, 15, in the 1487 act forbad anyone to retain the king's tenants "contrary to the statutes". Royal tenants were to appear "only in the king's livery and sign, and to serve him only." Furthermore, no one was to call them to any field or assembly except at the king's command and then "always in the king's livery or sign, with a cognizance of him that so conveys them by the king's commandment." Here, indeed, was an attempt by legislation to establish over his own men the sovereign's superior and exclusive control.[11] Seven years later, in 1494, Henry's council enjoined three men, Hunter, Picrofte, and Aylmer (probably the king's or the prince's feed men) "to wear no man's livery, neither serve any man but the king and my lord prince."[12]

[8] John Fortescue, *The Governance of England, ed. Charles Plummer*, p. 153.
[9] British Museum MS. Harley 433, fols. 270, 274. Sir Marmaduke was also to "see that no liveries or cognizances be given within the said honour contrary to the law and to the statutes thereof made." The date was probably October 1484. Lord William Hastings had been appointed steward of Tutbury and constable of the castle on 30 March 1474. MS Harley 3881, fol. 21 v.
[10] *S. R.,* 3 Henry VII, c. 15 [xv].
[11] In 1498 the council of the duchy of Lancaster ordered the mayor and his brethren of Leicester, parcel of the duchy, to enforce the acts against livery and retaining and to prevent the inhabitants from being retained "except only with us to do us service when they thereunto shall be required, in the retinue of our stewards there ... " Mary Bateson, *Records of the Borough of Leicester,* II, p. 354.
[12] C. L. Scofield, *A Study of the Court of Star Chamber*, p. 17.

The same policy underlay Henry VII's proclamation of 1502; and two years later, when the king's political and administrative power had become preponderant, an act of parliament forbad "unlawful retainors" —but only for Henry VII's lifetime "and no longer."[13]

Heretofore, the king, his councillors, and his judges had fenced gingerly with the problem and had attacked it only obliquely. Several acts of Tudor parliaments mention retaining, along with livery and maintenance, among the many different causes of disorder. The mis-named star chamber act of 1487, which Caxton in his edition of the statutes labelled more appropriately, but no more accurately, "Against Liveries", attributed the subversion of good rule to unlawful maintenances, liveries, bribes, riots, embraceries, and "retainders by indenture". This statute called for the execution of old laws against these offenses, and it provided a committee of seven councillors to punish misdoers. Even in 1495, after the council had tried to check retaining, parliament attacked it only indirectly through the law requiring military service of every man, especially of those bound to the king by offices and fees. But in the statute of 1504, chapter 14 entitled "Illicit Retainings" dealt with the practice in most emphatic words. No one, it declared, should "unlawfully retain privily or openly". However, the word "unlawfully" admits of ways, besides the two customary exceptions for household servants and men of law, to retain men lawfully. Yet this act, by omitting the 1468 "lawful service" clause, may have blocked up one loop-hole; and though the peers were not named expressly, it forbad any one to "name or cause himself to be named servant or to be retained to or with any person". The statute also nullified "all manner of writings or indentures between any person herebefore made, whereby any person is retained contrary to this act". Despite its verbal vigor and its apparent comprehension of all persons, the act of 1504 still failed to state explicitly that a peer's retainder of non-residents constituted "illicit retaining."

What this statute did do, however, was to bring retaining under the king's control. It served to make him beneficiary of the institution, and a proviso (section 10) allowed the king to grant men licenses under the sign manual, the signet, or privy seal. The statute's penalties were not to apply to any person whom the king might authorize to "take, appoint, or indent with any persons to do, and to be in a readiness to do, the king service in war or otherwise at his commandment". But those whom the king so licensed should not use their retainers for their own purposes; nor should the men retained, for their part, give ser-

---

[13] *S. R.,* 19 Henry VII, c. 14.

vice or attendance to him with whom they had indented—except at the king's command. The license, or placard as the statute styled it, was "to endure during the king's pleasure and no longer".

One such placard, apparently drafted after the act of 1504 and before Henry VII's death in 1509, conforms to the letter of this law.[14] It is unduly long, but its very verbosity amplifies the proviso and elaborates Henry's policy. The prolix preamble explains that England was "in good and honorable peace, liege, comity, and confederation with all Christian princes," and that the king's realm and subjects were "in good obedience, rest, peace, and tranquility without any likelihood of war". And yet, the preamble continues,

"forasmuch as to wise providence and good policy it appertaineth in time of peace to foresee the remedy against the dangers of war, as well to resist outward attempts of hostility when the case shall require, as also to conserve our realm and subjects in good order of justice, tranquility, and good obedience... [the king, by advice of his council, intends] to provide a good, substantial, and competent number of captains and able men of our subjects to be in readiness to serve us at our pleasure when the case shall require..."

In other words, Henry VII sought to establish in time of peace, a skeleton, if not a standing, army subject to his call and at no cost to himself. To accomplish this he resorted to retaining and gave "full power and authority" to some men "to take, appoint, and retain by indenture or covenant" a specified number of able men, his subjects, "to do us service in the war in your company under you and at your leading at all such times and places and as often as it shall please us to command or assign you . . ." Here, certainly was the king's attempt to outbid the peers, and perhaps, if successful, to bring all retaining indirectly under the sovereign's control.[15]

The king was not unmindful, the placard makes clear, of the potential dangers in permitting even this legalized and restricted kind of retain-

---

[14] P.R.O. E101/59/5. This appears to be a draft form for a placard conforming to the specifications provided in the statute 19 Henry VII, c. 14, par. 10. Though the manuscript bears a later ascription to Henry VIII's reign, its preamble sounds more in Henry VII's (see Appendix D). In any event, it was probably drawn up before the 1512–1514 war with France.

[15] In May 1492, Henry VII had requested Sir Robert Plumpton to put himself in a surety of his menial servants and tenants to ascertain how many of them would serve the king. He was to certify the earl of Surrey "of the number of such assured men." *The Plumpton Correspondence*, Camden Soc., 1839, pp. 96–91, *note*. See also, C. G. Bayne, *Select Cases in the Council of Henry VII*, pp. 80 (livery given "to do you service" at the battle of Stoke, 1487) and 85–86 (the king's authority to give liveries, 1487).

ing. Besides relying upon the captain's "faith and truth", the king required him to send to his secretary a certificate setting forth the names and number of his retainers. The captain might fill vacancies in his company, but not "above the said number", and he was not to recruit men retained by other licensees or "reserved" for the king's own companies. He was to equip his retinue, or "cause them to be arrayed", and he might "view and review" his men as often as he wished but "at the least once or twice yearly". For the musters before the king's commissioners, each retainer was to wear a jacket of the king's colors bearing his cognizance and also the leader's. Then, "whensoever the case shall so require", the captain was, upon warning, to bring up his men, "sufficiently horsed and harnessed", to serve the king at his wages.

The contract contained further safeguards against the temptation for the captain to abuse this opportunity and to use the retainers for his own part and quarrel. They were not to wear their jackets or cognizance "but only at the time of the said view, review, and musters, or when we [the king] shall command you [the captain] to bring them to do service unto us as above". Also, the licensee must not, "under color hereof or by virtue of these our letters of placard, retain" more men than his contract specified. If he did so, contrary to the king's "authority and license", he would fall under the penalty of the statutes —but only for the number of retainers in excess of his quota. Otherwise, this placard gave to both the captain and his retainers a "sufficient discharge" to retain and to be retained "any act, statute, prohibition, or other ordinance in the time of us or any of our noble progenitors or predecessors by authority of parliament or otherwise heretofore made, enacted, passed, or ordained to the contrary notwithstanding."

Henry VII's license to retain potential soldiers is more akin to Hastings' contracts than to the conventional military indenture. Like them, it was for an indefinite term (the king's pleasure), not for just six months or a year; it had force and effect in time of peace as well as war; and the men were to serve the king wherever, even overseas, and "whenever the case shall so require"—not for only a single campaign in a specified land. By using such a contract the king might convert the old practice of retaining, at least in law and theory, to his own advantage. But his success would depend upon his ability to control the licensees by enforcing the contracts through courts of common law or conciliar tribunals. Administrative agencies would supplement the retainer's "faith and truth" as the operative force to make the system work. All depended, of course, upon the power and effectiveness of the regal government. Although the hazards were great and the loss of control over the licensees might prove disastrous, the success of

7

Henry VII's foreign policy by 1503—peace with Scotland by his daughter's marriage to King James IV—and the efficiency of his civil administration would seem to justify the risk. The need for military preparedness against future contingencies, as the placard's preamble declares, and perhaps Henry's parsimony prompted him to use, rather than to abolish, the system of retaining. Unauthorized, unlicensed retaining the statute of 1504 tried to stop. Then the proviso to the act enabled the king to extend the right to retain to his own patentees. Finally, Henry VII's policy required every subject to put his allegiance above all his other loyalties—above even that to the captain with whom he might covenant to serve his sovereign.

For ill or good the practice of retaining continued despite the Tudor principle of repression. Most often king and council acted only against men politically or socially inferior—the king's own dependants, tenants on his lands, and the inhabitants of corporate boroughs. Like Richard III, the first two Tudors ordered mayors and aldermen to prevent burgesses from being drawn, by the magnet of aristocratic influence both at court and in the country, into the system of retaining. Within two months of his usurpation, King Richard had issued a proclamation "against retainers in Northampton;" and the next year he sent orders, after a riot there, to the mayor and bailiffs of Bedford. They were to see that the inhabitants did not "take or receive any retainders, liveries, clothings, or cognizance of any person or persons of what estate, degree, or condition soever they be." The borough officers were to hold any offenders against this proclamation until the king's pleasure became known. Similarly, Henry VII, between 1500 and 1504, wrote under the signet to the mayor and corporation of Gloucester and charged them to put "in plenary execution" the ordinances that they had made "for setting apart of liveries, retainders, night walking, and other enormities". No burgess or inhabitant, the council of Gloucester had ordained, was to be "of open retaining, livery, or otherwise by oaths or promise to any gentleman dwelling without the said town, upon pain to be discommoned [disenfranchised] and put out of the said town". Any offender should not buy or sell until he had "refused his said retaining [and] made fine with the sheriffs".[16] Two decades later, Henry VIII, in 1523 at the hey-day of Wolsey's power, applied the same policy to the city of Carlisle. The king, in a letter under the signet to the "mayor

16 *Tudor and Stuart Proclamations, 1485–1714*, ed., R. R. Steele, I, clxxvi; *Letters and Papers . . . of Richard III and Henry VII*, ed. James Gairdner (Rolls Ser.) II, 288 (from MS. Harley 433, fol. 188 v) 28 Sept. 1484; *H. M. C. Reports*, vol. XII, part ix, 436, 437.

and his brethren", forbad the retainder of any inhabitants. This time no citizen was

"to be from henceforth retained with any man, be he spiritual or temporal lord or other, by livery, badging, clothing, cognizance or in any otherwise ... but to be abiding and attending at all seasons, both of war and peace, in the same our city for the defense and surety thereof against the Scots."

For anyone who disobeyed this command, the king would provide "sharp punition".[17]

Although no indentures dating after 1483 are at hand, there is evidence that the lords continued to have, "over and beside" their household servants, non-resident retainers. The roll of "Fees and Annuities" kept for the second Lord Hastings contained the names of men whom he "retained" and yet were not "of his council"; nor were they household servants.[18] The roll for 1500—01 lists the yearly salaries paid to Hastings' chief officers and "others" as Dugdale euphemistically described them. Two men, Maurice Berkeley, knight, whose annuity was £5, and Thomas Entwysell, esquire, with a fee of £3.6.8, were probably the first Lord Hastings' retainers, or their sons of the same name. Lord Edward Hastings paid annuities to one peer, St. Amand, 3 knights, 3 esquires, and 8 men to whom the roll did not ascribe either offices or functions. These 15 retainers, obviously not household servants, were non-residents; and since Dugdale merely sampled Hastings' roll, and did not transcribe all of it even for the year 1500—01, the presumption is that this lord had many more retainers. Unlike his father, whose office of chamberlain carried with it influence at court, the son had to provide cash fees for his adherents. The second Lord Hastings may have retained these men lawfully with the king's permission, but no license for him to do so has been found. Other peers, too, like Lord Burgavenny and the earls of Oxford and Northumberland, kept retainers during Henry VII's reign; and even Empson and Dudley, the king's notorious ministers, were accused in 1509 of having called up their servants, adherents, and other men "secretly retained."

On through Henry VIII's reign, allusions to retaining, casual as they are, indicate that its continuance was taken for granted. The extraordinary event, the one worth recording, was not the existence of retaining, but one of the intermittent attempts to suppress it. At the end of

[17] J. O. Halliwell-Philips, *Letters of the Kings of England,* (1846), I, 273–274.

[18] Huntington Library MS. Dugdale, *History of the Family of Hastings,* pp. 31–32. From the *compotus* of Richard Sacheverell, the receiver-general of Edward, Lord Hastings, 15–16 Henry VII.

his war with France in 1514, Henry VIII re-affirmed his father's policy against retaining. A proclamation of 12 October 1514, issued "by the advice of his council" and sent to the sheriffs of Middlesex and London, forbad anyone to retain or to be retained contrary to the form of existing statutes.[19] This order, put forth in flamboyant phrases, coincided with Wolsey's advent as Henry's chief-councillor. Its grandiloquence heralded the cardinal's campaign of smoke and thunder against various kinds of disorder; and it declared void all forms of royal license to keep retainers. But the 1514 proclamation went further than earlier ones for it deprived offenders of any hope of pardon. No person henceforth was to retain or be retained.

"contrary to the said statutes; nor that any person or persons heretofore in any wise retained by [permission of] the king's letters missive, placards, patents, or otherwise from henceforth use or wear any livery, badge, token or otherwise call himself servant to any such person to whom he or they have been so retained ... without any manner [of] hope, trust, or confidence of any pardon or release to be obtained of our said sovereign lord for any such unlawful demeanor; any commandment, letters missive, placards, commissions, or letters patent under the king's great seal to the contrary made in any wise notwithstanding. All which commandments, letters missive, placards, commissions, and letters patent of what date or nature soever they be, or to whom or for what cause soever they were granted, the king's highness utterly hath revoked and by this proclamation utterly declareth them now and from henceforth to be void and of no force, strength, nor effect. And God save the King."

This ostensible profession of the principle of abolition actually constituted, however, a confession of its compromise. The frank admission that the king had granted to some men permissions, in various forms and under various seals, to keep retainers and even to give livery meant that Tudor practice was still one of connivance. The king's control through licenses to retain might mitigate the risk he ran when he allowed a man to have a company of retainers and to give them livery. No matter how slight this check might be, still the formality of licensing at least preserved the principle of royal consent. In practice, however, both Henry VII and Henry VIII had to tolerate retaining. Ample proof remains that men, especially peers and courtiers, continued to keep retainers for their own service, as well as for their sovereign's, both with and without his express permission.

Normally, retaining by peers went on, and when a lord was threatened with punishment, the accusation itself attests the practice. In 1517 Lords Burgavenny, Dorset, Hastings, and Shrewsbury were assumed to be re-

19 British Museum MS. Harley 442, fol. 15. A copy in a late-sixteenth, or seventeenth-century hand.

taining men, or at least more men than they should; and the same year the duke of Buckingham, Henry VIII's rival for the throne, sought his sovereign's consent to retain men for service in the west. He sent his chancellor, Robert Gilbert, to the king and his council to procure a license to keep retainers in the counties of Hereford, Gloucester, and Somerset. At both London and East Greenwich Gilbert had labored and made suit to the king "that the duke might obtain from the same lord king the said authority and license." Buckingham desired, so Gilbert testified against his master in 1521, to have these men and to transport arms into Wales "with this intention, that the duke himself ... should assume the crown of England and the regal power of the same realm." Regardless of the truth of the charges alleged against Buckingham in 1521, he had planned in November 1520 to take to Wales with him the next February "300 or 400 men who will be his own servants." Perhaps because Buckingham's large retinue, combined with his Plantagenet blood, frightened Henry Tudor, Gilbert failed to procure for him a license. But the duke's efforts to recruit retainers were not the cause of the king's action against him, they were cited only as evidence of his treasonable intent.[20]

Two years before his trial and execution, Buckingham had enticed a retainer away from Henry. Sir William Bulmer, a king's knight, had sworn to be only "the king's man" and "not to be retained to any of the king's subjects by oath, promise, badge, or otherwise." But despite this solemn obligation, Bulmer had broken his promise and had become the duke of Buckingham's retainer; and to make matters worse, he had worn the duke's livery in Henry VIII's presence. For this offense, Wolsey called him up before the king's whole council in 1519 and then and there gave him "a lesson to be remembered."[21] Other peers, too, continued to retain, and when the earl of Northumberland went to arrest Wolsey in 1529, he arrived with "a great company of gentlemen as well of the earl's servants as of the country"—men who, the cardinal believed, would be true and faithful and would live and die with their lord. Even the conscientious Sir Thomas More had retainers, and when he resigned the chancellorship in 1532, he acted like a good lord and

---

20 P.R.O. KB8/5/ mem. 4 v *(Baga de Secretis)* for the record of the trial, 13 May 1521, Cf., *The Third Report of the Deputy Keeper,* Appendix II, p. 231, no. 6: Gilbert labored etc. *ut idem dux dictam auctoritatem et licentiam de eodem domino rege optineret.* Buckingham had sought falsely and traitorously to destroy the king *contra legiancie sue debitum, ac coronam Anglie et regalem potestatem eiusdem regni Anglie super se assumeret; Letters and Papers of Henry VIII,* III, part i, no. 1070 (p. 392); *Year Book* 13 Henry VIII, plea no. 1.

21 Huntington Library MSS. Ellesmere 2655, fols. 14v, 15, 15v; and 2654, fols. 24v, 25. Cf., *American Hist. Rev.,* XLIX (1944), 654–655.

"placed all his gentlemen and yeomen with bishops and noble men, and his eight watermen with the Lord Audley."[22]

Nevertheless, some men actually were prosecuted for retaining or being retained. Justices of the peace at their quarter sessions would indict them and send the indictments on to the court of king's bench. The cases already cited, and there are many more on the King's Bench Rolls, of prosecutions during Henry VII's reign prove that the statutes against livery and retaining were by no means dead letters. On only a very few occasions did Henry VII's council, however, act against retaining—not at all as frequently as the champions of Tudor conciliar rule, then and today, would like one to belive. True, the council in 1494 enjoined Hunter, Aylmer, and Picrofte to wear no man's livery and to serve no one save the king or prince. But this was not a "star chamber" prosecution, and Bayne, after his exhaustive search of Henry VII's council records, found "no record . . . of any government prosecution [for retaining] in the star chamber." He concluded that the first Tudor merely copied the practices of Edward IV and Richard III and that towards retaining "no new departure was made in his reign."[23]

When the council, in 1504, heard the "great matter at variance" between the archbishop of York and Henry, earl of Northumberland, the king indirectly took cognizance of retaining. Each lord was bound in £2,000 to keep the peace, and they were enjoined to "cause their servants to lay down and not to use their said weapons; and also that they should not use to come to Westminster with so much company as they used to do . . ." But the council did not forbid the earl to retain men. Despite this settlement, the earl's troubles continued, and his name appears with frequency in Sir Edmund Dudley's "Account Book" between 1504 and 1508. Sizeable sums are listed against his name, but finally in November 1507 he procured a pardon at the cost of £10,000 —£5,000 of which he was to pay in annual installments and the rest "to hang at the king's pleasure by recognizance." Retaining, however, was by no means Northumberland's only fault. In February 1507 he had paid £50 of ready money and £50 by obligation in return for "the king's gracious favor" that he might "be dismissed out of the starred chamber" in his matter with Sir John Hotham. The reasons for the

[22] George Cavendish, *The Life of Cardinal Wolsey,* ed. S. W. Singer, (1827) I, 39, 86, 276, 280; William Roper, *The Life . . . of Sir Thomas More,* Early English Text Soc., vol. 197 (1935), 52.

[23] For the cases cited, *supra,* pp. 83–86; for additional cases of retaining brought before the king's bench, see C. G. Bayne, *Select Cases in the Council of Henry VII,* pp. cxix–cxxvi, citing references to P.R.O., KB9/385; KB27/913, 914, 916, 921, 941 etc.

earl's misfortunes are not clear; but troubles between the archbishops of York and the earls of Northumberland had recurred since 1443 when their servants rioted.[24]

Equally obscure is the king's motive in prosecuting George Neville, Lord Burgavenny. He is the only peer in Henry VII's reign, or in Edward IV's, the record of whose prosecution under the statutes against retaining has been found. Henry had a deeper reason than just retaining for bringing this suit since an indictment in June 1506 refers to Burgavenny's treason and misprision during the Cornish rebellion of 1497, nine years back; and in his final settlement with the king, Burgavenny had to guarantee, by a £5,000 bond, his allegiance for the rest of his "natural life." A jury of twelve, in January 1507, at Maidstone, presented charges of retaining against him to a panel of justices of the peace which included Fineux, the chief justice of the king's bench, a puisne justice, Read, and two of the king's councillors. The indictment accused Burgavenny of having "excited, requested, solicited, and retained" 471 men for the 30 months after 10 June 1504. These men came from 86 towns and villages in the middle of Kent, and the little army was made up of 25 gentlemen, 4 clerks, 440 yeomen, a cobbler and a tinker. Each of them had, Burgavenny confessed, bound himself for life to be obedient to him, to execute his orders, to be his helper [*auxiliator*], and "to do both on foot and on horse, lawfully and unlawfully" whatever the lord might command. Each man also agreed to belong to his retinue and to be retained "with no other person." Since these men were not knights and esquires, Lord Burgavenny had violated the act of 1390 for he had recruited them without the king's license.

The two indictments presented at Maidstone were brought immediately, in Hilary Term 1507, before the king's bench, and Burgavenny was ordered to appear. This he did in Michaelmas Term, 1507, "in his own person." To the charges he answered "that he could not deny that he was guilty of retaining each and all of the aforesaid persons for the whole aforesaid time." For this offense, "he put himself in the lord king's mercy." Then the court judged his forfeit to be 100 shillings for each month's retaining of each of the men—as the statutes of 1468

[24] C. G. Bayne, *idem*, pp. 41, 42 and *n.* 1; for a later copy of extracts from Dudley's *Account-Book*, British Museum MS. Lansdowne, 127, fols. 37, 50v, 58v.

Northumberland was accused of maintenance against Robert Snaynton through Thomas Neville, one of his household servants. *Yorkshire Archeol. Soc.* (Record Ser.) LI, 96–99. Bayne corrected the date of this case to Henry VII's reign. Although this is a star chamber case, Northumberland was charged with maintenance and not retaining since Neville, as a household servant, was retained lawfully.

and 1504 required. The sum of the fines for the men named in the first indictment was £41,550; for those in the second, £28,250; and for those in a third indictment presented at Dartford, Kent, in July 1507 but judged the same day in Michaelmas Term, £750—making a grand total of £70,550.[25]

From this point on, the case became a financial matter, a question of Burgavenny's ability to bargain with the king. The Fine Roll for December 1507 records 3 recognizances between them. One, dated 23 December for £5,000, records the names of 27 men who were "bounden by recognizances [of £100 or £200 each] for the good and true demeanor of the said Lord Burgavenny in his allegiance during his said life against our said sovereign lord, the king, and his heirs, kings of this realm of England." The second recognizance, dated 24 December 1507, was for 5,000 marks. In this Lord Burgavenny agreed not to enter the shires of Kent, Surrey, Sussex, or Hampshire "during his life natural" without first procuring "the especial license of our said sovereign lord, the king, for the same cause by his highness in writing and signed with his most gracious hand to the same lord given."

The same day Burgavenny signed a third recognizance, one that brought both his person and his property completely under Henry VII's power. The conditions prescribed therein show how preposterous was Henry's action; they attest its political and mercenary ends; and they explain why many a man felt relief at this king's death. Lord Burgavenny acknowledged that he was "indebted to our sovereign lord in the sum of £100,000 or thereabouts . . . for . . . unlawful retainers . . . contrary to certain laws and statutes." But what really gave the king his power over Burgavenny was his recognition of Henry's right to collect this enormous fine or any part thereof; and to do this, he agreed, the king might, "and at all times may, as well attach the body of the said lord and him in prison to keep and hold as to take and receive the whole issues, revenues, and profits of all the lands and tenements of the said Lord Burgavenny." At this point, Henry's mercy entered in, and he, "of his most gracious and merciful disposition," accepted the peer's proposal to pay £5,000 in ten annual and equal installments. Still, "all the residue of the said sum of £100,000 was to be at all times by our said sovereign lord at his most gracious and high pleasure demandable and leviable." To this indenture Burgavenny put his seal and sign manual, and its counterpart the king "signed with his most gracious hand." Exemplifications of Lord Burgavenny's "confession and condemnation" were sent to Sir Edmund Dudley whose "Account Book"

[25] C. G. Bayne, *idem*, pp. cxxi–cxxii, citing P.R.O., KB9/441/ no. 4; P.R.O., KB27/985 (Rex) mems. 7–9.

records on 28 December 1507 the indenture for £5,000. The appearence in Dudley's accounts from 1504 to 1508 of a few other entries involving retainers, such as Sir Edward Stanley's bond for £200 for having retained 56 men in 1502 in Yorkshire, suggests that the mercenary motive often attributed to Henry VII lay behind these prosecutions, and, perhaps, behind the statute of 1504 against illicit retainers.[26] Doubtless Henry VII should be commended for having, at long last, turned the statutes against a peer of the realm. But he enforced the law, not for the law's sake, but rather for his own, and his sordid ends deprive his deed of virtue. Despite the "strict legality" for which the Tudors are famed, they governed according to the rule of politics more than by the rule of law.

Grim as was Lord Burgavenny's fate when Henry VII put into play the judicial process prescribed by the acts of 1468 and 1504, the Fine Roll records for him a happy ending. The marginalia thereon tell that the gay young king, Henry VIII, "cancelled and annulled" the three recognizances through a warrant under his sign manual in 1509. Within five years, Lord Burgavenny was again retaining men, this time lawfully for the king's service. When the royal commissioners held a muster of his retinue at Canterbury in May 1514, his company contained 984 men whom he led as chief captain and lieutenant of the king's army.[27] Despite his rehabilitation, Burgavenny was to be one of the peers whom Wolsey threatened in 1517 to prosecute for having too many men in their livery. Thomas Allen, the earl of Shrewsbury's faithful man, was scared at the rumors he had heard and warned his master of what was going on at London. In a state of high excitement, he wrote to the earl:

"The king's sollicitor showed me the lord marquess [Dorset], the Lord Hastings, Sir Richard Sacheverell, the Lord Burgavenny, Sir Edward Guilford, by information put into the king's bench, are like to be in great danger for retaining of servants. At the reverence of God, my lord, take heed of it, for Bulkely which is ... commanded to Fleet, at his first coming (unto such time as some of ... spied it and gave him warning of the same) wore your badge upon ... Here is great trouble betwixt the lord marquess, the Lord Hastings, and Sir Richard Sacheverell: both parties stand bound to appear in star chamber, and, as they say, shall be bound to be of good bearing. My Lord Hastings and Sir Richard Sacheverell be here examined because they had so many in a livery at the meeting of the Scottish queen. I heard my lord cardinal command them to bring in every man's name which was with them in their livery at the said time." [28]

[26] P.R.O., C54/373/ mems. 11, 12; British Museum MS. Lansdowne 127, fols. 17, 46v, 53, 53v, 56.
[27] *Letters and Papers of Henry VIII,* II, part i, no. 471.
[28] Edmund Lodge, *Illustrations of British History* (1791), I, 23–24.

The alarm Allen exhibited has led to the belief that the cardinal constantly hailed men guilty of livery and retaining before the council or their committees. But the paucity of such cases suggests only spasmodic bursts of law enforcement, efforts more ostentatious than effective. In fact, the magnitude and magnificence of Wolsey's own retinue, his gentlemen in livery coats of crimson velvet and his yeomen in scarlet, perhaps provoked the lords temporal to outshine him in pomp, to envy his power, and so to keep more, rather than fewer, retainers. As archbishop of York, Wolsey gave his retainers for their badge "the crossed keys;" and in 1523 he had to placate his royal master's jealousy by writing Henry "that neither the said earl of Northumberland, nor any of his retinue, wore the crossed keys, but that they wore your highness' cognizance only, and under that his own badge.[29] For the cardinal, the acts against retaining were surely statutes, not of conviction, but of convenience. He might apply them against a peer or two, but hardly against the peerage without disaster to his royal master. By binding a few men "to be of good bearing," as Henry VII's council had done, Wolsey might temporarily restrain their conduct and that of their retainers; but this was not enough to eradicate a habit so ingrained in the aristocracy as was retaining. And so despite the Tudor prosecutions, whether of dukes or drapers, and despite the admonitions set forth in statutes and proclamations, the retaining of non-residents survived. But why?

Custom, vanity, and the peer's grasp upon a prescriptive right, on the one hand, and the king's own necessity, on the other, may account for the institution's continuance. Some slight control over retaining, and not its abolition, seems the most that any Tudor monarch seriously hoped to obtain. The extent to which the Tudors connived at the practice depended upon the political and military exigencies of the day. The sovereign's need of the magnates' support really determined the survival of retaining even in Elizabeth I's reign. By then the king had converted what the peers once held to be their right into a royal privilege—one requiring in law the sanction of a regal seal. In the end, the rule of politics, as retaining under Henry VIII, Edward VI, Mary, and Elizabeth I makes evident, overtook the rule of law. But the parti-coloured velvet uniforms worn by the great lord's retinue worked to transmute his followers into the *dramatis personae* for parades and pageants— except in time of foreign war or domestic crisis when they reverted to companies of men "defensibly arrayed."

As early as 1525, before parliament's religious revolution had provoked

29 *The State Papers ... of Henry VIII,* I, 146. Wolsey to Henry VIII, 26 Nov. 1523.

rebellions, the dukes of Norfolk and Suffolk had used their retainers to suppress riots at Cambridge and Lavenham and in Essex. Afterwards they reported to Henry VIII's council that they would so arrange that if any further confederacy of evil-disposed persons be made, "their servants and the king's shall be ready to withstand it." The popular risings in the 1530's, when the king and his government needed loyal adherents, enabled some peers to maintain their natural place in the governing class. To put down the Lincolnshire rebellion in the autumn of 1536, Henry VIII's council again fell back upon the system of retaining. Although the duke of Norfolk might think that only "noblemen" could give good service, other privy councillors willingly accepted aid from "gentlemen and their servants and friends" against the "cankered commons". Lord Montague received letters in the king's name, dated 6 October, ordering him to see to the quiet of his country and to be ready to advance, on a day's notice, with those under his rule; and similar orders went to Christopher More, esquire, to raise his friends, tenants, and servants against the Pilgrimage of Grace. The earl of Shrewsbury, already apprised of the rebellion, replied on 6 October to the king's request to assemble his servants, tenants, and friends that he had moved to Sherwood forest to be "nearer the king's servants in Derbyshire". Among them was the earl's son and heir, Francis Talbot, whom he described as "the king's servant" and who was, presumably, a king's knight, the sovereign's own retainer.[30]

After all, the Tudor king himself was the lord who had by far the largest number of retainers and who set the pace for the peerage. Until he stopped retaining servants, in one form or another, the lords would imitate the royal establishment. The term, retainer, when applied to men in the king's service, was ambiguous and no more precise than the word, servant. Yet there were, besides the countless employees on the king's pay roll, men listed on his "exchequer roll" who were his exclusive servants and not to be retained by those lords who had licenses to keep retainers. Such perhaps were the king's retainers in the East and Middle Marches about whom the privy council wrote, 12 March 1537, to the duke of Norfolk: "his majesty, retaining all the gentlemen and headmen, as he doth, shall not be evil served"[31]. Closer to the sovereign were the "king's knights" whose antecessors appear back before 1399. They were men whom the king personally knighted at his coronation or on

---

[30] *Letters and Papers of Henry VIII,* IV, part i, no. 1329; *Hardwicke State Papers,* I, 30,41; *Letters and Papers of Henry VIII,* XI, nos. 556, 560, 562, 565; Huntington Library MS. HM 382 original letter missive under the stamp and signet of Henry VIII to Christopher More, 6 Oct. 1536.

[31] *Hardwicke State Papers,* I, 40–41.

some other festive occasion. They formed an élite whose loyalty to their sovereign was intensified through the oaths and ritual of knighthood. The names of the king's knights, including peers and sons of peers, in the fifteenth century are known, and the record of their services, military and civil, to their kingly lord is indeed impressive.[32] Such a companionage, whether styled king's knights or retainers, who supported the monarch in war and politics and who appeared periodically at court, set a tone and a pattern for the peers to emulate. When King Ferdinand of Spain, in 1511, asked Henry VIII to send him 1500 archers, he granted Lord Thomas Darcy's request to be their captain. Thereupon, "many lords and knights made suit to be in the same journey, but the king answered them that he retained them still for other great considerations and purposes"—his impending invasion of France. Then "Lord Darcy and all the other captains took their leave of the king and went into their countries to provide for all things mete and necessary for the voyage"—such as calling up and enlisting their own retainers for this expedition.[33]

Right here in the king's military needs, Henry VIII's, as well as Henry VII's, is a clue to the Tudors' tolerance of retaining and their reluctance to enforce effectively the statutes against it. As long as foreign wars and domestic discords compelled the king to raise military forces, so long had he to depend upon loyal lords and knights to recruit his armies. In 1513 Henry VIII commanded David Owen to raise troops for his French War "any act, statute, or ordinance heretofore made to the contrary, concerning retainers, notwithstanding." And as late as 1544 he commanded the earl of Huntingdon to accompany him to France and to bring along 150 footmen, including 29 archers, and also 70 horsemen.[34] In order that peers might produce, on short notice, such companies of warriors, they had to have available the man-power which the system of retaining supplied. Until a civilian lord-lieutenant with a shire militia was enough to keep England tranquil, and until justices of the peace could maintain order, a potential army organized around the lords and their retainers had a place in even the Tudors' system of government.

However, as politics began to supersede force and arms as the means of governance, the king's own retainers began to serve him more and

[32] This estimate of the significance of the king's knights is based on the unpublished doctoral dissertation of Dr. Frances Huntington Winkler in the Yale University Library entitled "The Making of King's Knights in England, 1399–1461."

[33] Edward Hall, *Chronicle of England,* ed. Charles Whibley, I, 27–28, 30.

[34] J. O. Halliwell-Philips, *Letters of the Kings of England* (1846), I, 202–04. For the earl of Huntingdon's order, see Appendix B.

more at court and in parliament. In 1523, Wolsey at the top of his power and prestige, failed to persuade, or to compel, the house of commons to vote the subsidy he demanded. After having debated his request for 15 days, "the house was like to have been dissevered;" but finally "the knights being of the king's council, the king's servants, and gentlemen, of the one part ... were spoken with and made to say, yea". Later, when "the more part, being the king's servants, gentlemen, were there assembled . . ., [they] gave to the king 2 shillings of the pound of goods or lands."[35]

The indispensability of retaining, whether directly by the king or indirectly through loyal lords and magnates, is equally apparent during Edward VI's, Mary's, and Elizabeth's reigns. Each of these sovereigns granted licenses to peers and councillors, to bishops and judges, and to members of the royal household to retain a set number of men. Henry VIII had not been dead four months when King Edward's uncle, Protector Somerset, procured a letter patent permitting him to retain, besides his household servants, up to 200 gentlemen and yeomen and to give them his "livery, badge, or cognizance." The game was on again, and the Patent Rolls from 1547 to 1563 record several dozen licenses to keep as many retainers as accorded with the patentee's rank and status, or with his ability to fee and robe his retinue. The number ranged from 10 to 200, and the lords spiritual, like the lords temporal, usually were allowed 100 or 200 retainers. Archbishop Cranmer was to have 100 men, and in Mary's reign Bishop Gardiner of Winchester was granted 200 and Heath of York 60 retainers. Those councillors, like Sir William Paget, and household officers like Sir Edward Hastings, the chamberlain, who could afford so many men might have up to 100. Judges, sergeants, knights, gentlemen of the privy chamber, esquires of the body, and lesser officers like the secretaries, were content with a smaller allowance, ranging from 10, 12, or 16 up to 50 or 60. In the spring of 1550, an entry in Edward VI's *Journal* tells that "licenses were signed for the whole council, and certain of the privy chamber, to keep among them 2,290 [corrected to 2,340] retainers."[36]

[35] Henry Ellis, *Original Letters*, 1st Ser., I (1824), 220–21: an anonymous letter written from London to the earl of Surrey, lieutenant of the North.

[36] For licenses granted between 1550 and 1563, P.R.O., Patent Rolls: 4 Edw. VI, pt. V, mm. 35, 36; pt. VIII, mm. 20, 21, 22; 7 Edw. VI, pt. III, m. 23; pt. IV, mm. 35, 36, 37; 1 Mary, pt. XV, mm. 16, 17, 44; 2–3 Ph. and Mary, pt. I, m. 29; pt. III, mm. 17, 18, 29; pt. VII, m. 5; 3–4 Ph. and Mary, pt. X, mm. 18, 51; 4–5 Ph. and Mary, pt. XIII, m. 46; 2 Eliz. pt. VII, m. 22; 4 Eliz. pt. VI, m. 51; 5 Eliz. pt. III, mm. 12, 13; pt. IV, m. 8.

For references to licenses between 1547 and 1563: *Cal. Patent Rolls, 1547–48,* p. 249; *1549–51,* pp. 312, 326, 327, 335; *1550–53,* pp. 7, 26; *1553,* pp. 42, 78,

With the granting of so many licenses in Edward VI's name, the
baronial triumph would seem complete. The stage was set for a revival
of fifteenth-century faction, for Wars of Religion if not of Roses. And
yet when Northumberland sent his rival, Somerset, to the Tower in October 1551, the Protector's 200 licensed retainers availed him nought—
despite his "100 horse, besides his friends which stood by and the idle
people which took his part".[37] Even in Mary's reign, once Lady Jane
Grey was despatched and Wyatt's futile rising suppressed, recourse to
arms was conspicuously absent. However, during her reign there was
an increase in the number of men licensed to keep retainers and in the
number of retainers a man might keep. Besides the peers and bishops,
some of whom were allowed 200 men, several councillors were permitted to keep as many as 100 retainers. The queen licensed her judges,
men-of-law like Anthony Brown, a queen's sergeant, numerous knights
and esquires of the body, and gentlemen of the privy chamber to retain
anywhere from 10 to 60 men.

Here is a clue to the policy that governed the granting of licenses
between 1547 and 1565. With hardly an exception, the patentees—at
least those whose licenses were entered on the patent rolls—held royal
appointments. Their offices ranged from the captain of Castle Portland
or a gentleman of the privy chamber, to the chief justice, the lord high
admiral, and other great officers of state. The monarch's motive in
encouraging retaining would seem to have been, in theory, that of
Henry VII—to provide the sovereign with force and arms. However,
the retainer was to do his service to the patentee and not directly to the
king; and often his function was no more than to appear in a lord's
gayly garbed retinue. The councillors, such as Sir William Cecil who, as
principal secretary, in April 1553 was allowed 50 retainers, took retaining for granted. In the mid-sixteenth century, men still assumed that
retaining was necessary, customary, and desirable—hence natural. What
was new was to have a royal license, or perhaps only to have it enrolled
as of record in chancery. The letters patent granted in the names of

92, 99, 100, 101 253, 254, 298; *1553* (1 Mary), pp. 15–19, 869, 878; *1553–54,*
pp. 174, 321, 390, 409; *1554–55,* p. 79; *1555–57,* pp. 18, 47, 66, 67, 73, 74,
168, 169, 181, 224, 228, 229, 252, 280, 294, 487, 510, 516, 517, 547; *1557–58,*
pp. 4, 192, 306, 311; *1558–60* (Elizabeth), p. 352; *1560–63,* pp. 130, 239, 334,
338, 510, 530, 533, 623.

This list by no means exhausts the entries of licenses on the Patent Rolls,
1547–63, but it seems sufficient to establish the fact of their use and suggests
the magnitude, extent, and spread of the practice. For examples of such licenses,
see Appendix D. *The Literary Remains of King Edward VI,* ed. J. G. Nichols,
I, 256.

[37] *The Literary Remains of King Edward VI,* I. 356.

Edward VI, Mary, and Elizabeth I afford a measure of the extent to which Henry VII's policy had succeeded. But they also show how the rule of politics, which so dominated the conduct of Henry VIII and his children regnant, compelled them to compromise the first Tudor's aspiration to over-ride the peerage.

The letters patent granted between 1547 and 1563 are very long and replete with legal verbiage. They are in English, except for a few in Latin from Mary's reign, and their purpose was to protect the patentee from prosecution. Hence, they dispensed with all the laws, statutes, and ordinances against livery and retaining. Most of the licenses follow a common form, or rather they contain common terms in common phrases which were used by all 3 monarchs. The monarch granted to the patentee "full authority, power, and license"—Mary and Elizabeth extended the grant to their heirs and successors, too—"lawfully" to retain and keep in his service, "during his life and at his pleasure," a specified number of persons, usually gentlemen and yeomen. These retainers were to be "over and besides" the patentee's household servants and his other officers on his lands and estates. He might even retain the king's tenants, and those of any subject, and the residents within the royal lands and franchises. Furthermore, the licensee might give these men "his livery, badge, or cognizance;" and in return they were "to do unto him their service." The sole safeguard for the sovereign was that the retainers were for his or her "better service and surety always to be employed." Commonly, Edward VI and Mary stipulated that the patentee was not to retain the sovereign's servants named in the exchequer roll or any others "sworn and retained to serve" the monarch. Except for these 2 saving clauses, the license was all to the recipient's advantage. It provided "sufficient warrant and discharge" for both lord and retainer, for the retaining, the giving and taking of livery, and for the retainers' "promise and doing of their service."[38]

In case this dispensation from the penalties of the laws was not adequate, the letters explained with legal redundancy, the privileges were granted any statute, act, article, or clause "heretofore made or hereafter to be made or provided to the contrary in any wise notwithstanding." A few licenses even specified those "statutes, laws, or customs made, or to be made, for retaining, to the contrary notwithstanding." To complete a dispensation from the acts of parliament that would have made even a James II blush, Edward VI and Mary frequently added a pardon for all trespasses and contempts committed, done, or perpetrated after a given date, often the sovereign's accession. Such a sell-out to the mem-

[38] The quotations from licenses in this and the following paragraphs are taken from the original Patent Rolls in the P.R.O. as cited above in note 36.

bers of the council, the court, and the government indicates the dread and fear of deposition that constantly haunted every Tudor and determined his or her political psychology—until faction at last burnt out itself in Essex's 1601 rebellion. After that had happened, then the 1628 House of Commons could repeal the statutes "concerning giving of liveries" without even debating the matter.[39]

Deviations from the common form of license reflect even more vividly the vitality of this revived retaining. The letter patent of Sir Robert Brooke, speaker in the 1554 parliament and then chief justice of the common bench, illustrates the extent to which the practice permeated Queen Mary's government. Enrolled in Latin in 1556, it starts with a long preamble, perhaps drafted by the judge himself. At any rate, Sir Robert was certainly conscious of the dispensation he had procured for his grant begins by telling that licenses were needed

"because in the statute in the parliament [of Edward IV in 1468 it was enacted]... that no person of whatsoever rank, degree, or condition he be, by writing or anything else, after [24 June] in the year of our Lord 1468, should give to anyone livery or sign or should retain anyone other than his menial or household servant, officer, or man learned in both laws, by any writing, oath, or promise..."

The letter continues to quote verbatim the terms of the 1468 act concerning the penalties—the 100 shilling fine—and forfeitures to be imposed upon its violators. Then begins the license proper in the conventional form. Brooke might "retain lawfully" 10 men who were neither his household servants "nor his officers serving him in his legal eyres and services." He might also lawfully give these 10 men his livery without fine or imprisonment. The retainers, too, were hereby discharged from any penalties, "the aforesaid statute or any other statute, act, ordinance, or provision to the contrary notwithstanding." The only reservation was that Sir Robert's retainers should not exceed 10 in number.

[39] *Statutes at Large,* 3 Charles I, c. 5, sec. 27. The Commons' Journals for 1628 indicate that the repeal of the statutes concerning livery was included in a bill for the continuance and repeal of divers statutes. The bill was read for the first time on 9 June, committed on the 13th, reported on the 23rd, and passed on the 25th when it was "sent up to lords by Sir Edw. Coke." That afternoon, Wednesday 25 June, it received first and second readings, and the next day, the third reading.

Several unpublished diaries of members of the house of commons for the 1628 parliament note the course of the bill. The only issue concerning it was whether the "short" or "long" bill to continue and repeal statutes should be used. None of the diarists even mentions the word, "livery." I am indebted to Hartley Simpson for a view of these diaries.

When Queen Mary's chief justice took to retaining, the ambition of Henry VII's justices to eliminate the institution would indeed seem dead. Even if only the loyal servants of the queen got these licenses, still they denied the principle of repression; and one may doubt the efficacy of this policy of control by licensing. But Mary Tudor, personally, was not alone to blame. Her brother and then her sister—and I suspect her father, too—all failed to accomplish Henry VII's objectives. Even Elizabeth I's chief justice, Sir Robert Catlin, procured a license on 25 June 1563 "to retain and keep in his service and retinue" 30 gentlemen and yeomen. He might recruit the queen's tenants (but not her servants and retainers nor those of her heirs and successors) any acts or statutes to the contrary "heretofore made or hereafter to be made" notwithstanding. The terms appearing in these letters patent not only prove that retaining flourished in the sixteenth century, but they attest the use of the prince's dispensing power, in favor of government officials and courtiers, to encourage the practice. Thomas Babington, an esquire in ordinary for the body of Queen Mary, and his son, William, her servant and justice, obtained a joint license in survivorship enabling them "during their lives and during the life of the longer liver of them" lawfully "to retain and keep in his or their service or services" 30 gentlemen or yeomen. To these retainers they might give "their or either of their livery or liveries, badges, or cognizance." A similar grant in survivorship to Lady Jane Dormer, duchess of Feria, and to her son, Sir William Dormer, permitted them "during their lives and the longer life of either of them" to retain 30 men, for Queen Mary's "better service and surety always to be employed".

The sovereign's surety and service was, of course, the rationalization used to condone, if not to justify, this breach in the doctrine of strong monarchy. Elizabeth I, however, recognized the danger and the fallacy in the theory that retaining by even loyal servants increased the sovereign's power. Although she used her sister's formula, for her "heirs and successors," and although she dispensed with statutes "hereafter to be made," Elizabeth I did limit the duration of a few of her licenses. Whereas, earlier letters patent were to endure for the recipient's lifetime, Chief Justice Catlin's was to run only "during the times and so long as he shall remain or be in that office and place of chief justice." The privilege of retaining (no longer a right taken for granted) was to continue concurrently with a royal office-holder's tenure. This new principle might mitigate the threat to the prince's political and social ascendancy—if only it could be maintained. Already in 1560, Elizabeth I had limited Sir Henry Sydney's license to the term he was to serve as president of Wales; and 2 years later, in 1562, when John le Weston, esquire, captain of Castle Portland, asked to retain 20 men ostensibly for the better security of the castle, the queen, with some misgiving, allowed him to do so. Also she let him give his livery to these men, "over and above" his household servants, but "for and during the time only that he shall continue and be captain and lieutenant of our said castle and isle and not otherwise." The queen went still further in an effort to control this license. She implemented Henry VII's policy by following Henry II's practice of using the royal justices as her administrative agents. An elaborate proviso required le Weston to

> "deliver or present ... to one of our justices of assize of the said county of Dorset, once in the year at the place [where the] assizes shall be kept in the said county, a roll containing in writing the names and surnames of all the said persons so retained, with their qualities and dwelling places to the intent that if the said persons shall seem to any of our said justices men not worthy to be retained that then the same may be altered."

Here, at last, was an effort to recapture the initiative and to devise a method, one worthy of her grandfather, to assert again royal control over retaining. But to Henry VII's high-flown ambition to suppress the practice, Queen Elizabeth I, in 1560—1563, did not yet aspire; and like him, she, perforce, had to pursue a policy of connivance and control.

The letters patent do not describe the kinds of services that these Tudor retainers were expected to perform. Presumably they continued the old custom—to ride and go with their lord, and his part to take, perhaps arrayed defensibly or maybe only in colorful apparel. Each lord's retinue still constituted, as the first Lord Hastings' had, a reservoir of potential soldiery; and in theory, their retainers were to serve the sovereign as Henry VII's policy prescribed. On one occasion, the day after Wyatt had raised his standard at Maidstone, 25 January 1554, Queen Mary and her government used the system. A letter under the signet to Sir Thomas Cawarden reads: "put yourself in full order with as many of your servants and tenants as you can make (both on horseback and foot), to be in readiness to march ... upon hour's warning ... and in the meantime to have good regard to the quiet order of the parts where you dwell."[40] Just why civil or religious war did not break out then and there remains a mystery, if not a miracle. Perhaps each magnate's knowledge that so many other men also had their retainers in readiness worked to neutralize their power and to give Queen Mary, who took a vigorous initiative against Wyatt, the whip-hand. Or possibly Henry VII's principle, that every retainer should act only in the sovereign's service, was a recognized premise of the new chivalry; or

40 A. J. Kemp, *The Loseley Manuscripts* (1835), pp. 131–32.

maybe the character of these gentlemen and yeomen whom the magnates retained explains the absence of belligerence.

Certainly a transmutation of values, or at least a change of clothes, was taking place. Instead of coming up at his lord's call to take his part and quarrel "defensibly arrayed," the retainer of the mid-sixteenth century more often was costumed for a pageant. The fifteenth-century retainer's second function, to satisfy his lord's vanity and his love of ostentation, was gaining an ascendancy over his martial duties. The pomp and ceremonial of Renaissance England required the noble, even if he was not yet a milord, to surround himself, and also his lady, with a bevy of adherents in parti-coloured costumes. On state occasions and for public ceremony, the lords' liveried retinues of gentlemen and yeomen—no longer knights and esquires some of whom now had their own retainers—supplied the back-drop for the central figures. When the queen mother of Scotland, Mary of Guise, rode through London on 6 November 1551 to Bishopsgate, the duke of Northumberland headed the escort with 100 great horses and men with coats of velvet embroidery, with white feathers in their velvet hats, and wearing gold chains. Then followed the earl of Pembroke and his 100 horse and men, each holding a new javelin and wearing his badge. Next came the lord treasurer with 100 horsemen in coats of marble, their badge a golden falcon. Lords, knights, gentlemen, and ladies in number followed after.

Six months later, in May, a "goodly muster" of lords and their men-at-arms in "each lord's colors" afforded the Londoners a dazzle. Besides coats of red and white, coats of black or yellow velvet, or of blue embroidery, there were banners, standards, and pencels bearing the magnates' badges. The lord grand master's standard of red damask bore a white lion silver, crowned gold, and with ragged staffs; the duke of Suffolk's a unicorn silver ermine in sun-beam gold, white and morrey; while the lord privy seal's tri-colored banner with a white goat was powdered with scallop shells. The marquess of Northampton's standard, yellow and black, had a maiden head crowned gold, and the earl of Warwick's guidon of red damask was a white lion crowned gold and powdered with ragged staffs of silver, but the kingmaker's bear was missing. The earl of Huntingdon carried on his standard the old Hasting's badge, a bayon, and his pencels had the bull's head, crown about his neck, both devices being those used by William, the first baron Hastings.[41]

The substitution of velvet and damask for plate armour, of javelin for sword and lance, signalled the swan-song of retaining as the first

[41] *The Diary of Henry Machyn, 1550–1563,* ed. J. G. Nichols (Camden Soc. 1848), pp. 11–12, 18–19.

Lord Hastings had known it. Form was fast supplanting substance, and function was giving way to fantasy. When Lord Berkeley and his lady moved up and down the country in 1559 with 150 servants in livery coats of white frieze lined with crimson taffeta for winter, of tawny cloth for summer, then the white lion rampant on his badge was all but tamed.[42] Faction was, however, not yet extinct—the revolts of Norfolk and Essex against Elizabeth I were to prove that—but the fiery fervour of fifteenth-century retaining was tempered. Loyalty to one's lord—to one's chief—in war or in politics was long to endure. But during Elizabeth I's time the new chivalry, refined through Castiglione's *Courtier,* first Englished in 1561, and the subsequent cult of Glorianna were to transform retaining from a basicly military institution into a pathway to preferment. The queen's letters patent might make into a royal boon what the peers once had taken to be their right. But magnates continued to find the privilege one worth both the price of a royal license and the cost of the good lordship that they tendered their retainers. Great lords still wanted indentured retinues in 1565, and on 30 July Sir William Cecil, none other, wrote from Richmond to the earl of Shrewsbury, the queen's lieutenant-general in Yorkshire:

"I have a bill signed for your lordship to license you to retain 100 persons; which bill I will deliver to my lord of Leicester, because his lordship required me to procure the like both for himself and for your lordship."[43]

Nuisance that the lord's company of liveried retainers might be, and had been, to the proponents of law, order, and strong monarchy, this social sin, if sin it was, was surely venial. The angels, after all, had worn and presumably still are wearing Richard II's badge, the White Hart, as the celestial livery.[44]

[42] John Smyth, *The Lives of the Berkeleys,* I, 284, 285.
[43] Edmund Lodge, *Illustrations of British History* (1791), I, 350.
[44]. Plates VI and VII.

APPENDIX A
THE HASTINGS AND OTHER INDENTURES

The H. E. Huntington Library Manuscript, HA Box 104, contains 67 original indentures and a small parchment scroll written in the late sixteenth or seventeenth century. One indenture from each of the 26 forms according to which they have been classified is transcribed, in modern spelling, below; the scroll, also in modern spelling, reads:

The names of such persons as by indenture, of their own free wills and mere motions covenanted, belaft, and faithfully promised to aid and assist the right honorable William, Lord Hastings, and his part to take against all persons within this realm of England during their lives as well in peace as wars, their allegiance to the king's majesty, his heirs and successors only reserved and excepted, with so many able persons as every of them might well make to be furnished and arrayed at the cost and charges of the said lord, for the which the said lord promised them to be their good and true lord in all things reasonable, and them to aid and succor in all their rightful causes so far forth as law, equity, and conscience required. *Anno Edwardi quarti decimoquarto.*[1]

John Blount, Lord Mountjoy.	John Aiton.
Henry, Lord Grey of Codnor.	John Bonington.
William Trussel, Knight.[2]	Ralph Longford.
Bryan Stapleton.	William Laughton.
Walter Griffith.	John Thirley.
Robert Tailbois.	Thomas Cokeyn, son and heir of
John Gresley.	John Cokeyn.
Simon Montfort.	John Danvers.
Thomas Stathom.	Thomas Green.
Nicholas Longford.	Richard Boughton.
Robert Harcourt.	Philip Leche.
Thomas Chaworth, Esquire.[3]	John Sacheverell.
John Harcourt.	Hugh Percehale.

[1] For discussion of the inapplicability of this date for all the indentures, see below, p. 122, and the Catalogue of Indentures by regnal years.

[2] After each of the following eight names the scroll adds "Knight."

[3] After each of the following 56 names, the scroll adds "Esquire."

Maurice Berkeley.
John Curson, son and heir of
                    Thomas Curson.
John Stanley.
Nicholas Knyveton.
William Nevill of Rolston.
William Palmer.
William Moton.
Thomas Entwisell.
Nicholas Knyveton. [*sic*]
Thomas Staunton.
Ralph Vernon.
Henry Longford.
Thomas Meverell, the elder.
Thomas Meverell, the younger.
Nicholas Meverell.
Ralph Shirley.
Richard Savile.
Thomas Curson of Coxhall.
James Blount.
William Griffith of North Wales.
Ralph Delves.
John Babington.
John Staunton.
John Cokeyn of Ashburn.
Thomas Danvers.
John Griffin.
Humphrey Bradbourne.
Henry Columbell.
Gervase Clifton.
William Basset.
Nicholas Montgomery.
Robert Leigh of Adlington.
Ralph Pool of Radbourn.
Robert Slingsby.

Robert Eyre.
Thomas Gresley.
John Wistoe.
Henry Vernon, esquire, son and
        heir of William Vernon,
                            knight.
Ralph Sacheverell.
Roger Draycote.
John Turville.
John Miners.
Henry Willoughby.
Nicolas Agarde, Gentleman.[4]
Henry Columbell of Darley.
Ralph Agarde, son and heir of
                    John Agarde.
Robert Brabazon.
Robert Bradshaw.
Richard Eyre.
John Agarde.
John Thurkily.
Henry Eyre.
William Staunton.
William Dethick.
Lawrence Lowe.
Humphrey Stanley.
John Knyveton of Underwood in
                    com. Derby.
Jasper Roskin.
Rainold Leigh, son of Robert
            Leigh of Adlington.
Ralph Fitzherbert.
William Woodford.
Nicholas Ruggeley.
Thomas Ruggeley.

The names of these three retainers are not on the list, but Box
104 contains their indentures:

John Shirley, Esquire.   John Leete of Sutton, Derby,
John Burdet, Esquire.   Esquire.

---

[4] After each of the following 19 names, the scroll adds "Gentleman" or "Gent."

Catalogue of Indentures by regnal years and forms.

Year		Form
1	William Griffith, Esq. 6 Nov.	A
4	Henry, Lord Grey of Codnor 30 May	Y
5	William Bassett, Esq. 6 Nov.	B
	Nicholas Knyveton, Esq. 6 Nov.	B
	Thomas Stathom, Knt. 20 Feb.	C
9	Simond Mountfort, Knt. 22 Nov.	D
14	Morris Berkeley, Esq. 18 Mar.	E
	Laurence Lowe, 13 Apr.	B
	John Bonington, Esq. 20 Apr.	F
	Thomas Entwisille, Esq. 20 Apr.	F
	Nicholas Kneveton, Esq. 20 Apr.	F
	John Shirley, Esq. 24 Apr.	F
	Robert Slingesby, Gt. 24 Apr.	F
	John Agarde, Gt. 28 Apr.	G
	Nicholas Agarde, Gt. 28 Apr.	G
	Robert Bradshawe, Gt. 28 Apr.	F
	Ralph Fitzherbert, Gt. 28 Apr.	G
	John Thyrkylle, Gt. 28 Apr.	G
	John Harecourt, Esq. 21 Oct.	H
	James Blount, Esq. 12 Dec.	I
15	William Trussell, Knt. 10 Mar.	B
	John Cokeyn, Esq. 10 Apr.	J
	Henry Columbell, Gt. 10 Apr.	G
	Ralph Pole, Esq. 10 Apr.	F
	John Knyfton, Gt. 12 Apr.	K
	Ralph Sacheverell, Esq. 12 Apr.	K
	Thomas Cokeyn, 14 Apr.	J
	Philip Leche, Esq. 14 Apr.	K
	Thomas Meverell, Esq. 14 Apr.	K
	Thomas Meverell, junior, Esq., 14 Apr.	K
	Nicholas Meverell, Esq. 14 Apr.	K
	John Leeke, Esq. 24 Apr.	K
	William Moton, Esq. 12 Dec.	K
16	William Langton, Esq. 18 Jun.	W
	John Davers, Esq. 20 Sep.	L
	Henry Columbell, junior 4 Oct.	M
	Richard Eyre, 4 Oct.	M
	Robert Eyre, Esq. 4 Oct.	M
	Robert Leghe, Esq. 4 Oct.	M

Year		Form
17	John Gresley, Knt. 8 Dec.	N
	William Neville, Esq. 14 Dec.	X
	Henry Willoughby, Esq. 28 Feb.	O
18	John Sacheverell 14 Oct.	Q
	John Wystow, Esq. 7 Dec.	Q
	John Griffon, Esq. 11 Dec.	Q
	Henry Bradbourne, Esq. 16 Dec.	Q
	Gervaise Clifton, Esq. 4 Feb.	R
19	Richard Boughton, Esq. 10 Apr.	Q
	Thomas Curson, Esq. 18 Apr.	S
	Thomas Gresley, Esq. 26 Apr.	S
	John Harcourt, Esq. 27 Apr.	S
	Hugh Perchale, Esq. 28 Apr.	S
	Ralph Vernon, Esq. 18 Dec.	T
	Bryan Stapleton, Knt. 15 Jan.	Q
	John Blount, Lord Mountjoy, 23 Feb.	Z
20	William Dethick, Gt. 30 Sep.	U
21	Henry Longford, Esq. 25 Apr.	V
	Ralph Longford, Esq. 25 Apr.	V
	Nicholas Ruggeley 3 May	V
	Thomas Ruggeley 3 May	V
	Ralph Shirley, Esq. 9 Aug.	S
	John Aston, Esq. 25 Oct.	V
	Ralph Delves, Esq. 25 Oct.	V
	Nicholas Montgomery, Esq. 25 Oct.	V
	Robert Tailboys, Knt. 4 Oct.	V
22	Roger Brabazon, Gt. 14 Dec.	T
	Richard Saville, Esq. 28 Dec.	T
	John Bordet, Esq. 6 Jan.	T
1	Edward V	
	Thomas Greene, Esq. 13 May	T

Summary.

Year	Retainers		Retainers by Ranks	
1	1		Peers	2
4	1		Knights	6
5	3		Esquires	43
9	1		Gentlemen	16
14	13 (14 a)		Total	67
15	13			
16	6			
17	3			
18	5			
19	7 (8 b)			
20	1			
21	9			
22	3			
1 Ed. V	1			
Total:	**67**			

a Kneveton's second Indenture, cf. 5 Ed. IV.
b Harcourt's second (?) indenture, cf. 14 Ed. IV.

Number of indentures following each form.

A	1		O	1
B	4		P	1
C	1		Q	5
D	1		R	1
E	1		S	5
F	7		T	5
G	5		U	1
H	1		V	8
I	1		W	1
J	2		X	1
K	8		Y**	1
L	1		Z**	1
M	4			69*
N	1			

* Two retainers, Kneveton and Harcourt, each had two indentures; hence there are 69 indentures extant for 67 retainers.
** From British Museum transcripts.

*Retainers whose indentures are now lost but which the Bodleian MS.
Carte 78, folios 227–230, assigns to the regnal years indicated.*

Regnal Year

1	Thomas Green, Esquire.
16	John Stanley, Esquire.
	Humprey Stanley, Gentleman.
18	Walter Griffith, Knight.
20	Ralph Agard, Gentleman.
	John Curson, Gentleman [*sic*].
	William Staunton, Gentleman.

Of these seven retainers, H. Stanley, Griffith, and Curson served as
sheriffs, and their names appear in the list of sheriffs in Appendix B.
None was a known M. P. so they do not affect the statistics about members of the House of Commons in Appendix B and above, pp. 30-36.
The assigment by MS. Carte 78 of Thomas Green's indenture to the year
1461 is probably in error since his indenture survives bearing the date
1 Edward V [1483]. If the years assigned to the indentures of the
other six retainers are correct, then they reinforce the conclusion reached
above that the vast majority of indentures date from 1474 and later.
Possibly, some retainers first had contracted with Lord Hastings in the
1460s and then later on, after 1474, made second indentures, as did
Nicholas Kneveton and John Harcout, which superseded the first and
explain their disappearance.

The date, 14 Edward IV [1474], attached to the Huntington Library
scroll suggests that Hastings had retained all of these men by that year.
However, the scroll is written in a hand seemingly of the late sixteenth
century, or later, and its inclusion of the expression, "the right honorable William, Lord Hastings," seems anachronistic. Furthermore, John
Blount, Lord Mountjoy, whose name heads the list, did not succeed to
his nephew's peerage until 2 January 1476. The unavoidable conclusion
is that the list was compiled from the indentures much later than 1474,
perhaps for the first time in 1622. MS. Carte 78 states: "This roll was
copied out of the indentures . . . 13 February A.D. 1622." The probabil-
ity is that most of the indentures dated in and after 1474 indicate the
date when the signer was first retained—unless, of course, one wishes
to believe that the men were retained originally in the 1460s (when
some certainly were under 18 yars of age) by oath or oral promise and
without written indentures. In that case, the indentures can have no
value as evidence of the date a man was retained. Then the conclusions
reached above, pp. 34-36 about the relation between a man's membership in Hastings' retinue and his service as a member of parliament or
as a sheriff become invalid.

Transcripts of the Indentures: Forms A to Z.

[A. William Griffith, Esq. 6 November 1461]

This indenture made at Westminster the vi day of November the first year of the reign of our sovereign lord, King Edward the IV, betwixt William Hastings, knight, Lord Hastings, our said sovereign lord's chamberlain, on that one part, and William Gruffith of North Wales, esquire, on that other part, beareth witness that the said William is withholden and retained with and toward the said lord for term of his life, promiting and binding him by the faith of his body and by these present indentures to be true, faithful, and diligent unto the said lord and with him for to be and his quarrel to take against all persons of what estate, degree, or condition so ever they be, his ligeance only except. In witness whereof to the part of this indenture with the said lord Hastings remaining the said William Gruffith hath put to his seal and to the other part with the said William Gruffith remaining the said Lord Hastings hath put to his seal. Given the day, place, and year abovesaid.
William Gruffith. [Seal attached]

[B. William Bassett, Esq. 6 November 1465]

This indenture made the vi day of November the fifth year of the reign of King Edward the fourth between William, Lord Hastings, upon the one part, and William Bassett, esquire, upon the other part, witnesseth that the said William is belaft and retained for term of his life with the said lord afore all other, his ligeance reserved,[1] to ride and go and him assist and aid against all persons, his said ligeance only except, within the realm of England with the said lord upon reasonable warning accompanied with such persons as is according to his degree at the costs and expenses of the said lord; for the which the said lord promiseth to be good and tender lord to the said William in all thing reasonable that he hath to do.[2] In witness whereof the parties abovesaid interchangeably have put to their seals. Given the day and year abovesaid.
William Bassett. [Seal attached]

[1] [Laurence Lowe, Gentleman. 3 April 1474] For *reserved* read: only except to be of his counsel [councelle] learned and.

[2] [Nicholas Knyveton, Esquire. 6 November 1465] After *do* add: And pay yearly to the said Nicholas at the feast of Michaelmas for term of his life £4 of lawful money of England to be taken of the revenues and profits of the manor of Ashby in the shire of Leicester by the hands of the receiver or bailiff of the said manor for the time being.

[Laurence Lowe]: For *hath to do* read: now hath to do and in all things reasonable that he hereafter shall have to do.

[William Trussell, Knight. 10 March 1475]: And shall pay yearly to the said Sir William Trussell £10 of lawful money.

[C. Thomas Stathom, Knight. 20 February 1466]

This indenture witnesseth that I, Thomas Stathom, knight, am retained, withholden, and promised to William Hastings, Lord Hastings,
for to be towards him before all other lords, my ligeance and also
Harry, Lord Grey, lord of Codnor only except. And if it fortune the
same Lord Grey to decease, which God defend, then I, the said Thomas Stathom, knight, promit and bind me by this same my present
writing to be towards and owe my service to the said Lord Hastings
next my ligeance before all other lords and with him to ride and go
within the ground of England at all such times as shall like his lordship to call upon me at his cost. In witness whereof I have set to this
indenture my seal and sign manual the xx day of February the fifth
year of the reign of King Edward the IV.

Thomas Stathom, k. [Seal attached]

[D. Simon Montfort, Knight. 22 November 1469]

This indenture made the xxii day of November the ix year of the
reign of King Edward the IV between William, Lord Hastings, on the
one part and his entirely beloved cousin, Sir Simon Montfort, knight,
on the other part, witnesseth that the said Sir Simon of his mere motion and free will granteth and by these presents faithfully promiteth
for term of his life to be retained and withholden with the said lord
as his servant and his full part and quarrel to take against all others
during the said term, the allegiance of the said Sir Simon only except
and reserved; and over that the said Sir Simon granteth and promiteth
to be ready at all times and places within this realm of England to
attend upon the said lord or there as he shall by the said lord be
appointed by his writing or commandment, as well in time of peace
as war, upon reasonable warning accompanied with such people as
thereto shall be requisite and as accordeth to the worship that the said
Sir Simon is of or shall be called unto. And in consideration of the premises the said lord accepteth and taketh the said Sir Simon according
to his desire and promiteth him to be his good and faithful lord and
him aid, assist, comfort, and fortify in all lawful and reasonable causes
as belongeth a lord to do. And moreover the said lord granteth by these
presents to pay and satisfy the reasonable expenses of the said Sir Simon
and company so laboring with him in time of war or otherwise coming
to the said lord by his commandment or writing. And the same Sir
Simon promiteth again to the said lord upon his faith and honor of
knighthood to perform the premises and every part of them, never in
his life to attempt the contrary. In witness whereof to the one part of
these indentures remaining with the said lord the said Sir Simon hath
set to his seal and sign manual, and the said lord to the other part of

these indentures remaining with the said Sir Simon hath set to his seal and sign manual the xxii day of November, the said ix year of the reign of our said sovereign lord, King Edward the IV.

Simon Montfort, k. [Seal attached]

[E. Maurice Berkeley, Esquire. 18 March 1474]

This indenture made the xviii day of March the xiv year of the reign of King Edward the IV between William, Lord Hastings, knight, on the one part and Maurice Berkeley, esquire, on the other part, witnesseth that the said Maurice of his own desire and motion granteth, agreeth, and as well by this oath made upon the Holy Evangelist as by this present indenture promiteth to be during his life true servant to the said lord and to him do faithful service and his part take against all men, saving his faith and ligeance which he oweth to the king and his heirs. And at all times when he shall be required come to the said lord with as many persons defensibly arrayed as he may goodly make or assemble, at the costs of the same lord. And the said [lord] promiteth to the said Maurice to be his good and favorable lord in such matters as he hath to do and him support, aid, and succor in his right as far as law and conscience requireth. In witness whereof the foresaid parties to these indentures interchangeably have put their seals the day and year abovesaid.

Maurice Berkeley. [Seal attached]

[F. John Bonington, Esquire. 20 April 1474]

This indenture made the xx day of April the xiv year of the reign of King Edward the IV between William, Lord Hastings, on the one part and John Bonington, esquire, on the other part, witnesseth that the said John of his own desire and motion is belaft and retained for the term of his life with the said lord afore all other, to ride and go with the same lord and him aid and his part take against all other persons within the realm of England, his ligeance only except. And at all times shall come to the said lord upon reasonable warning accompanied with as many persons defensibly arrayed as he may goodly make or assemble, at the costs and expenses of the said lord. For the which the same lord promiteth to be good and tender lord to the said John in all thing reasonable that he hath to do, and him to aid and succor in his right as far as law and conscience requireth. In witness whereof the foresaid parties to these present indentures interchangeably have set their seals and signs manual. Given the day and year abovesaid.

John Bonington. [Seal attached]

[G. Nicholas Agarde, Gentleman. 28 April 1474]

This indenture made the xxviii day of April the xiv year of the reign of our sovereign lord, King Edward the IV, between William, Lord Hastings, on the one part and Nicholas Agarde, gentleman, on the other part, witnesseth that the said Nicholas of his own desire and motion is belaft and retained for term of his life with the foresaid Lord Hastings afore all other, to ride and go with the same lord and him assist, aid, and his part take against all other persons within the realm of England. The ligeance and faith which he oweth to our said sovereign lord the king and to my lord prince and to their heirs only except. And the said Nicholas at all times shall come to the said Lord Hastings upon reasonable warning, accompanied with as many persons defensibly arrayed as he may goodly make or assemble, at the costs and expenses of the same lord. For the which the same lord promiteth to be good and tender lord to the said Nicholas in all thing reasonable that he hath to do, and him to aid and succor in his right as far as law and conscience requireth. In witness whereof the foresaid parties to these present indentures interchangeably have set their seals and signs manual. Given the day and year abovesaid.

Nicholas Agarde. [Seal attached]

[H. John Harcourt, Esquire. 21 October 1474]

Be it known to all Christian people to whom this present writing shall come that I, John Harcourt, esquire, son and heir of Robert Harcourt, knight, of mine own motion and desire am belaft and retained for term of my life with William Hastings, knight, Lord Hastings, to do him service in the realm of England in peace and in war, sufficiently accompanied, furnished, and arrayed as belongeth unto my degree, and his part take against all manner men at all such times as I shall be required, my faith and ligeance which I owe unto our sovereign lord, King Edward the IV, and to my lord, the prince, only except. In witness whereof to this my present writing I have put my seal and sign manual. Given the xxi day of October the xiv year of the reign of our sovereign lord the king.

John Harcourt. [Seal attached]

[I. James Blount, Esquire. 12 December 1474]

This indenture made the xii day of December the xiv year of the reign of King Edward the IV betwixt William Hastings, knight, Lord Hastings, on the one part and James Blount, esquire, on the other part, witnesseth that the said James granteth to the said lord, as well by the faith of his body as by this present indenture, of his own free will and motion is retained [*sic*] with the said lord to be his true and faithful servant and to do him true service during his life, and his part take against all earthly creatures, his ligeance and the lord Mountjoy, his nephew, when he cometh to full age, except. And the said James shall at all times be ready to go and ride with the said lord whensomever he shall thereto be required within the land with all such men as he may make at the costs and charge of the said lord. And for this thus doing the said lord promiteth and granteth to the said James that where the town of Derby hath granted and ordained the said lord to have the rule and governance of the said town, that the said James shall occupy and have the rule in his absence of the said town in manner and form as the said lord and the said James between them be agreed. And over that to be his good and favorable lord and him to aid, help, and succor in all such things as to him shall belong of right according to the king's laws. In witness whereof the said parties have set their seals and subscribed their names the day and year abovesaid.

James Blount. [Seal attached]

[J. John Cokeyne, Esquire. 10 April 1475]

This indenture made the x day of April the xv year of the reign of our sovereign lord, King Edward the IV, between William, Lord Hastings, on the one part and John Cokeyne of Ashburn in the country of Derby, esquire, on the other part, witnesseth that the said John at his own request and desire is belaft and retained with the said lord for term of his life to ride and go with the same lord within the realm of England, and him assist, aid, and his part take against all other persons, his ligeance only reserved. And the said John at all times shall come to the said lord upon reasonable warning accompanied with as many persons defensibly arrayed as he may goodly make or assemble, at the costs and expenses of the same lord. In witness whereof to this part of this indenture remaining with the said lord the foresaid John hath set his seal and sign manual, the day and year abovesaid.

John Cokeyne. [Seal attached]

[K. John Knyveton, Gentleman. 12 April 1475]

This indenture made the xii day of April the xv year of the reign of King Edward the IV between William, Lord Hastings, on the one part and John Knyveton of Underwood in the country of Derby, gentleman, on the other part, witnesseth that the said John of his desire and motion is belaft and retained for term of his life with the said lord, and him to aid, assist, and his part take against all manner of persons, his ligeance only except. To ride and go with the said lord[1]

1 [William Moton, Esquire. 12 December 1475] Insert: in all places.
[Philip Leche, Esquire. 14 April 1475] *do.*
[John Leeke, Esquire. 24 April 1475] *do.*

within the realm of England at all times when he shall be required, accompanied with as many persons defensibly arrayed as he may goodly make and assemble, at the costs and expenses of the said lord. For which the same lord promiseth to be good and tender lord unto the said John in such things as he hath and shall have to do as far as right, law, and conscience requireth. In witness whereof the foresaid parties to these indentures interchangeably have put their seals and signs manual. Given the day and year abovesaid.

John Knyveton. [Seal attached]

[L. John Davers, Esquire. 20 September 1476]

This indenture made the xx day of September, the year of the reign of King Edward the IV, xvi, between William, Lord Hastings, of the one part and John Davers, esquire, of the other part, witnesseth that the same John is retained with the said lord of his own motion and desire to do him service for term of his life, and the part of the foresaid Lord Hastings to take against all earthly creatures except his faith and allegiance which he oweth to the king and his heirs. And also his service which he oweth to Dame Elizabeth Ferrers, wife to Sir John Bourchier, for term of her life. To ride and go accompanied with as many men defensibly arrayed as he may make at such times as he shall thereto be required by the said lord, at costs and expenses of the same lord. In witness whereof the abovesaid parties to these indentures interchangeably have set their seals and signs manual, the day and year aforesaid.

John Davers. [Seal attached]

[M. Robert Eyre, Esquire. 4 October 1476]

This indenture made the iv day of October the year of the reign of King Edward the IV the xvi, between William Hastings, knight, Lord Hastings, on that one part and Robert Eyre of Padley, esquire, on that other part, witnesseth that the said Robert of his own motion and desire is retained with the said lord to do him service for term of his life and his part take against all persons except the king and his heirs. And the said Robert granteth that he shall at all times as he shall be reasonably required come unto the said lord with as many persons as he may bring defensibly arrayed at the costs and expenses of the said lord. And the said lord promiseth to be good lord unto the said Robert, in such as he hath to do, as law and conscience requireth. In witness whereof to these said indentures interchangeably as well the said lord as the said Robert have set hereunto their seals the day and year abovesaid.

Robert Eyre. [Seal attached]

[N. John Gresley, Knight. 8 December 1477]

This indenture made the viii day of December in the year of the reign of King Edward the IV, our sovereign lord, the xvii, between William, Lord Hastings, on the one part and Sir John Gresley, knight, on the other part, witnesseth that the same Sir John Gresley is retained and belast with the said lord for term of his life and his part shall take and him to do service within the realm of England at the pleasure and commandment of the said lord against all earthly creatures, his ligeance reserved, and shall be at all times ready to come unto the said lord or his assign [assigne] at such time and to such place as he shall be by the said lord or by his authority commanded, warned, or desired with him to ride and go with as many defensible men as he may make at the costs and charges of the said lord. For the which service the same lord promiteth by these presents to be unto the said Sir John Gresley good and tender lord and to help him to his power in all matters and causes lawful and reasonable as far as right and conscience shall require. In witness whereof to the one part of this indenture remaining with the said Lord Hastings, the foresaid Gresley hath put to his seal and sign manual, the day and year abovesaid.

Sir John Gresley. [Seal attached]

[O. Henry Willoughby, Esquire. 28 February 1477]

This indenture made the xxviii day of February the xvii year of the reign of King Edward the IV between William Hastings, knight, Lord Hastings, on the one part and Henry Willoughby, esquire, on the other part, witnesseth that the said Henry agreeth and promiteth and by this present granteth unto the said lord to be unto him faithful and true servant and to do him faithful, true, and diligent service, and his part take against all men saving the allegiance which the same Henry oweth unto the king and the prince. And for this the same lord granteth unto the said Henry to be his good, loving, and favorable lord, and him aid, help, succor, and support in all his matters according to the law. In witness hereof either party to this present indenture have interchangeably set their seals, the day and year abovesaid.

H. Willoughby. [Seal missing]

[P. John Sacheverell, Esquire. 14 October 1478]

This indenture made betwixt William Hastings, knight, Lord Hastings, on that one part, and John Sacheverell, son and heir of Ralph Sacheverell, on that other part, witnesseth that the [said] John by his own special desire and labor is retained with the said lord to do him

9

service, and by these presents granteth that he at all times shall be ready when he shall be reasonably required with as many men as he may make, shall come to the said lord and his part take against all persons, except his ligeance, at the costs of the said lord. For the which the said lord promiteth to be good lord unto the said John. In witness whereof either party to this present indenture interchangeably have put their seals the xiv day of October, the xviii year of the reign of King Edward the IV.

John Sacheverell. [Seal attached]

[Q. John Wystow, Esquire. 7 December 1478]

This indenture made the vii day of December the xviii year of the reign of King Edward the IV, between William, Lord Hastings, knight, on the one part, and John Wystow, esquire, on the other part, witnesseth that the same John of his own desire and motion is belaft and retained for term of his life with the said lord him to do service in peace and in war within the realm of England, with as many persons defensibly arrayed as he can or may make or assemble, at all times when he shall be required, at the costs and expenses of the said lord. And the part of the said lord he shall take against all manner of men, his ligeance only except. For which the said lord promiseth unto the same John to be his good lord. In witness whereof the parties abovesaid to these indentures interchangeably have put their seals and signs manual the day and year abovesaid.

John Wystow. [Seal attached]

[R. Gervase Clifton, Esquire. 4 February 1478]

This indenture made the iv day of February the xviii year of the reign of King Edward the IV between William Hastings, knight, Lord Hastings, on the one part, and Gervase Clifton, esquire, on the other part, witnesseth that the said Gervase agreeth, promiteth, and by these presents granteth unto the said lord that he shall be faithful and true unto him, and to the same lord do faithful and true service. And himself to be ready with as many men as he may goodly make defensibly arrayed at all time and times that he shall be required by the same lord during his life, at the costs and charges of the same lord, and his part take against all men saving his allegiance. For which promise the same lord granteth unto the same Gervase to be his good lord, and to him owe his special favor as law, right, and conscience requireth. In witness hereof the parties abovesaid to these present indentures interchangeably have set to their seals the day and year abovesaid.

Gervase Clifton. [Seal attached]

[S. Thomas Gresley, Esquire. 26 April 1479]

This indenture made the xxvi day of April the xix year of the reign of King Edward the IV between William, Lord Hastings, knight, on the one part and Thomas Gresley, esquire, on the other part, witnesseth that the same Thomas of his own desire and motion is belaft and retained for term of his life with the said lord to do him service in peace and in war within the realm of England, at all times when he shall be required with as many persons defensibly arrayed as he can or may make or assemble, at the costs and expenses of the foresaid lord. And the part of the same lord he shall take at all times against all manner of men, his ligeance only except. In witness whereof the parties aforesaid to these indentures interchangeably have put their seals and signs manual the day and year abovesaid.

T. Gresley. [Seal attached]

[T. Roger Brabazon, Gentleman. 14. December 1482]

To all men to whom this present writing shall come, Roger Brabazon, gentleman, sendeth greeting. Know you that I, the said Roger Brabazon, have agreed, granted, and by this my present writing promited to William Hastings, knight, Lord Hastings, to be retained with the said lord and to do to him faithful and true service during my life, in war and peace, with as many persons defensibly arrayed as I can or may make, whensoever I be by the said lord or any other in his name thereto required, at the costs of the said lord, and to take the part of the said lord during my life against all persons, saving my ligeance to the king[1] and my lord prince.[1] In witness whereof to this my present writing, I, the said Roger, have set my seal and sign manual the xiv day of December, the xxii year of the reign of King Edward the fourth.

Roger Brabazon. [Seal attached]

[U. William Dethick, Gentleman. 30 September 1480]

This indenture made betwixt William, Lord Hastings, on that one part, and William Dethick, gentleman, on that other part, witnesseth that the said William is become servant and belast with the said lord, him to serve and to take his part against all creatures living, his ligeance only except. And the said William shall be ready at all times with such power as he can make to do service unto the said lord as well in time of peace as in time of war, when he shall be required at the costs and charges of the said lord. In witness whereof either party have to these

---

[1] [Thomas Green, Esquire. 13 May 1483 (1 Edward V)] read: our sovereign lord.

indentures interchangeably put their seals. Given at Tutbury the last day of September, the year of the reign of King Edward the fourth the xxth.

[No signature and the seal is missing, but a red mark therefrom remains on the parchment]

[V. Ralph Longford, Esquire. 25 April 1481]

This indenture made the xxv day of April the xxi year of the reign of King Edward the IV between William Hastings, knight, Lord Hastings, on the one part, and Ralph Longford, esquire, on the other part, witnesseth that the said Ralph agreeth, granteth, and by these present indentures bindeth him to the said lord to be his retained servant during his life, and to him to do faithful and true service, and the part of the same lord take against all men in peace and war with as many persons defensibly arrayed as the same Ralph can or may make at all times that the said lord will command him, at the said lord's costs and charges, saving the allegiance which the same Ralph oweth to the king our sovereign lord and to the prince. And the said lord granteth to the said Ralph to be his good and favorable lord and him aid and support in his right according to the law. In witness hereof the foresaid parties to these present indentures have interchangeably set their seals and signs manual the day and year foresaid.

Ralph Longford. [Seal attached]

[W. William Langton, Esquire. 18 June 1476]

This indenture made the xviii day of June the xvi year of the reign of King Edward the IV between William, Lord Hastings, knight, on the one part, and William Langton, esquire, on the other part, witnesseth that the same William Langton, esquire, of his own desire and motion is belaft and retained for term of his life with the said lord, with him to ride and go and to do him service in all places within the realm of England at all times when he shall be required with as many persons defensibly arrayed as he may make and assemble, at the costs and expenses of the said lord, and also he shall take at all times the said lord's part against all other persons, his ligeance only except. In witness whereof the foresaid lord and William to these indentures interchangeably have put their seals the day and year above rehearsed.

William Langton. [Seal missing, but a red mark therefrom remains on the parchment]

[X. William Nevill, Esquire. 14 December 1477]

This indenture made the xiv day of December the xvii year of the reign of King Edward the IV betwixt William, Lord Hastings, knight, on the one part, and William Nevill of Rolston in the country of Nottingham, esquire, on the other part, witnesseth that the said William Nevill, of his own desire and motion, is belast and retained for term of his life with the said lord, him to do service and his part take against all manner of men, his faith and ligeance which he oweth unto our sovereign lord the king and his heirs only except. And also the said William Nevill granteth that he shall be ready and come to the said lord at all times when he shall be required by the same lord, or by any other in his name, with as many men defensibly arrayed as he may make or assemble at the costs and expenses of the said lord. And the same lord promiseth to be good and tender lord to the said William Nevill as far as law and conscience shall require. In witness whereof to the one part of this indenture remaining with the said lord, the foresaid William Nevill hath put his seal and sign manual the day and year abovesaid.

William Nevill. [Seal attached]

[Y. Henry, Lord Grey of Codnor. 30 May 1464. From a seventeenth-century transcript in British Museum MS. Cotton, Titus B VIII, folio 329]

This indenture made the xxx day of May the iv year of the reign of our sovereign lord, King Edward the IV, witnesseth that Henry, Lord Grey [of] Codnor, in the consideration of the faithful, true heart, love, and kind cosinage which William, Lord Hastings, hath showed and done to the said Henry, Lord Grey, trusting always of continuance of the same, promiteth and by these presents faithfully bindeth him from henceforth to the said William, Lord Hastings, for to owe and bear good will to the said Lord Hastings, always taking his full part and quarrel and to be with him against all manner persons, his ligeance, my Lord of Clarence of [*sic*] and Sir Thomas Burgt, knight, only except. In witness whereof as well the said Lord Grey as the said Lord Hastings to these indentures interchangeably have set their seals and signs manual the day and year abovesaid.

Harry, Lord Grey.

[Z. John Blount, Lord Mountjoy. 23 February 1480. From a seventeenth-century transcript in British Museum MS. Cotton, Titus B VIII, folio 329]

This bill indented made at London the xxiii day of February the xix year of the reign of King Edward the IV showeth that I, John Blount, of my free will and motion promise and fully determine myself to be faithful and loving cousin to William Hastings, Lord Hastings, and his part take, mine allegiance reserved. And for the same, the said Lord Hastings promises to be good and loving cousin unto the said Lord Mountjoy in any matter that he hath or shall have to do as may stand with reason and convenience [conscience?]. And for the more surety of the promises upon both parties aforesaid to be performed and kept, we, the said William, Lord Hastings, and John, Lord Mountjoy, these presents indentures interchangeably have subscribed with our own hands.

L. Mountjoy [*sic*]

Miscellaneous Indentures among the Hastings Manuscripts.

[1. Hastings MSS. Family Papers, Box 44. Indenture between Sir Ralph Fitzwilliam and Sir Nicholas Hastings, 21 August 1311.]

Ceo covenaunt fu fet le samedy procheyn apres la feste del assumpcione de nostre dame lan du regne le Rey Edward fiz le Rey Edward quint, enter Sire Rauf le Fiz William de une parte e Sire Nichol de Hastyngges de auter part, cest a saver qe levauntdit Sire Nichol demorera ove levauntdit Sire Rauf en pees e en guerre a terme de lure deux vyes, issint qe levauntdit Sire Nichol irra ove levauntdit Sire Rauf en guerre la hou sun corps demeyn irra e qe levauntdit Sire Nichol vendra a le dit Sire Rauf a cheskune foyz qe renablement serra garny en temps de guerre ove deux vallets e lure munture e dis garcuns. En temps de pees ove deux vallets e quater garcuns. E qe levauntdit Sire Rauf trovera a levauntdit Sire Nichol covenable munture pur sun corps demeyn e deux Robes par an e une sele solum ceo qe apent a chivaler e sil aveygne qe le dit Sir Nichol perde nul graunt chival de armes en le servis de dit Sire Rauf qe le dit Sire Rauf seyt tenuz a fere a dit Sire Nichol allouuance solum ceo qe le dit chival par deux homes serra presee. E de quel lyu en le cunte de Everwyke qe le dit Sire Nichol seyt movaunt vers le dit Sire Rauf a sun maundement qe le dit Sire Rauf trovera a le dit Sire Nichol ses renables mises e despenses, e qe les gents le dit Sire Nichol avaunt nomez eyent lure guages en temps de guerre e de pees de le dit Sire Rauf solum ceo qe apent. En temeygnaunce de quel covenaunt cheskun de eux a auter endenture ad mis sun seal. Done a Hildirskelf le iour a lan avauntdits.

[Seal attached. The tag contains writing and was probably an old indenture: Rauf en pees . . .; sun corps demeyn . . . e lur; en alaunt . . .]

[2. Hastings MSS. Seals. John of Gaunt's confirmation of an indenture between his father-in-law, Henry, duke of Lancaster, deceased, and Ralph Hastings. 31 March 1362.]

Johan fuitz au noble Roi dengleterre, counte de Lancastre, de Riche-mond, de Derby e de Nicole, Seneschale dengleterre [blot] [space] y ceux qi cestes presentes lettres verront ou orront salutz. Come notre trescher piere Duc de Lancastre qi dieux absoille, granta nadguaires par ses lettres endentez a son bien amez Bach[elo]r monsieur Rauf de Has-tingges par cause de sa demoere pardevers lui sibien en temps de pees come de guerre un annuale Rent de quarrante marcz desterlings a terme de sa vie a prendre de sun Manoir de Pikerynge par les meyns des baillifs ou provostz illoeqes qi pur le temps y serroient as deux termes de lan, cest assavoir as les festes de Pasqz e de la seint michiel par oweles poy ... s come es as [sic] avauntdites lettres endentez piert plus au plein. Nous desirantz le bon acomplissement des voluntez e desirs notre dit piere le Duc, grantoms, confermoms, e ratifioms a dit monsieur Rauf la dite annuelte de quarrante marz a voir e prendre des nous e de noz heirs a terme de sa vie solent leffect e purporte des lettres en-dentez avauntdites. En tesmoignance de quelle chose nous avoms fait faire cestes noz lettres patentes enseallez de notre privez seale. Done a notre Chastelle de Hertford le derrein iour de Marz lan du regne notre dit S[eignur] le Roi et piere, Trentisme sisme.

[Seal attached. Parts of this manuscript are badly blurred and required the use of violet ray to read.]

[3. Hastings MSS. Accounts. Box 13, 1326—1391. A receipt by Ralph Hastings to John of Gaunt for his retainer's fee. 1391.]

Noveruit universi per presentes me Radulphum de Hastynges, chiva-ler, recepisse de Roberto de Mortone, receptore domini Johannis, ducis dacquitanie et Lancastrie viginti marcas sterlingorum de termino Miche-lis ultimo preterito videlicet in parte[?] solutionis cuiusdam annualis feodi quadraginta marcarum michi dicto Radulpho per dictum dominum Johannem, ducem dacquitanie et lancastrie ad terminus vite mee con-cess[ati]. De quibus quidem viginti marcis de termino supradicto fateor me fore solutum et dictos dominum Johannem et Robertum inde esse acquieti per presentes sigillo meo signatas. Datum apud Allerstane, die dominica proxima ante festum Translationis Sancti Johannis Beverlaci, Anno regni Regis Ricardi secundi post conquestum Anglie, quinto-decimo.

[Sealed]

[4. Hastings MSS. Accounts. Box 13, 1326—1391. John de Beaumont to Giles Jordan, bailiff, regarding the payment of fees. 1391.]

Johan de Beaumont, seignour de Folkyngham a Giles Jurdon, notre baillife de [D]ughtburghe, saluz. Nous mandoms e chargeoms qe vous paiez a Coke Hensemane e Walran a chescun deux 1 *d.*, 1 *ob.* le iour pour lour gages, e a chescune deux pour lour vesture par an v. *s.* e a chescune deux pour lour fee par an xiii *s.,* iiii *d.*

Item, a dit Coke pour son fee qest aderer tanque a Nouwelle derrein passe v. *s.*

Item, lour lez costages de noz chivalx soiournants a [D]ughtburghe, ceste assavoir, feyn, liter, e provandre a touz autres costages necessariez a noz ditz chivalx.

Item, paiez a Johan Burton, notre Stodehird, pour son fee par an, xx *s.* et pour gages ii *d.* le iour qant il serra occupie en notre service. Et ceste lettre patente ent vous serra garrant s[ur] votre acompte. En tesmoignance du quel chose a ceste lettre nous avoms mys notre seal adiurer tanque notre revenue en Engleterre. Escrit a Londres le xxxme Iour de Ianyuer lan de Roi Richard second apres la conqueste, quatorszime.

[Seal *en placard* missing]

[5. Hastings MSS. HA, Family Papers, 1400—1462. Military indenture between King Henry V and Nicholas Montgomery, Richard Hastings, and John Osbaldeston, 30 May 1416.]

Ceste indenture faite parentre notre sovereign seignur le Roy, dune part e Nichol Moungomery e Richard Hastynges e Johan Osbaldestone, Chivalers, dautre part, tesmoigne que les ditz Chivalers sont retenuz devers notre dit seignur le Roy pour luy accompaignier en un son viage en sa propre persone dieu devant affaire sur la meer e illoeques luy faire service de guerre ovesque noef hommes darms lour mesmes accontez e dys e oyt archers ben e covenablement armez e arraiez selonc lour estatz par le quarter dun an a comencer lundy le vynt e second iour de Juyn prochein venant. Et prendront les ditz chivalers pour chescun de eux mesmes deux souldz pour chescun de les autres hommes darmes dousze deniers e pour chescun des ditz archers sys deniers le iour pour lour gages durant le susdit quarter dont averont les ditz chivalers assignement destre paiez de les quinszisme e dysme des layes paiables a le Pentecost prochein venant en tielx lieux come parentre les ditz Chivalers e le Tresorer de les guerres de notre dit seignur le Roy pourra estre accordez. Et averont les ditz Chivalers pour eux e leur ditz gentz eskippesone as costages de notre dit seignur le Roy. Et seront tenuz les ditz Chivalers destre au port de Southamptone le susdit lundy prestz pour y faire lour moustre deinz la Nief des ditz gentz darmes e archers devant celuy qui par notre dit seignur le Roy a ce sera deputez e assignes.

Et de les gaignes de guerre e de la prinse des grandz Chieftains si
aucuns aviegnent en dit viage desouz la fortune des ditz Chivalers et de
lour ditz gentz, avera notre dit seignur le Roy ce qa [*sic*] luy appar-
tiendra par manere come ad estee cy devant usez e accustumez dauncien
temps. En tesmoignance de quele chose a la partie de ceste endenture
demorante devers les ditz Escuiers [*sic*] notre dit seignur le Roy ad fait
mettre son privie seal. Done a Westmoustre le xxx Iour de May lan du
regne de notre dit seignur le Roy quart.

[Seal missing, red mark remains]

[6. Hastings MSS. HA, Accounts, Box 16, 1403—1484. Richard
Hastings' receipt for wages. 12 April 1419.]

Ceste endenture fait le xii iour daprille lan notre seignur le Roy
Henry quint puis le conquest septisme, testmoigne qe Richard Hastynges, Chivaler, ad resceu de Johan Rochevale, Tresorer dez guerres notre
dit seignur xlii *li.*, ix *s.*, iiii *d.*, *ob.* sur les gages e regardes de luy v
homes darmes e xviii archers pur un demy quarter dun an. En tesmoignance de quelle chose lez parties avantditz ount mys lour sealx lez iour
e an suisditz.
[Seal attached]

[7. Hastings MSS. HA 6711. King Henry VIII to the earl of Huntingdon. 1544.]

Right trusty and well-beloved cousin, we greet you well and let you
wit that being determined to invade the realm of France this summer
with a royal army in our own person, for the good opinion we have of
your earnest good will and desire to serve us, we have appointed you
to attend upon us in your person with such number of horsemen and
footmen as ensueth to be by you furnished in their best array. And
therefore do require you and also command you to put yourself in readiness for this purpose, bringing with you as well the number of cl able
footmen, whereof xxix [xxxix?] to be archers, every one furnished
with a good bow in a case to carry it in, with xxiv good arrows in a
case with a good sword and dagger. As also 1[?]xx horsemen well
furnished upon able horses or geldings, either demi-lances or javelins
and well harnessed for that purpose, foreseeing that if any other man
having tenants within your rooms and offices be by our letters appointed
to make us [four-letter tear] men, he shall have the preferment of the
making of the same his tenants to serve us in this journey, not failing
to have number of ... footmen and also of horsemen in such order as
you and they may be ready to set forward immediately [twenty-letter
tear] warning to be given you by proclamation or otherwise by our right
trusty and well-beloved councilor, the lord [twenty-letter tear. John
Russell, Lord Russell] our privy seal, in whose company we have ap-

pointed you to serve us in the rear ward of our said army [twenty-letter tear] you shall be advertised of our pleasure as well touching such colors as you shall give to your men in the [twenty-letter tear] as also of the time and place they shall repair unto for their embarking. Requiring you to bring [thirty-five letter tear] and able men as we specially trust you. Given under our signet at our palace of Westminster [forty letter tear] year of our reign.

Verso: To our right trusty and . . .
    The earl of Huntingdon

[Seal on lower left-hand corner of verso. Upper left-hand corner of recto contains the stamp of Henry VIII. *Cf. Letters and Papers of Henry VIII,* XIX, Part i, pp. 150, 165.]

Miscellaneous Indentures in other Libraries.

[8. Bodleian Library, MS. Dugdale 2, p. 261. A transcript in Dugdale's hand. Indenture between Henry, prince of Wales, and Walter Devereux, 15 November 1408.]

Ceste indenture faite parentre le hault et puissant Prince Henry, prince de Gales, duc de Guyen, de Lancastre, et de Cornewaille, et conte de Cestre dune parte, et son bon ame escuier, Waulter Dewrose, dautre part, tesmoigne que mesme le Waulter est retenuz et demurrez devers mon dit seignur le prince pur lui servir en temps de pees come de guerre a pees et a guerre si bien de par decea come de la ou sur la mere pur terme de sa vie et pur estre ovec mon dit seignur le prince a pees et a guerre en contre *touz* genz de monde excepte notre tres doubte seignur le roy, pere a mesme monseignur le prince, pur le quel service prendra le dit Waulter de mon dit seignur le prince dys marcz pur an pour terme de sa vie par les maynes de le chamberleyn de Southgales pour le temps y esteant as termes de Pasque et de Seynt Michel par oveles porcions.

Et avera mon dit seignur le prince de lavantdit Waulter quant il serra en son service de guerre en sa presence ou de son commandement la tierce partie de lui et la teire [*sic*] partie de lez tierces de touz sez genz de lour gaignez de guerre.

Et si le dit Waulter ou aucun de sez genz prendat [*sic*] ou prendront aucun cheiftain, chastiel, ou forteresse en aucun voiage quant il serra as gages de mon dit seignur le prince, il serra tenuz pur lez ditz cheiftein, chastel, ou fortresse liverer a mon avantdit seignur le prince faisant a luy resonable gree pur le cheiftain, chastel, ou forteresse avantditz.

Et outre ce si mon dit seignur le prince envoie au dit Waulter pur venir devers luy soit il deins le royaume ou dehors ou sur la meer ovec aucun nombre de gens pur luy servir en sa presence ou aillours a son commandement, le dit Waulter serra tenuz pur venir a mon dit seignur le prince et pur les gentz queux il ainsi amesnent, il avera gagez tieulx come autres genz prendront de lours estatez et come le besoigne de lour venue requiert etc. Done a Westm. xv° Novembre, x H. v^ti [written over, meaning iv].

[A similar indenture between Henry, prince of Wales, and Geoffrey Arden, esquire, with a fee of 10 marks a year, dated 15 November, 10 Henry IV, 1408, appears on p. 264.]

[9. Bodleian Library, MS. Dugdale 2, p. 266. A transcript in Dugdale's hand. Indenture between Henry, prince of Wales, and Richard, earl of Warwick, 2 October 1410.]

Ceste indenture faite parentre le hault et puissant prince Henry, eisne filz au noble roy d'Engletcrre et de France, prince de Galez, duc de Guyene, de Lancastre, et de Cornwaile, et conte de Chestre d'une parte, et son treschier et tres ame cousin, Richard, counte de Warrewyk, d'autre parte, tesmoigne que mesme le conte est retenuz et demourez devers mon dit seignur le prince pur luy servir si bien en temps de pees come de guerre a peez et a guerre si bien de par decea come de la ou sur la meer, pur terme de sa vie, e pur estre oves mon dit seignur le prince a pees e a guerre encontre toutz gentz de monde excepte notre tres redoubte seignur le roy Henry, pere a monseignur Henry, le prince, pur le quel service prendra le dit conte de mon dit seignur le prince deux centz e cynquantz marcs de an a son eschequer de Kermerdyn a termez de Pasque e de St. Michel par ovellez porcions.

Et avera le dit conte quant il serra deins le hostel de mon dit seignur le prince avec luy quatre de sez escuiers e syz vadlets a bouche de court de monseignur le prince avantdit. Et avera mon dit seignur le prince de le avantdit conte pur tout la vie le dit conte quant il serra az gagez de mon dit seignur le prince la teirce partie de luy e la teirce partie de la teircez de toutz les gentz de lour gaignez de guerre. Et si le suis [?] dit conte ou daucun de sez gentz prendra ou prendront auscun cheiftein, chastell, ou fortresse en ascun voiage quant il serra as gagez de mon dit seignur le prince quil serra tenuz a liverer a mon dit seignur le prince faisant a luy resonable gree etc.

Done en le manoir de Lambehith ii^do Octobre, xii H. 4^ti.

[10. Bodleian Library, MS. Dugdale 2, p. 261. A transcript in Dugdale's hand. Military indenture between King Henry V and Sir Richard Hastings, 1 May 1421.]

Cette indenture faite parentre le roy notre sovereign seignur d'une parte, e Richard Hastyngges, chivaler, d'autre parte, testmoigne que le dit Richard est demorez devers notre dit seignur le roy pur lui faire service de guerre en lez partiez pardela par un demy an e avera le dit Richard continualment demorantz ovec luy durant le dit temps dys homez d'armes lui mesmes a coutez e trent archiers montez, armez, e arraiez come a lour estatez il appartient. Et prendra le dit Richard gagez assavoir pur lui mesmez deux soulds, pur chacun des ditz autrez homez d'armez dousze deniers le iour ovesque regard a custumez.

Et pur chescun des ditz archiers syz denyers le iour durant le temps susdit, desqueux gagez e regard serra le dit Richard paiez pur le primer quarter en main etc.

Et serra le dit Richard tenuz d'estre ove les genz de sa dicte retenue au port de la ville de Dovorre le vynt e teirce iour de ceste presente moys de May pur faire la moustre entierre diceux sur les dounez [*downs?*] pres dilloeques etc. Done a Westm. i May ix H. v^ti.

[11. Transcript provided by Dr. N. B. Lewis of an indenture between Richard, duke of Gloucester, and Henry, earl of Northumberland, at Alnwick Castle. 28 July 1474. (Spelling modernized by me). Northumberland MSS. Y. II. 28. Summarized in H.M.C. Report VI, part i, p. 223b.]

This indenture made the xxviii day of July, the xiv year of the reign of our sovereign lord, King Edward fourth, betwixt the right high and mighty prince, Richard, duke of Gloucester, on the one part, and the right worshipful lord, Henry, earl of Northumberland, on the other part, witnesseth that the said earl by these presents promits and grants unto the said duke to be his faithful servant, the said duke being his good and faithful lord; and the said earl to do service unto the said duke at all times lawful and convenient when he thereunto by the said duke shall be lawfully required, the duty of the allegiance of the said earl to the king's highness, the queen, his service and promise to Prince Edward, their first begotten son, and all the king's issue begotten and to be begotten, first at all times reserved and had.

For the which service the said duke promits and grants unto the said earl to be his good and faithful lord at all times; and to sustain him in his right afore all other persons, except tofore except. Also the said duke promises and grants to the said earl that he shall not ask, challenge, nor claim any office or offices or fee that the said earl hath of the king's grant, or of any other person or persons, at the making of these presents, nor interrupt the said earl nor any of his servants in executing or doing of any the said office or offices by him or any of his servants in time to come. And also the said duke shall not accept nor retain into his service any servant or servants that was or any time sith hath been, with the said earl retained of fee, clothing, or promise according to the appointment taken betwixt the said duke and earl by the king's highness and the lords of his council at Nottingham the xiith day of May in the xiv year of the reign of our said sovereign lord, except John Wodryngton. In witness whereof the said duke and the said earl to these indentures interchangeably have set their seals the day and year above said.

[Seal missing]

APPENDIX B
LORD HASTINGS' RETAINERS

Tables of Lord Hastings' retainers who served as members of the house of commons and as sheriffs, 1461–1483.

TABLE I

Parliament	No. of M.P's Known	Retainer	Date of Indenture	Constituency
1461	78 out of 288	John Gresley	8 Dec. 1477	Staffordshire
1463–65	71 (26 doubtful) of 292	Simon Montfort	22 Nov. 1469	Warwickshire
1467–68	280 out of 294	? Maurice Berkeley	18 March 1474	Gloucestershire
		? Thomas Danvers	—	Hindon, Wilts
[1470–71 Henry VI]	121 out of 295	? Henry Vernon	—	Derbyshire
1472–75	283 (2 doubtful) out of 295	? Maurice Berkeley	18 March 1474	Southampton
		James Blount	12 Dec. 1474	Derbyshire
		Richard Boughton	10 Apr. 1479	Warwickshire
		? Thomas Danvers	—	Downton, Wilts
		Nicholas Longford	—	Derbyshire
		Robert Tailboys	4 Oct. 1481	Lincolnshire
		William Trussel	10 March 1475	Leicestershire
1478	291 out of 295	? Thomas Danvers	—	Downton, Wilts
		John Gresley	8 Dec. 1477	Derbyshire
		Thomas Gresley	26 Apr. 1479	Stafford Borough
		Simon Montfort	22 Nov. 1469	Warwickshire
		William Moton	12 Dec. 1475	Leicestershire
		? John Staunton	—	Westbury, Wilts
		Robert Tailboys	4 Oct. 1481	Lincolnshire

Parliament	No. of M.P's Known	Retainer	Date of Indenture	Constituency
		William Trussel	10 Mar. 1475	Leicestershire
		? Henry Vernon	—	Derbyshire
		John Wigston (Wystow)	7 Dec. 1478	Leicester Borough
1483 (20 Jan. –18 Feb.)	120 (62 doubtful) of 296	? Henry Vernon	—	Derbyshire
		Simon Montfort	22 Nov. 1469	Warwickshire
		? Thomas Danvers	—	Downton, Wilts

SUMMARY

Number of M.Ps known: 1123 out of 1760 = 63.8 %
Minus Doubtful cases: 90
Number of M.Ps certain: 1033 out of 1760 = 58.3 %

Number of Hastings' Retainers
MPs. one or more parliaments: 14 = 63.8 %: conjectured 100 % = 22 retainers.
              Doubt.   4
              Certain   10 = 58.3 %:   ,,   ,,   = 17 retainers.

Number of Hastings M.Ps at Single Parliaments:

          25 = 63.8 % — conjectured 100 % = 40
Doubtful   10
Certain   15 = 58.3 %   ,,   ,,   = 26

Hastings Retainers: % of total M.Ps.

Including Doubtful = 14 out of 1123 = 1.2 %
Certain: = 10 out of 1033 = .97 %

Hastings M.Ps. at Single Parliaments: % of total M.Ps.

Including Doubtful = 25 out of 1123 = 2.2 %
Certain: = 15 out of 1033 = 1.5 %

Hastings Retainers who sat in Parliament (? = Doubtful).

	Number of Parliaments		Number of Parliaments
? Maurice Berkeley	2.	Simon Montfort	3.
James Blount	1.	William Moton	1.
Richard Boughton	1.	? John Staunton	1
? Thomas Danvers	4.	Robert Tailboys	2
John Gresley	2.	William Trussel	2
Thomas Gresley	1.	? Henry Vernon	3
Nicholas Longford	1	John Wigston (Wystow)	1

Individual Retainers:		M.Ps. at Single Parliaments.	
Total:	14	Total:	25
Doubtful:	4	Doubtful:	10
Certain:	10	Certain:	15

TABLE II

Summary of Hastings Retainers as Sheriffs by Counties and Years.

Year	Counties	Number of Sheriffs
Nov. 1461	Staffs	1
1463	Staffs (?)	1 (?)
1464	Lincoln	1
1466	Notts & Derby; Staffs	2.
1467	Staffs	1.
11 April 1471	Warwick & Leic.	1.
9 Nov. 1471	Notts & Derby; Staffs; Warwick & Leic.; Wilts (?)	4 (?)
1472	Notts & Derby; Staffs	2
5 Nov. 1475	Notts & Derby; Staffs; Warwick & Leic.; Northants	4
1476	Notts & Derby	1
1477	Notts & Derby	1
1478	Notts & Derby; Staffs	2
1479	Staffs; Warwick & Leic.	2
1480	Notts & Derby; Staffs; Lincoln; Rutland (?)	4 (?)
1481	Staffs	1
5 Nov. 1482	Notts & Derby; Staffs; Warwick & Leic.	3

Sheriffs of Nottinghamshire and Derbyshire.			Staffordshire.	
9 for 22 years, 1461–1483.			12 for 22 years.	
Date	Hastings' Retainers	Date of Indenture		Date of Indenture
7 Nov. 1461			John Harcourt, esq.	1474
1466	Nicholas Knyveton, esq.	1465	John Harcourt, esq.	1474
1467			John Acton (Aston)	1481
9 Nov. 1471	Gervase Clifton, esq.	1478	Walter Griffith, knt.	—

Date	Hastings' Retainers	Date of Indenture		Date of Indenture
1472	John Curson, esq.	—	William Bassett, esq.	1465
5 Nov. 1475	William Bassett, esq.	1465	John Aston, esq.	1481
1476	Ralph Pole, esq.	1475		
1477	Gervase Clifton, esq.	1478		
1478	John Babington, esq.		Nicholas Montgomery, esq.	1481
1479			John Aston	1481
1480	Robert Eyre, esq.	1476	William Bassett, esq.	1465
1481			Humphrey Stanley, gt.	—
1482	Gervase Clifton, esq.	1478	Nicholas Montgomery, esq.	1481
6 Nov. 1483	John Babington, knt.			
5 Nov. 1484	Nicholas Montgomery, esq.	1481		
1485			Humphrey Stanley	
1486	John Curson, esq.		Henry Willoughby	1477
4 Nov. 1487	Gervase Clifton, knt.			
1488	John Leak, esq.		Hugh Persall, knt.	1479
5 Nov. 1489	Nicholas Knyfton, the elder	1465	Thomas Gresley, knt.	1479

Warwickshire and Leicestershire.

5 for 22 years, 1461–1483

Date		Date of Indenture
11 Apr. 1471	Simon Montfort, knt.	1469
9 Nov. 1471	William Moton, esq.	1475
5 Nov. 1475	William Trussel, knt.	1475 (March)
1479	Richard Boughton, esq.	1479 (April)
1482	Thomas Entwysell, esq.	1474
5 Nov. 1484	Richard Boughton, esq.	1479

Wiltshire.

Maurice Berkeley, knt   1474

Lincolnshire 1461—82/3.

	Date of Indenture
5 Nov. 1464	
Brian Stapilton, knt.	1479
5 Nov. 1480	
Robert Tailboys, knt.	1481

Rutland.

5 Nov. 1480
William Palmer, esq.

Northamptonshire.

Mich. 1475. William Bassett, esq. [T. Wake (5. Nov.) died]   1465

SUMMARY

Hastings Retainers as Sheriffs:

19 certain + 3 Doubtful = 22

	No. of men	No. of years
Nottingham & Derby	7	9
Staffordshire (1 doubtful)	8	12
Warwickshire & Leicestershire	5	5
Lincolnshire	2	2
Northamptonshire	1	1
Rutland (Doubtful)	1	1
Wiltshire (Doubtful)	1	1

10

APPENDIX C

THE RECORD OF HUGH PESHALE'S PROSECUTION

[Public Record Office, KB 27/865, Membrane 123v. King's Bench Roll. Michaelmas Term, 17 Edward IV (1477).]

Salop. Alias, scilicet, die Martis proximo post festum Sancte Trinitatis anno regni domini regis nunc decimo septimo apud Ludlowe in comitatu predicto coram Ricardo Grey, filio precarissime consortie domini regis, et sociis suis justitiariis domini regis ad pacem in [comitatu] predicto conservandam necnon ad diversa felonias, transgressiones, et alia malefacta in eodem comitatu perpetrata audiendum et terminandum assignatis per sacrum xii juratorum extitit presentatum quod Hugo Peshale de Knyghtley in comitatu Staff., armiger, videlicet, decimo die Augusti anno regni domini regis nunc sexto decimo apud Newport in comitatu Salop. ad tunc et ibidem dedit et liberavit diversas liberationes pannorum sive togarum, scilicet, Thome Peshale de Newport in comitatu Salop., wever, Reginaldo Peshale de Newport in comitatu Salop., wever, Rogero Burton de Newport in comitatu Salop., hewster, Ricardo Mon' de Newport in comitato Salop., sadler, Maurice Taylor alias dicto Maurice ap Jeam ap Atkin, taillour, de Newport in comitatu Salop., taillour, [sic] Thome Burton de Newport in comitatu Salop., husbondman, Thome Wright de Newport in comitatu Salop., hosteler, Henrico Rise de Newport in comitatu Salop., ffyssher, Edwardo Lee de Egemondene in comitatu Salop., yoman, Johanni Gaynant de Egemondene in comitatu Salop., laborer, Johanni Adams junior de Egemondene in comitatu Salop., husbondman, Eade Vawer de Egemondene in comitatu Salop., husbondman, et Willielmo Shutte de Egemondene in comitatu Salop., laborer, contra ordinationem et provisionem diversorum statutorum in hoc casu editorum et provisorum et contra pacem domini regis etc. de causis venire fecit terminandum etc.

Quodquidam inditamentum dominus rex nunc coram eo postea certis venire fecit terminandum etc.

Postea quod preceptum fuit vicecomiti quod non omittat etc. quam venire facet eos ad respondendum etc. Et modo scilicet, die veneris proximo post quindenam Sancti Michaelis isto eodom termino coram domino rege apud Westmonasterium veniunt predicti Hugo Peshale, Thomas Peshale, Reginaldus Peshale, Rogerus Burton, Ricardus Mon',

Maurice Taylor, Thomas Burton, Thomas Wright, Henricus Rise, Edwardus Lee, Johannis Gaynant, Johannis Adams junior, Eada Vawer, et Willielmus Shutte per Simonem Hadyngtone, attornatum suum. Et habito auditu premissorum, dicunt separatim quod inditamentum predictum non est sufficiens in lege ad ponendum ipsos seu eorum aliquem responsuro eidem inditamento per eo, videlicet, quod per idem inditamentum non fit mentio qualem liberationem pannorum sive togarum predictus Hugo Peshale dedit prefatis Thome Peshale et aliis nec quod iidem Thomas Peshale et omnes alii eandem liberationem pannorum et togarum predictorum de prefato Hugone Peshale receperunt prout per legem fieri deberet et pro insufficientia eiusdem petunt separatim quod ipsi inde per curiam dimittantur etc. Super quo vicecomiti inditamento producto et per curiam hic intellecto quod idem inditamentum non est sufficiens etc. Consideratum est quod iidem Hugo Peshale, Thomas Peshale, Reginaldus Peshale, Rogerus Burton, Ricardus Mon', Maurice Taylor, Thomas Burton, Thomas Wright, Henricus Rise, Edwardus Lee, Johannis Lee, Johannis Gaynant, Johannis Adams junior, Eada Vawer, et Willielmus Shutte eant inde sine die etc.

[In the margin;] Sine Die.

APPENDIX D
LICENCES TO RETAIN MEN AND TO GIVE LIVERY

[1. Form for a license to retain men for the king's service. Time of Henry VII [?]. P.R.O., E101/59/5. Spelling modernized.]

Henry, by the grace of God, king of England and of France and lord of Ireland, — — — — — — greeting. Albeit that our Lord be thanked, by our great study, labor, costs, and policy, we be in good and honorable peace, liege, comity, and confederation with all princes Christian, and that in likewise we have established and put our realm and subjects in good obeisance, rest, peace, and tranquility without any likelihood of war, YET forasmuch as to wise providence and good policy it appertaineth in time of peace to foresee the remedy against the dangers of war, as well to resist outward attemptates of hostility when the case shall require, as also to conserve our realm and subjects in good order of justice, tranquility, and good obeisance, and forasmuch also as there is a mutual bond betwixt us and divers other right mighty princes, our friends and allies and confederates, whereby for the maintenance of the estate of us and them and our and their subjects, every of us is bound to assist and defend the other in case we or they be invaded by any other, which our confederates have heretofore and may fortune to require assistance of us hereafter according to our mutual bonds in that behalf; And also for the more ready furniture of a crew to our town and marches of Calais after the old manner in time of need, and when the case shall so require, WE, for these considerations, by the advice of our council intending to provide a good, substantial, and competent number of captains and able men of our subjects to be in areadiness to serve us at our pleasure when the case shall require, and trusting in your faith and truth, will and desire you, and nevertheless command you, and by these presents give unto you full power and authority from henceforth during our pleasure to take, appoint, and retain by indenture or covenant in form and manner as hereafter ensueth, and none otherwise, such persons, our subjects, as by your discretion shall be thought and seemeth to you to be able men to do us service in the war in your company under you and at your leading at all such times and places and as often as it shall please us to command or assign you, to the number of — — — persons whose names be contained in a certificate by you made in a bill of parchment indented betwixt us and you, and interchangeably signed by us and subscribed with your hand and to our secretary delivered. And as often and whensoever it shall fortune any of the said persons to decease or by any manner of ways be of that condition that by virtue of this our license, he or they cannot nor may not longer be retained with you or withdraw him or them and depart into strange places to you unknown, or otherwise be unable to serve us in the war or that for any cause moving you, you list to discharge him or them so that it be without color or defraud, that then and so often it shall be lawful [lieful] to you in the place and places of every of them to retain other able persons for the furniture of the said number. PROVIDED always that you retain not above the said number which you shall indent for in form and manner hereafter ensuing. PROVIDED also the same able persons shall not be chosen, taken, nor retained but only of your own tenants or of the inhabitants within any office that you have of our grant, or of the grant of any other person or persons or community [cominaltie], or of the tenants or servants of other our subjects not retained nor authorized by our letters of placard to retain as you be, which tenants or servants or others of their good free wills will be agreeable to do unto us service in your company and at your leading. PROVIDED always that you retain no manner [of] person or persons within any city or town incorporate which we have reserved to ourself to be at the leading of such a person or persons as we shall assign and appoint thereunto. And also to array and cause them to be arrayed and put them in all manner harness necessary and convenient for the war and the same by yourself or deputy to view and review as often as it shall seem good, and at the least once or twice yearly. Every of them having a jacket of our colors with our cognizance and yours, and to keep them in such areadiness that upon any reasonable warning hereafter to be given unto you by our letters under our signet, you may muster them and every of them before our commissioners for that purpose to be appointed at any time when we shall command the same to be done. And over that whensoever the case shall so require and warning shall be given unto you by our letters to come to serve us with them, forthwith and with all diligence, in your own person, bring the said able men by you retained to us at our wages and lead them to such place as we shall appoint you, sufficiently horsed and harnessed. At which time we authorize you to furnish, or cause to be furnished, the said able persons with horses and not to put any man to charge for the said horses before that time, having jackets and cognizances as above, to do unto us service. PROVIDED always that under color thereof you neither exact, levy, nor take any sums of money for the harnessing, jacketing, or horsing of yourself or any of your retinue of any man, but we can be contented that such that be not mete nor able to do unto us service personally in the war, which of their good, free wills can be contented to do the same, shall furnish any of your retinue with harness, jackets, or horses when the case shall require, without that, that you or any for you take or retain any money of them or any of them, but only jackets, harness as above. PROVIDED also that you make no common cessing or contributions of any villages or townships for the provision of any horse or harness, or any other thing to the charging of our poor subjects in that behalf. And if it shall fortune us in our person to make any voyage into the parts of beyond the sea, then in your own person with as many of them as you can bring to come and do unto us service accordingly. And that you give unto your company straight commandment and injuction not to wear or use any such jackets or cognizances but only at the time of the said view, review, and musters, or when we shall command you to bring them to do service unto us as above. And these our present letters shall be unto you and all and every the persons by you to be retained in form above specified and indented for with us, and such other as you shall retain in the place of any of them died, avoided, or discharged as above is specified, sufficient discharge in this behalf at all times hereafter; any act, statute, prohibition, or other ordinance in the time of us or any of our noble progenitors or predecessors by authority of parliament or otherwise heretofore made, enacted, passed, or ordained to the contrary notwithstanding. PROVIDED always that you, under color hereof or by virtue of these our letters of placard, retain no more in number by word, promise, or otherwise than is contained in your said certificate indented and indented for with us as above under the pains specified in our statutes made and ordained in that behalf. And in case it can may be proved that you retain above the said number of —— —— —— persons contrary to this our authority and license, then you to fall into the penalty and damages of the said statutes only for such persons as above the said number shall be by you retained and for no more and none other. WILLING and straightly charging and upon their allegiance commanding, all and every such persons as by this our placard you have license and authority to retain to do us service in the war, to be unto you at all times for the due execution of the same placard and as far as the license and authority that you have of us by the same doth extend, answering, assisting, obeying, and attending.

[Statutes of the Realm, 19 Henry VII—De retentionibus illicitis—chapter 14, par. x, authorizing such licenses, reads:]

Provided also that this act extend not to the punishment of any person or persons, the which by the virtue of the king's placard or writing signed with his hand and sealed with his privy seal or signet, shall take, appoint, or indent with any persons to do and to be in readiness to do the king service in war, or otherwise at his commandment, so that they that shall have such placard or writing for their part use not by that retainer, service, attendance, or any otherwise, the person or persons that they shall take, appoint, or indent with; nor the persons that so do indent to do the king service, use not themselves for their part in doing service or giving attendance to them that shall have authority by reason of the king's writing to take, appoint or indent with them, in anything concerning the said act otherwise than shall be comprised in the same king's placard or writing, and that placard or writing to endure during the king's pleasure and no longer.

[2. License for Lord Cobham to retain 100 persons, 11 July 1550. Patent Roll 4 Edward VI, Part V, Membrane 35.]

Pro Domino Cobham de Licentia.

[In English]

Edward the sixth etc. To all men etc. Know you that of our especial grace, certain knowledge, and mere motion, and by the advice of our council, we have given and granted full authority, power, and license, and by these presents do give and grant unto our right trusty and right well-beloved councillor, the Lord Cobham, our deputy of Calais, full authority, license, power, and liberty that he during his life at his pleasure may lawfully and without offense, loss, damage, forfeiture, or other penalty retain and keep in his service from time to time by way of retainder over and beside all such persons as daily attend upon him in his household and to whom he giveth meat, drink, livery, fee, or wages, and also over and besides all such persons as be or shall be under him in any office or offices of any stewardship, understeward-ship, bailiwick, keeper of parks, houses, warrens, or other games of venery, pheasants, partridges, and other fowl of what kind soever they be of as well of such office or offices which he hath or shall have of us or of any our subjects for term of life or at pleasure, or otherwise as of other his own proper offices, hereditaments, or possessions, the number of one hundred persons, gentlemen or yeomen, whatsoever albeit the same person or persons so retained or to be retained be the tenants of us or of any other our subjects, or dwelling or resident within our honours, manors, dominions, leets, towns, or hundreds, and to the same to give at his will and pleasure, his livery, badge, or cognizance, or to as many of the said number of one hundred persons as will receive the said liveries, badges, or cognizances and grant to do unto him their service when he shall appoint and require the same for our better service and surety always to be employed. The said persons to be reputed, taken, and accepted by virtue of this our grant and license to all instructions, constructions, and intents as they were daily attendant on the said Lord Cobham in his household and as though they had meat, drink, livery, wages, and lodging in his house as his household servants daily attending upon him have or shall have.

Provided always that this our grant and license unto the said Lord Cobham shall not extend or authorize him to take or retain into his service any of our servants being named in our Chequer Roll, nor any other being [Ms. thing] sworn or retained to serve us as our servant or servants. And this our license shall be a sufficient warrant and discharge as well to the said Lord Cobham for the retaining of the said number of one hundred persons as also to the said persons so to be retained by way of retainer and to every of them for the taking of his said livery, badge, and cognizance and the promise and doing of their service in form expressed in any act, statute, provision, article, or clause heretofore made or hereafter to be made or provided to the contrary in any wise notwithstanding. And that the said number of one hundred persons so retained or to be retained and every of them shall be discharged and exonerated of all forfeitures, losses, and penalties that in anywise may or shall rise or grow to us, our heirs or successors by force or virtue of any statutes, laws, or customs made or to be made for retaining to the contrary notwithstanding. And furthermore of our especial grace and by the advice aforesaid, we have pardoned, remised, and released, and by these presents do pardon, remise, and release to the said Lord Cobham all and every trespass, offense, contempt, violation, or forfeiture, losses, penalties, sum or sums of money by him committed, done, or perpetrated since the five and twenty day of January last past contrary to any act or acts of retainer or retainers heretofore had, made, or established. That express mention etc. In witness whereof etc. T. R. apud Leighes, xi die Julii. per breve de privato sigillo.

[Membranes 35 and 36 contain similar licenses, in English, for Sir Peter Carewe, knight, 29 June 1550, to retain 40 persons; for Sir Gawyn Carewe, knight, 11 June 1550, to retain 40 persons, under the same terms. Their pardons date from 25 January last past.]

[3. License for Sir William Cecil to retain 50 persons, 12 April 1553 P.R.O., C66/853, Patent Roll 7 Edward VI, Part III, Membrane 23.]

Edward the sixth etc. Know you that We of our grace especial, certain knowledge, and mere motion have given and granted, and by these presents do give and grant, full authority, power, and license to our trusty and right well-beloved councillor, Sir William Cecil, knight, one of our two principal secretaries, that, he, during his life at his pleasure may lawfully and without offense, loss, and damage, forfeiture, or other penalty, retain and keep in his service, from time to time by way of retainer, over and besides all such persons as be or shall be under him in any office or offices or any stewardship, under-stewardship, bailiff-wick, keeper of parks, houses, warrens, or other games of venery, pheasants, partridges, and other foul of what kind soever they be of, as well of such office or offices which he hath or shall have of us or of any other our subjects, for term of life or at pleasure or otherwise as of other his own proper office, hereditaments, or possessions, the number of fifty persons whatsoever. Albeit, the same person or persons so retained, or to be retained, be the tenants of us or of any other our subjects, or dwelling or resident within our honours, manors, dominions, leets, towns, or hundreds, and to the same to give at his will and pleasure his livery, badge, or cognizance, or to as many of the said number of fifty persons as will receive the said liveries, badge, or cognizance and grant to do unto him their service when he shall appoint and require the same for our better service and surety always to be employed. The said persons to be reputed, taken, and accepted by virtue of this our grant and license to all instructions, constructions, and intents as they were daily attendant on the said Sir William Cecil, knight, in his household and as though they had meat, drink, livery, wages, and lodging in his house as his household servants daily attending upon him have or shall have, and this our license shall be sufficient warrant and discharge, as well to the said Sir William Cecil, knight, for the retaining of the said number of fifty persons, as also to the said persons to be retained by way of retaining and to every of them for the taking of his said livery, badge, or cognizance, and the promise and doing of their service in form expressed. Any statute, act, provision, article, or clause heretofore made, or hereafter to be made or provided to the contrary in any wise notwithstanding. That express mention etc. In witness whereof etc. *T[este] R. apud Westmonasterium xii die Aprilis. per breve de privato sigillo.*

[4. License for Henry, earl of Arundel, to retain 200 gentlemen or yeomen, 20 November 1553. P.R.O., C66/878, Patent Roll I Mary, Part XV, Membranes 16—17.]

Pro Henrico Comite Arundell de licentia.

Mary by the grace of God etc. To all men to whom etc. greeting. Know you that we of our especial grace, certain knowledge, and mere motion have given and granted for us, our heirs and successors full authority, power, and license, and by these presents do give and grant, unto our right trusty and right well-beloved cousin and councillor, Henry, earl of Arundel, full authority, license, power, and liberty that he, during his life at his pleasure, may lawfully and without offense, loss, damage, forfeiture, or other penalty, retain and keep in his service from time to time by way of retaining, over and besides all such persons as daily attend upon him in his household and to whom he giveth meat, drink, livery, fee, or wages, and also over and besides all such persons as be or shall be under him in any office or offices of any stewardship, understewardship, bailiffwick, keeper of parks, houses, warrens, or other games of venery, pheasants, partridges, and other fowls of what kind soever they be, as well of such office or offices which he hath or shall have of us or of any other our subjects for term of life or at pleasure or otherwise as of other his own proper offices, hereditaments, or possessions, the number of two-hundred persons, gentlemen or yeomen, whatsoever. Albeit the same person or persons so retained or to be retained be the tenants of us or any other our subjects, or dwelling or resident within our honours, manors, dominions, leets, towns, or hundreds, and to the same to give at his will and pleasure his livery, badge, or cognizance, or to as many of the said number of two-hundred persons as will receive the said livery, badge, or cognizance and grant to do unto him their service when he shall appoint and require the same for our better service and surety always to be employed; the same persons. to be reputed, taken, and accepted by virtue of this our grant and license to all instructions, constructions, and purposes as they were daily attendant on the said earl of Arundel in his household, and as though they had meat and drink, livery, wages, and lodging in his house as his household servants daily attending upon him have or shall have. Provided always that this our grant and license unto the said earl of Arundel [m. 17] shall not extend to authorize him to take or retain unto his service any of our servants being named in our exchequer roll, or any other being sworn or retained to serve us as our servant or servants. And this our license shall be a sufficient warrant and discharge as well to the said earl of Arundel for the retaining of the said number of two-hundred persons as also to the said persons so to be retained by way of retaining and to every of them for the taking of his said livery, badge, or cognizance and the promise and doing of their service in form expressed in any statue or provision, article, or clause heretofore made or hereafter to be made or provided to the contrary in anywise notwithstanding. And that the said number of two-hundred persons so retained or to be retained and every of them notwithstanding that they be not herein particularly and expressly named, shall be discharged and exonerated of all forfeitures, losses, and penalties that in anywise may or shall rise or grow to us, our heirs or successors, by force or virtue of any statute, laws, or customs made or to be made for retainers to the contrary notwithstanding. And furthermore of our especial grace and mere motion, We have pardoned, remised, and released, and by these presents do pardon, remit, and release to the said earl of Arundel all and every trespass, offense, contempt, violation, or forfeiture, losses, penalties, sum or sums of money by him committed, done, or perpetrated since the first day of September last past contrary to any act or acts of retainer or retainers heretofore made or established. That express mention etc. In witness whereof etc. Witness ourself at Westminster the xx day of November. *per ipsam Reginam etc.*

[5. License for Sir Robert Brooke, C. J., to retain ten men, 27 May 1556. P. R. O., C66/899, Patent Roll 2 and 3 Philip and Mary, Part III, Membrane 17.]

De licentia pro Roberto Broke, milite.

Rex et Regina omnibus ad quos presentes littere prevenerunt, salutem. Cum in statuto in parliamento domini Edwardi nuper regis Anglie quarti, progenitoris nostri, tento apud Westmonasterium anno regni sui octavo stabilitato et inactitato existit inter alia quod nulla persona cuiuscumque status, gradus vel conditionis fuerit per scriptum vel aliquem alium pro illa post festum Natalis Sancti Johannis Baptiste quod tunc esset in anno domini nostri dei millimo quadringentesimo sexagesimo octavo daret alicui aliquam liberaturam vel signum vel retineret aliquam personam aliam quam suum menialem seu familiarem servientem, officiarum, vel hominem eruditum in una lege vel altera per aliquod scriptum, juramentum, aut promissionem. Et quod si aliquis incontrarium fecerit quod tunc incurreret penam et forisfacturam pro qualiter tali liberatura vel signo dato centum solidorum. Et retentor vel acceptor talis juramenti, scripti, aut promissionis vel retentor per indenturam pro qualiter tali retentione aut acceptione talis juramenti vel promissionis aut retinens per indenturam incurreret penam et forisfacturam centum solidorum pro quolibet mense quo aliqua talis persona esset sic secum retenta per juramentum, scriptum, indenturam, aut promissionem. Ac etiam quod quelibet persona sic retenta per scriptum, indenturam, juramentum, aut promissionem pro quolibet tali mense quo ipse esset sic retenta forisfaceret et deperderet centum solidos prout in statuto predicto inter alia plenius continetur. Sciatis nos de gratia nostra speciali quam ex certa scientia et mero motu nostris concessimus et licentiam dedimus ac per presentes pro nobis et heredibus nostris dicte regine concedimus et licentiam damus dilecto et fideli nostro, Roberto Broke, militi, quod ipse licite retinere possit de tempore in tempus durante vita sua decem homines aut pauciores licet non fuerunt sui meniales aut familiares servientes nec officiarii sui ad sibi deserviendum in legalibus itinerantibus et servitiis suis et quod idem Robertus licite dare possit eis de tempore in tempus liberaturas absque aliquo imprisonamento, pena, penalitate, deperdito, aut forisfacturo alicuius summe pecunie aut alia pena seu deperdito per ipsum Robertum pro tali retentione hominium seu eorum alicuius aut pro tali donatione liberaturo, reddendo, solvendo, levando, aut sustendo. Et absque aliquo imprisonamento, pena, penalitate, deperdito aut forisfacturo per tales homines sic retinendis seu eorum aliquem pro tali retentione aut acceptione liberaturae, reddendo, solvendo, levando, aut sustentando, statuto predicto aut aliquo statuto actu ordinatione seu provisione in huiusmodi casu edito et proviso vel in contrarium presentium edito seu proviso in aliquo non obstante. Proviso semper quod idem Robertus vigore presentium nullo tempore habeat ultra numerum decem huiusmodi hominium sic retentorum ultra familiares servientes et officiarios suos. Eo quod expressa mentio etc. In cuius rei etc. T[este] Rege et Regina apud Westmonasterium xxvii die Maii. per breve de privato sigillo etc.

[6. License for Francis, earl of Bedford, to retain 60 men, 19 November [1562]. P. R. O., C66/990, Patent Roll 5 Elizabeth, Part IV, Membrane 8.]

Elizabeth by the grace of God etc. To all men to whom these presents shall come, greeting. Know you that we of our especial grace, certain science, and mere motion, have given and granted full authority, power, and license, and by these presents for us, our heirs and successors do give and grant unto our right trusty and right well-beloved cousin and councillor, Francis, earl of Bedford, full power, authority, license, and liberty that he, during his life at his pleasure, may lawfully and without offense, damage, forfeiture, or other penalty retain and keep in his service from time to time by way of retaining over and beside all such persons as daily attend upon him in his household and to whom he giveth meat and drink, livery, fee, or wages, as also over and beside all such persons as be or shall be under him in any office or offices of any stewardship, understewardship, bailiffwick, keeper of parks, houses, warrens, or other games of venery, pheasants, partridges, or other fowl of what kind soever they be of as well of such office or offices which he hath or shall have of us or any other our subjects for term of life or at pleasure, or otherwise as of other his own proper offices, hereditaments, or possessions, the number of three score persons. Whatsoever albeit the same person or persons so retained or to be retained be the tenants of us or any other our subjects, or dwelling or resident within our honours, manors, dominions, leets, towns, or hundreds, and to the same to give at his will and pleasure his livery, badge, or cognizance, or to as many of the said number of three score persons as will receive the said livery, badge, or cognizance and grant to do unto him their service when he shall appoint and require the same for our better surety and service always to be employed, the said persons to be reputed, taken, and accepted by virtue of this our grant and license to all instructions, constructions, and intents as they were daily attendant upon the said Francis, earl of Bedford, in his household as though they had meat and drink, livery, wages, and lodging in his house as his household servants daily attending upon him have or shall have. And this our license shall be a sufficient farrant and discharge as well to the said earl for the retaining of the said number of three score persons as also to the said persons to be retained by way of retaining and to every of them for the taking of the said livery, badge, or cognizance, and the promise and doing of their service in form expressed, any act, statute, provision, article, or clause to the contrary heretofore made or hereafter to be made or provided in any wise notwithstanding. That express mention. In witness etc. Witness ourself at Westminster the xix day of November. *per breve de privato sigillo.*

INDEX

Oath: of allegiance, 17 n. 2, 91 n. 1, 94, 108; of fealty, 58 n. 11; of king's councillor, 58, 59 and n. 12; of king's justices, 69 n. 6; of king's retainer, 58 n. 10; of lords' to aid prosecution of wrong-doers, 72, 73 n. 14; of lords not to retain unlawfully, 90, 91; of commons, the same, 91 and n. 1; not to give livery, 92; sworn to Edward IV, 92; to be king's retainer only, 81, 94; illegal, sworn by retainers, 86; the retainer's, 48, 49, 53 n. 4, 57, 58 and nn. 10, 11, 59, 73, 77, 91, 98, 101, 103, 108, 112, 122, 125, 155

Offices: in gift of king, 93–95, 110, 113, 140, 149, 151–157; of the lords, 99, 111, 112, 140, 149, 151–156

Officers of the judges, 112, 155

Osbaldeston, Sir John, 55, 136, 137

Otway, Richard, 62

Outlawry, 88 and n. 33, 91

Owen David, 108

Oxford: earls of, 99; county, 29, Provisions of, 59

Padley, 128

Palmer, William, 40, 118, 144

Paget, Sir William, 109

Parades of liveried retainers, 11, 115–116

Pardon, 86, 100, 102, 111; general, 87, 88, 89 and n. 34, 152–157

Parliament: 10, 79, 109, 155; acts of *see* Statutes; authority of, 92, 97, 150; bills in, 78 and n. 23, 91 and n. 1, 112 n. 39; chamber, 72; Edward IV's, 10, 20, 30–36 *see* Parliaments; house, 30 n. 7; packing of, 10, 11, 30–36, 33 n. 9; summons to, 20

Parliament – the house of commons: 10, 30–36, 67, 71, 78, 109, 122; membership in [1461–83], 30, 32, 122, 141–143; nomination and election of members of, 30–36; Lord Hastings' retainers members of, 30–36, 122, 141–143; independence of, 34; esprit of members of, 36, 37; expenses of members of, 33 n. 9, 36; speaker of, 75–76; in 1628, 112 and n. 39; *Journals* of, 112 n. 39; diaries of members of, 9 n. 1, 112 n. 39; commons' petitions, 68 n. 4, 70–71, 78

Parliament – house of lords: 10, 112 n. 39; the lords of, 10, 30, 31, 46, 75, 82, 85, 88; their control over the house of commons, 32, 34 *see* Peers

Parliaments of: *1305*, 58, 68; *1327*, 59; *1331*, 59; *1377*, 69; *1399*, 71; *1461*, 30 n. 6, 32, 72, 92, 141; *1463–65*, 32, 141; *1467–68*, 32, 79, 80, 141; *1472–75*, 30 n. 7, 31, 32, 34, 35, 46, 141; *1478*, 33–36, 46, 141–142; *1483*, 32, 142; *1485*, 91 and n. 1; *1523*, 109; *1554*, 112; *1628*, 112 and n. 39

Parson of Beeston, 78 n. 22.

Partridges, 151–156

Paston: Sir John, 27, 30 n. 6, 31, 41–44; John the youngest, 30 n. 7, 31, 32, 36, 41–44; Margaret, the mother of, 41, 43, 44; Margery, the wife of John, 44; William, 43

Patronage, political, 45 *see* Good Lordship, Influence, Preferment

Peers of the realm: 10, 12, 13, 23, 24, 30 and n. 6, 39, 40, 42, 45, 46, 49, 50, 61, 62, 66, 69, 77, 79, 88, 100, 105, 106, 115, 116, 121; the king's counsellors-born, 46, 88; wars between, 25; their service owed the king, 56, 61, 79, 80; the king's dependence upon, 42, 79, 80, 92, 106, 108; territories of, 46; the retainers of, 10, 11, 25, 30, 39, 40, 45, 46, 50, 61–64, 75, 76, 78, 96, 99, 101, 106, 108; as retainers of other peers, 27, 28, 52, 72 n. 14; their right to retain, 70, 72 and n. 14, 75, 76, 78, 79, 82, 85, 87, 90–92, 95, 106, 116; licensed to keep retainers, 80, 81, 109, 110, 115, 116, 151–154, 156–157; forbidden to use livery, 72–73; exempted from act of *1468*, 79, 88; as king's knights, 108; their duty to retain men, 69, 70, 73, 76; their obligations to retainers, 50, 65, 66 and n. 20, 67, 77; limitations on same, 65, 66, 77; prosecutions of, for livery and retaining, 75, 102–106; no prosecution of, for same, 75, 82, 87, 102

Pembroke: Aylmer de Valence, earl of, 59; Sir William, earl of, 79 n. 24; William Herbert, earl of, 115

Pencels, 115

Penreth, 64

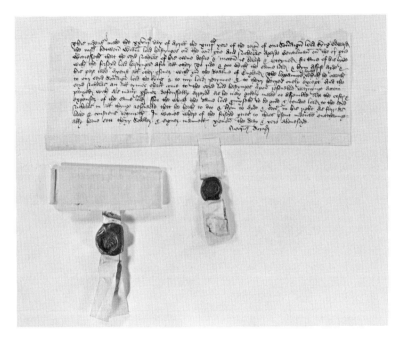

Plate I. Lord Hastings' part of the indenture with Nicholas Agarde, one of the 67 original indentures at the Henry E. Huntington Library. Reproduced by courtesy of the Librarian.

Plate II. The badges of the lords Bourchier and Hastings from British Museum MS. Additional 40742, folio 11, dated by the cataloguer *c.* 1466–70. The manuscript contains annotations by Sir John Fenn, the eighteenth-century antiquary, who presumably cut out the badges from a fifteenth-century paper manuscript and mounted them in this volume. Reproduced by courtesy of the Trustees, the British Museum.

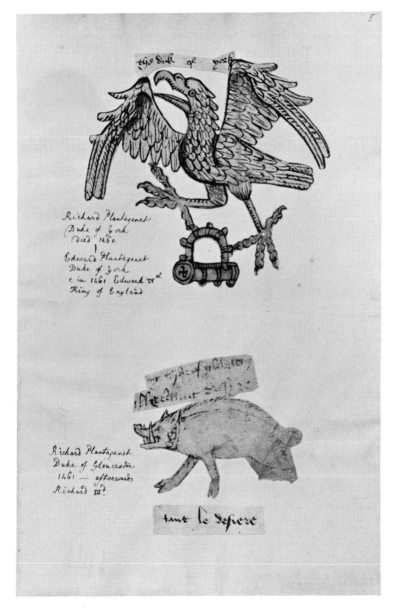

Plate III. The badges of the dukes of York and of Gloucester, from British Museum MS. Additional 40742, folio 5. Reproduced by courtesy of the Trustees, the British Museum.

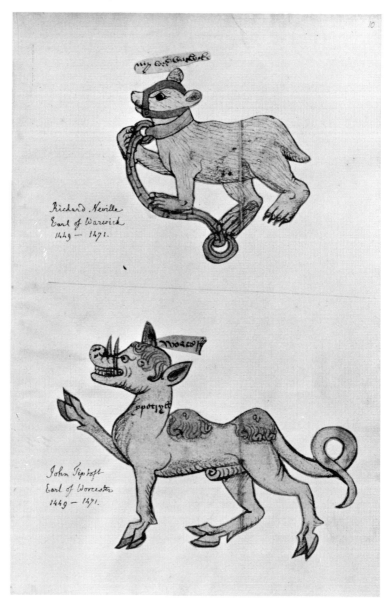

Plate IV. The badges of the earls of Warwick and of Worcester, from British Museum MS. Additional 40742, folio 10. Reproduced by courtesy of the Trustees, the British Museum.

Plate V. The badges of the dukes of Norfolk and of Suffolk, from British Museum MS. Additional 40742, folio 7. Reproduced by courtesy of the Trustees, the British Museum.

Plate VI. The Wilton Diptych, the National Gallery, London. "Richard II is kneeling under the protection of Saints John the Baptist, Edward the Confessor, and Edmund King and Martyr; on the right the Virgin stands holding the Child in the midst of a group of Angels." Note King Richard II's badge, the white hart crouching, embroidered on the left sleeve or shoulder of each angel. Dated 1395–1399 (?). Reproduced by courtesy of the Trustees, the National Gallery, London.

Plate VII. The Wilton Diptych, the National Gallery, London. Detail from the right front panel showing angels wearing King Richard II's badge, the white hart crouching, on their left sleeves or shoulders. Reproduced by courtesy of the Trusters, the National Gallery, London.

Plate VIII. The seal of William, Lord Hastings, 1461–1483, from one of his charters in the British Museum, Additional Charter 19808. Reproduced by courtesy of the Trustees, the British Museum.